The Story of Western Furniture

Phyllis Bennett Oates

Illustrated by Mary Seymour

ICON EDITIONS

HARPER & ROW, PUBLISHERS, New York

Cambridge, Hagerstown, Philadelphia, San Francisco
London, Mexico City, São Paulo, Sydney

1817

FIRST U.S. EDITION

ISBN: 0–06–436350–3

LIBRARY OF CONGRESS CATALOG CARD NUMBER: 81–47246

Designer: Judith Allan

81 82 83 84 85 10 9 8 7 6 5 4 3 2 1

To the memory of my father

The author is indebted to Brenda Herbert for her constructive suggestions and patient help in editing this book.

Contents

Egypt, Greece and Rome

Our knowledge of the furniture of early civilizations comes mainly from stone carvings or paintings, which give an idea of its form and proportion but not of its details and construction. From ancient Egypt, however, we have both illustrations in art and actual pieces of furniture.

The peculiar geographical situation of Egypt, its unique climate and the character of Egyptian beliefs created the exceptional circumstances which made it possible for pieces of furniture made five thousand years ago to survive to the present day. The valley and delta of the Nile, protected from the outside world by natural barriers, was an attractive area for ancient man to settle in. The air was dry and clear and the river provided fertile alluvial land and easy transport. By 3200 BC towns had sprung up along its length and Upper and Lower Egypt were united under one king.

The culture of Egypt developed during the Old Kingdom, from c.2700–2200 BC. The king was considered divine and was believed to be the only intermediary between people and gods. His survival after death depended upon the preservation of his earthly body in an airtight, sealed and indestructible tomb. The Fourth Dynasty pyramids were built solely for this purpose and were filled with replicas of all the objects the Pharaoh had used in this life and might need in the after-life. The dry airless condition of the tombs has preserved intact the richly decorated furniture, fine cloth and delicate jewelry for thousands of years.

During the Old Kingdom ordinary people began to believe that not only the Pharaoh and other gods but they too had a 'ka', an individual personality. All who could afford to do so built and furnished tombs. For the Egyptian, his tomb was a record of his life and the gateway to an after-life: for us it is a time-capsule which has preserved the artefacts of a fascinating civilization and a record of its way of life.

Egyptian houses varied greatly according to the economic and social prosperity of the owners. The huts of the working classes contained little or no furniture. Low benches of mud, covered with rush mats or linen rolls served as beds and seats; there might be a three-legged stool or a rough table. Even at the height of Egypt's prosperity any but the simplest furniture was a status symbol.

9

A rich man's villa had thick walls of well-baked clay and carefully laid out gardens with trees and ponds. In the cool centre of the house a tall room served as the principal living area and the reception room for guests. The ceiling was supported by wooden pillars, probably shaped like palm trunks, and clerestory windows let in light and air. There would have been a raised altar in a niche with a stone basin for ceremonial washing. Behind this room lay the principal bedroom with a raised dais for the bed. Other bedrooms were at the rear of the house. There were bathrooms and lavatories, for importance was attached to cleanliness and sanitation. Some houses had upper storeys with loggias facing north where people could sleep in the open during the heat. Patterned fabrics were hung on the walls or used as room-dividers, and rush mats covered the floors. Stucco murals of delightful scenes from nature added richness. Egyptians had a great love and knowledge of natural history and depicted it sympathetically. Women enjoyed a high status in Egyptian society, playing an important role in the planning and organization of their houses, gardens and tombs.

By modern standards the amount of furniture in these houses was not excessive, but it was comfortable and well made. The Egyptians standardized the pattern and form of many pieces of furniture still in use today; for example beds, chairs, stools, chests, the basic pieces found in the well-to-do home. The bed was of simple form with a rectangular frame, often raised higher at the head on longer legs so that it sloped to the foot, sometimes at quite a steep angle. The frame was usually spanned by corded grass or fibre slotted through its rails. There was commonly a decorated foot-board but never a head-board. Egyptian beds were narrow and rarely more than a foot (30 cm) high. It was not common for man and wife to sleep together: love-making was kept for the correct days and was dictated by the calendar. Craftsmen drew inspiration from nature, and better quality beds often had legs carved in the form of animal feet (bull or lion were the most common), and floral motifs such as the lotus or papyrus flower were used as decorative features. Some fine examples of bull's feet carved in ivory have been found. The small beaded cylinders supporting the feet were obviously intended to protect the fine details by raising them off the ground but came to be generally adopted for many types of furniture and were sometimes sheathed in metal. Early legs had holes pierced around the top through which leather thongs were passed to lash them to the frame. The leather was used wet, and tightened as it dried to form very firm joints.

Folded pieces of linen formed mattresses, and linen cloths and skins were used as covers. Some beds do appear to have had stuffed mattresses, probably filled with straw. Pillows were not used – the head was supported by a head rest made of wood, iron or ivory, often highly decorative. A linen pad provided extra comfort. The head was regarded as the source of life which must be preserved to ensure life after death. Tutankhamun's head was supported by an iron rest placed in the linen wrappings of his mummy.

Stools were of two kinds, folding and rigid, with many varieties ranging from the simple to the richly ornate, often with animal legs. Chairs were a development of the basic stool. There was considerable variation in the height of stools

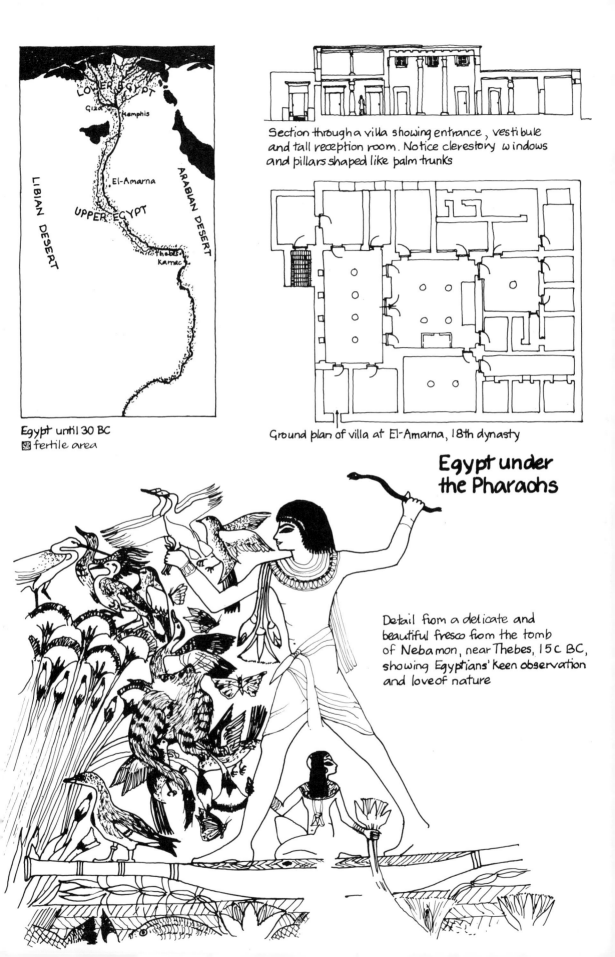

Egypt until 30 BC
▨ fertile area

Section through a villa showing entrance, vestibule and tall reception room. Notice clerestory windows and pillars shaped like palm trunks

Ground plan of villa at El-Amarna, 18th dynasty

Egypt under the Pharaohs

Detail from a delicate and beautiful fresco from the tomb of Nebamon, near Thebes, 15c BC, showing Egyptians' keen observation and love of nature

Constructional details of Egyptian furniture

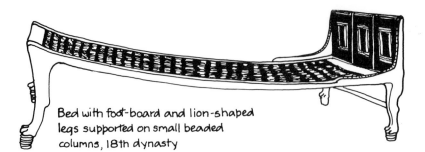

Bed with foot-board and lion-shaped legs supported on small beaded columns, 18th dynasty

Detail of a wooden bed with bull's legs, showing method of joining

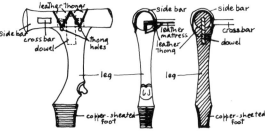

leather thong

side bar

cross bar
dowel

thong holes

side bar

leather
mattress
leather
thong

side bar

cross bar
dowel

leg

leg

copper-sheathed
foot

copper-sheathed
foot

Construction of a bed, 1st dynasty

Bull's leg made of ivory, showing holes for thonging. 1st dynasty

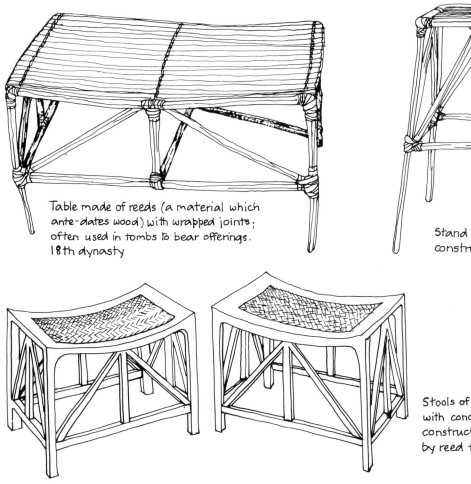

Table made of reeds (a material which ante-dates wood) with wrapped joints; often used in tombs to bear offerings. 18th dynasty

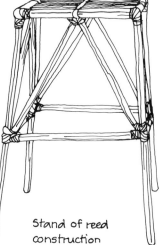

Stand of reed construction

Stools of lattice design with concave seats, construction influenced by reed furniture and chairs; some were low by European standards, with the seat barely nine inches (23 cm) from the floor. The Egyptians sat with equal ease either in the oriental manner with legs crossed underneath or the western way with feet resting on the floor. There were also double stools or chairs to seat a man and wife. Cushions of woven linen or leather, stuffed with the feathers of water fowl, were draped over the backs and seats of chairs.

For storage, baskets made of grass, rushes and palm fibres were used for a variety of purposes, particularly food; and chests and boxes with metal hinges held clothing, personal belongings and linen. Locks and keys were unknown in Egypt until Roman times. There is no evidence of chests-of-drawers or cupboards for domestic use, despite the fact that toilet boxes and gaming boards often had drawers and there were cupboard-like shrines in the temples and tombs.

Small pedestal tables were developed to keep things off the ground, probably derived from earlier stone or pottery plates or bowls placed on low pottery stands on which food was served. A dining table to seat several people was unknown. There were few other pieces of furniture. From the many illustrations of feasts it is apparent that the Egyptians liked to eat and drink well in a convivial atmosphere of flowers, music and dancing. Oil lamps lit the rooms and braziers on stands provided warmth on cool evenings.

The best evidence of stools of the earlier periods comes from the carvings on stelae found in private tombs. In Egypt a stele was considered to be a magical aid by which the dead man could continue to enjoy his earthly pleasures. He is usually illustrated sitting on a stool in front of a pedestal table bearing offerings. The tomb of Hesy-Ra, a royal official named as 'scribe and acquaintance of the king' provides the best examples of furniture in use during the Third Dynasty, about 2650 BC. A wooden panel shows him sitting upon a very fine stool with slender rounded side-rails and elegant gazelle-type legs. Other illustrations in the tomb show four cabinets on slender legs similar to the ones found in the tomb of Tutankhamun some 1300 years later. There were also a number of stools, head-rests, games, games boxes, vessels and rich wall hangings, which indicate a high standard of living.

The contents of the tomb of Queen Hetepheres of the Fourth Dynasty give an idea of the high peak that design and technical skill had reached at this time and of the richness and elegance of palace furniture. Her armchair is the most ancient existing wooden armchair so far discovered. It was completely covered in gold except for the seat and back panel. Although most of the wood had crumbled to dust, the metal sheathing and inlays retained their shapes and it was possible to reconstruct the chair. It has a low, wide, deep seat sloping down slightly from front to back. The leg supports are the fore and back legs of a lion standing on beaded drums covered with gold sheets. A bold motif of three lotus flowers is used in each side panel. The parts are joined by mortise and tenon joints secured with wooden pins and the flowers are dowelled into the supporting parts.

The bed is of standard design supported on lion's legs with claws, with a solid board fitted into the frame rails to form a base for a mattress. The rails terminate in papyrus flower heads. Legs and rails are sheathed in gold. To enclose the bed

Wooden panel from tomb of Hesy-ra,
3rd dynasty, showing stool with
gazelle legs and slender rounded
side-rails

Queen Hetepheres' chair

The Old Kingdom—
high standards
of design and
technical skill

Bed canopy of Queen
Hetepheres with bed and chair,
4th dynasty

Queen Hetepheres'
carrying-chair

and give privacy there is an ingeniously constructed gold covered canopy. Copper hooks around the top of the frame had supported curtains and roofing cloth. Some remnants of these survive, also a very fine linen cloth which was probably used as a mosquito net. The canopy was kept in a curtain box when not in use.

There is also a carrying chair, a gift from the Queen's son, King Cheops, framed and ornamented with gold and supported on carrying poles which terminate in heavy gold ornaments representing palm leaves.

No furniture has survived from the period between Hetepheres and Tutankhamun but pieces represented in sculptured reliefs show that the traditions of the Old Kingdom persisted with little change. The last great creative period of Egyptian artists and craftsmen was the Eighteenth Dynasty (c.1575–1310 BC) and the most impressive furniture yet discovered came from this time, when Egypt was at the height of its power and prosperity. Tutankhamun, the most renowned of the Pharaohs, owes his fame to the discovery of his tomb, intact, in the Valley of the Kings in 1922 by Howard Carter. Packed into four small rooms was the most incredible treasure, including articles of furniture on which an astonishing variety of precious materials had been lavished with consummate skill. The throne, one of the most ornate pieces, was lined with gold and inlaid with silver, multi-coloured glass, precious stones and majolica. Other pieces made of less precious materials were equally fine examples of the cabinet-makers' skill. The little ornate cabinet on long slender legs has a timeless quality and is reminiscent of the best designs of the eighteenth century AD.

Most cabinet-making techniques were perfected by the Egyptians. Egypt had little wood and craftsmen learned to make the best of what was available. None of her native woods – acacia, almond-fig, date-palm, persea, sycamore-fig, tamarisk, willow, sidder and poplar – were suitable for fine cabinet work; some were used for simple domestic furniture or coffins. For wide boards timber had to be imported. Ebony from the south was highly prized and often inlaid with ivory and gold; cypress, juniper and cedar came from Syria; pine and cedar from the forests of the Lebanese mountains. The Egyptians were superb craftsmen, in spite of, or perhaps because of, the lack of good indigenous wood. Only small panels could be produced from native wood so they devised a patchwork technique. They invented a number of joints, from mortise and tenon to dove-tailing. Small irregular pieces were joined together, flaws were filled and patched. As far back as the First Dynasty, veneering and inlay were introduced to cover inferior wood. Ebony, ivory, faience, coloured glass and coloured stones were all used for inlay. Thick veneers were held in place with small wooden pegs. With the introduction of glue in the Eighteenth Dynasty, thin veneers became possible. Veneering and inlay are seen at their best in the furniture of Tutankhamun.

Many Egyptian pieces were gessoed and painted, some elaborately decorated and gilded. The Egyptians had large supplies of gold and it appears to have been prized less than silver. Leaf gold was used on gesso, gold foil for inlay was glued into position, and sheet gold was rivetted into place. Varnish, both a colourless transparent kind and an opaque black, came into use in the Eighteenth Dynasty.

15

Ceremonial chair and footstool. The chair has an unusual curved seat imitating cow-hide; the back is inlaid with precious stones set in sheet gold

The throne of Tutankhamun: carved wood lined with gold and inlaid with silver, majolica, multi-coloured glass and precious stones

Furniture from the tomb of Tutankhamun, 18th dynasty

Ornate stool with animal legs, painted white, with gilded grille

Chair with padded seat and tasselled back (detail from scene on golden shrine)

Folding stool with loose cushioned seat (detail from scene on golden shrine)

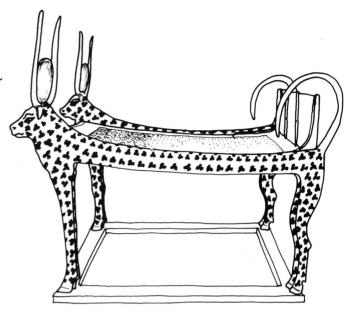

Bed of the Divine Cow, made
of wood, coated with gesso
and gilded

Ivory head-rest with symbolic
decoration. The head, thought
to be the seat of life, was
preserved with great care to
ensure continued existence
after death

Cabinet of ebony
and (probably) cedar

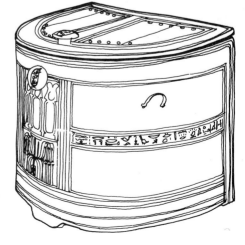

Gaming-board inlaid with
ivory, mounted on ebony stand.
The paws have ivory claws and
rest on gilded drums

Bow-fronted chest
veneered in ebony

The early Egyptian carpenter's tools were simple, with wooden handles and copper blades. Egypt was never eager to adopt new technology. Although bronze, a mixture of tin and copper, was known at Byblos in the Eleventh Dynasty, it was not used for tools in Egypt until 500 years later. Not until the sixth century BC did Greek smiths work in iron on Egyptian soil. Once bronze tools for woodworking came into common use in the Eighteenth Dynasty the harder cutting edges facilitated the making of much finer furniture.

The early axe was a flat semi-circular plate with a straight back bored with a row of holes to take the leather or hempen thongs used to bind the head to a long wooden handle. The most important and versatile tool was the adze, a cutting blade of bronze or copper lashed at right angles to a wooden haft, which was used both for hewing and trimming rough timbers and for shaping and smoothing the surface. A variety of chisels hit with a wooden mallet were used for finer work. Pull-saws were used for cutting timber, awls for punching small holes and bow-drills for making holes in seats and bed rails to take the cord or rush. Hammers, plumb-rules, cubit measures and wooden nails completed the tool bag. Metal nails were not used for carpentry until the Eighteenth Dynasty although they had been used earlier for attaching metal to wood.

How the rounded legs of Egyptian stools were formed is not known, as the true wood-turning lathe was not then in use. There is a tradition that the Greeks invented the plane, but it was introduced into Greece sometime about the seventh century BC from the Middle East. As yet the earliest known planes are those found in Pompeii. A fairly smooth surface could be obtained with the adze, a finer surface by rubbing down with stone blocks, using sand as an abrasive.

The rich Egyptians, with their comfortable life-style rooted in tradition, were unwilling to assimilate new ideas. They showed little interest in the outside world, despite increasing contact. All real progress took place in the lands to the north and east which were eventually to bring Egypt's civilization to an end.

The rich interiors of ancient Greece disappeared long ago and virtually no movable pieces of furniture survived. We have to turn to other sources for our knowledge of the Greek way of life. Fortunately a kaleidoscopic picture can be built up from its literature, its sculptural reliefs and the paintings on the many pottery vessels which survive. From Homer we know of the splendours of ancient palaces, from Plato, Aristotle and Xenophon of everyday life in the home, the women who ran it, and the business of men outside. From vase paintings we can visualize the furniture and furnishings. The early history of Greece is so romanticized and so enmeshed in myth that it is virtually impossible to piece together. We know that there was a Bronze Age civilization of some magnificence, dominated by the Minoans and Mycenaeans, who built splendid fortified palaces. This was overrun by the Dorian invasion of c.1150 BC, plunging Greece into a Dark Age for the next two or three hundred years. It was not until the fifth century BC that Greek civilization reached an intellectual and artistic peak, the flowering of the great classical period centred around Athens.

The Greeks built splendid public buildings but paid comparatively little attention to their own houses, which were used mainly for eating and sleeping.

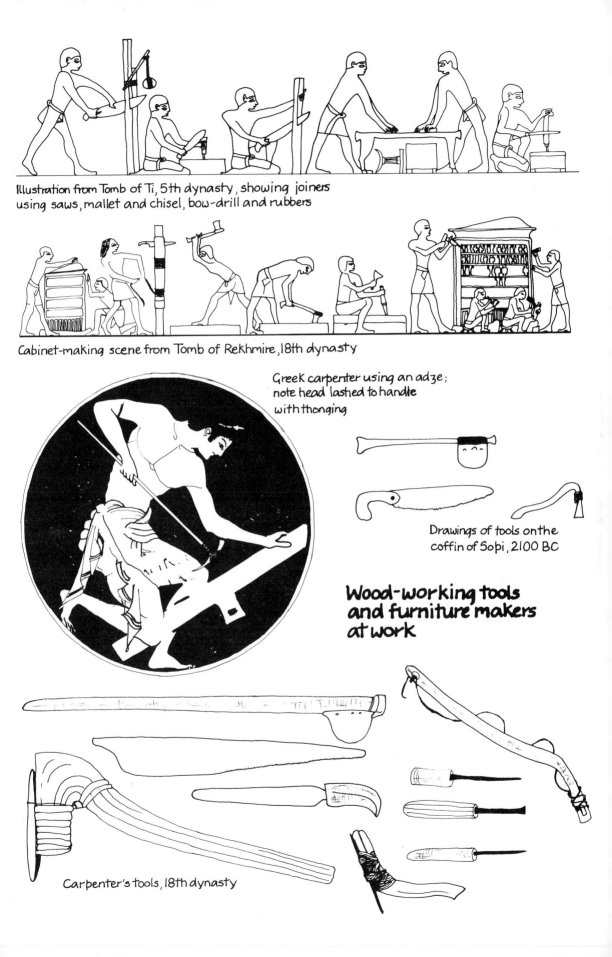

Illustration from Tomb of Ti, 5th dynasty, showing joiners using saws, mallet and chisel, bow-drill and rubbers

Cabinet-making scene from Tomb of Rekhmire, 18th dynasty

Greek carpenter using an adze; note head lashed to handle with thonging

Drawings of tools on the coffin of Sobi, 2100 BC

Wood-working tools and furniture makers at work

Carpenter's tools, 18th dynasty

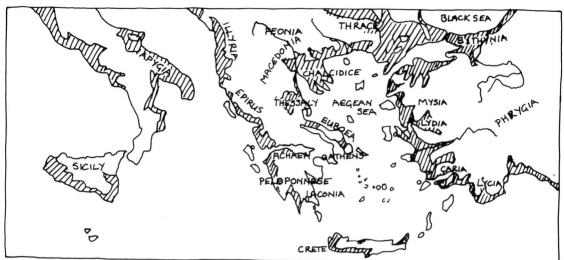

Greek expansion 8-3 CC BC

The Greek home

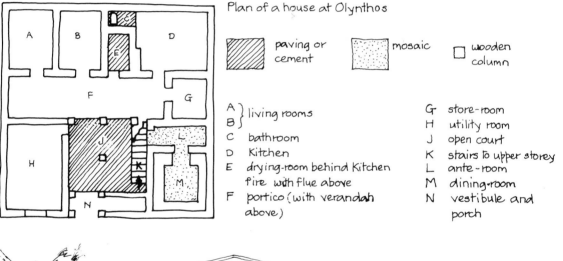

Plan of a house at Olynthos

▨ paving or cement

▦ mosaic

□ wooden column

A ⎫ living rooms
B ⎭
C bathroom
D Kitchen
E drying-room behind Kitchen fire with flue above
F portico (with verandah above)

G store-room
H utility room
J open court
K stairs to upper storey
L ante-room
M dining-room
N vestibule and porch

Courtyard to house at Priene showing porch and door to hall behind

Much of their time was spent out of doors. Excavations at Olynthos, a flourishing town of the fifth century BC, destroyed by Philip of Macedon in 348, give a fair picture of the average house of the classical period. A considerable part of the middle class area of the town has been uncovered. The houses, built of sun-baked brick on stone foundations, looked inwards to avoid the heat and glare of the sun and the noise of the streets. A porch and vestibule led into an open courtyard which usually had a shallow pool to catch rainwater and conduct it to an underground reservoir. Beyond was a portico off which were living rooms, kitchen and bathroom. Within the courtyard was placed an altar to the god Zeus. Lamps were set in niches in the walls of the court and charcoal braziers were used for heating on cool nights. The second storey, usually the women's part of the house, did not extend round the south side of the court, so that the winter sun could reach the portico. The interior walls were decorated with coloured plaster. The floors of the main rooms would have been cemented or paved with mosaics, those of the bathrooms had tiles, slate or cement. Other ground-floor rooms normally had pressed earth floors. In the upper rooms either floor boards or clay pressed on reeds supported on the joists would be used. Windows had shutters but no glass.

This plan was not necessarily followed in farmhouses and country villas. In Athens there were also apartment blocks housing several families of the citizen class, and less salubrious tenements for the workers.

The wives of wealthy Greeks led cloistered lives centred around the home, while the men were preoccupied with politics, business and the functioning of the city-state. Men of the citizen class had a considerable amount of leisure, mostly spent at the gymnasium where they participated in sport and conversation. The gymnasia of Athens became centres for political and philosophical discussion.

The symposium or formal dinner party provided another occasion for discussion. It took place in the dining-room, the male domain, and the ladies of the house were not present. The diners, probably nine in number, reclined on couches placed around the walls. The heterae – those fascinating, flimsily-clad females of the vase paintings, the *demi-mondaines* of the ancient world and the only women who might be invited to a party – would also recline. (Ladies always sat on chairs.) Little rectangular tables supported on three legs were brought in, laden with food, and placed before each couch.

The most elaborate furniture was in the dining-room. There would be between three and nine couches, usually five, ranged around the walls. The Greek couch was a development of the Egyptian bed – many Egyptian forms of furniture were adopted and modified by the Greeks – but the bed's foot-board and separate head-rest had disappeared. The legs were longer and mainly rectangular in form rather than turned or carved, and projected above the seat, higher at the head to form a support. Some couches had detachable bronze head-rests. The frame was strung with plaited cord or leather thongs and supported a thick mattress which draped over the end supports and helped to keep the pillow in position. Mattress and pillows were covered with richly patterned wool or linen fabrics. These might be perfumed before a party. The legs and rails of the couches were richly

Couches from vase paintings 7-5 cc BC

Couches with turned legs, and three-legged rectangular tables with lion paws, 625-600 BC

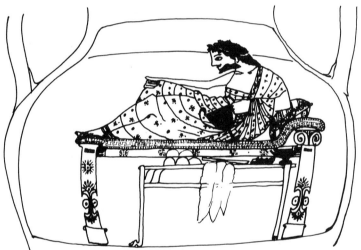

Couch with rectangular legs deeply incised at sides; a double volute forms a capital at head of leg. Note decorative mattress and pillow. 5 C BC

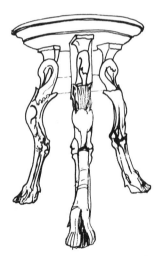

Round wooden Greek table from Egypt with three animal legs surmounted by bird heads. Hellenistic

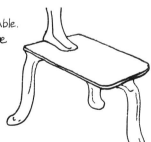

Bronze model of a three-legged table. The legs on a couch-table were arranged in a similar way

Elegantly proportioned couch with gracefully curved head-board and lively goat's legs. Late 6 C BC

painted or inlaid with wood (no shortage of wood in Greece), gems or metal; a favourite motif was the palmette. The feet could be of ivory or silver. Couches with turned legs did still occur and, after the introduction of the lathe in the seventh century BC, often became very elaborate. Some of the legs illustrated on the vases look perilously slender in places.

The Greeks used tables rather more than the Egyptians but there was still no large dining-table. As well as the little rectangular couch-tables, housed under the couches when not in use, the Greeks introduced an attractive small round table supported on three deer legs with hooves. The only other furniture to appear in the dining-room would be the lampstands, usually made of brass and supported on three bandy animal legs. Additional richness was achieved by the use of draperies and cushions, coloured walls and mosaic floors.

Elsewhere in the house would be additional couches or beds for sleeping. Seats ranged from portable folding stools to the formal upright chair with arms called *thronos*. *Thronoi* were the seats of deities or notables and were richly adorned with precious inlays of palmettes, rosettes and volutes, or elaborately carved in a sculptural way. They could be high-backed or backless, with or without arms.

One of the most attractive and popular chairs developed by the Greeks was the *klismos*, an elegant, beautifully proportioned chair with a curved back-rest at shoulder level and sabre-shaped legs supporting a plaited seat. After its heyday in the fifth century BC it became clumsier, with a deeper, heavy backboard.

Among a wide variety of stools, a favourite was the *disphros okbadias*, a light folding stool which was handy for slaves to carry around for their master's use. It was often supported by bandy, crossed animal legs terminating either in hooves turning outwards or lion's feet turning inwards. The *disphros*, another popular stool, had four turned legs sometimes strengthened by stretchers. There were many low stools to match the chairs or couches, usually supported by tiny bandy animal legs with lion-paws.

Stout chests resembling their Egyptian forerunners were still used for all forms of storage. Cupboards and chests-of-drawers had not yet evolved and articles not in immediate use were hung on the walls, either in the kitchen or living rooms. Food was kept in crocks and large storage bins. Women had a variety of small boxes and wickerwork baskets for trinkets, mirrors, jewelry, embroidery materials, wool for spinning, games and other small household articles.

The Macedonians invaded and took control of Greece by the mid-fourth century BC. In an extraordinary campaign their leader Alexander conquered all the territory from Greece to the Indus. Greek art followed in his wake and became the pictorial language of a large part of the known world, remaining when the empire collapsed and split into a number of warring city-states after Alexander's death. Peace was restored when Rome took over and established provinces throughout the Mediterranean towards the end of the second century BC. The Roman Empire was a single state stretching from the Atlantic to the Euphrates, the Black Sea, the Danube and the Rhine, and from the North Sea to the Sahara and Arabian deserts.

Romans cherished the cultural and intellectual achievements of the Greek

Chair with incised and painted legs,
rosette and palmette decoration

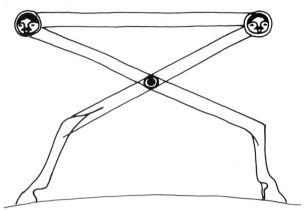

Folding stool with goat's legs turning outwards,
ornamented with circular lion-mask

Greek seats
from 5c vase paintings

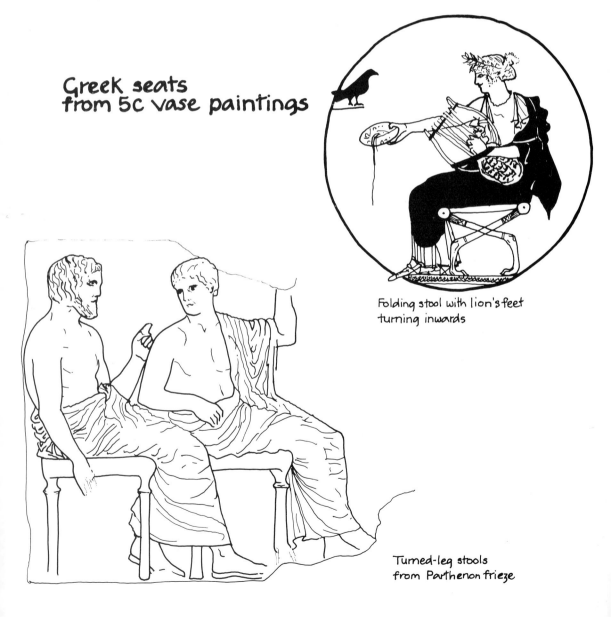

Folding stool with lion's feet
turning inwards

Turned-leg stools
from Parthenon frieze

Development of the Greek chair

Decorative chest with animal feet; armchair with turned legs, and back terminating in bird head, with two thick cushions. Household implements hanging on wall. (Terracotta relief from Locri 5C BC)

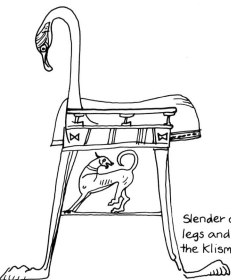

Slender chair with slightly curved legs and back; a forerunner of the Klismos. 6C BC

The Klismos – one of the most beautiful of Greek chairs

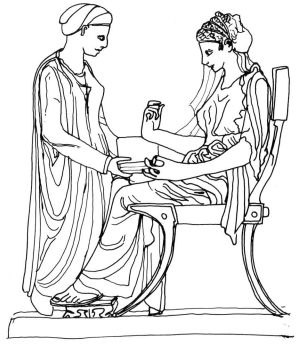

Detail from vase painting showing construction of the Klismos – front rail attached by dowels, cane seat, central vertical banister in back

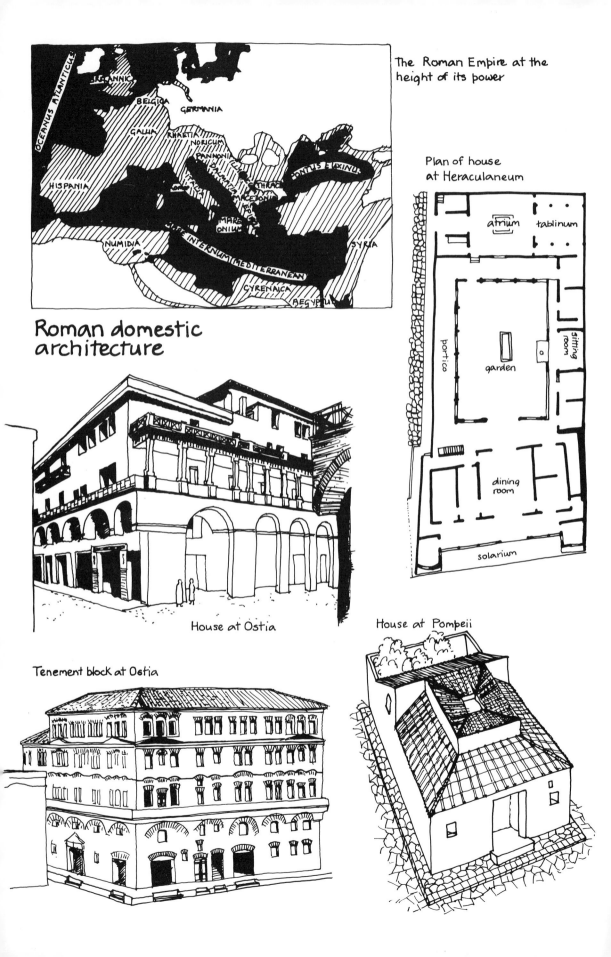

The Roman Empire at the height of its power

Plan of house at Heraculaneum

atrium tablinum

portico

garden

sitting room

dining room

solarium

Roman domestic architecture

House at Ostia

Tenement block at Ostia

House at Pompeii

world they had conquered and became the great patrons of art in the ancient world. They embellished their houses and gardens with old and modern Greek sculpture, and employed Greek artists to decorate their homes. Private houses were large and comfortable: a good middle-class house with a terrace might occupy a block 180ft (55m) square with a main reception room 48ft (15m) long. In Pompeii, a provincial watering place and trading centre, archaeologists have uncovered street after street of mansions with mosaic floors, fresco painted walls, colonnaded courts, running water, heated bathrooms and latrines, and glazed windows. The Romans were little concerned with the external appearance of their town houses; no windows opened on to the street and sometimes the frontage on either side of the entrance was let off as shops. The inward-looking house was built as two squares joined together. The first, the lofty atrium which housed the family altar and the ancestral statues, was half court and half reception room with an unroofed space in the centre and the *impluvium* beneath it to catch the rainwater. Beyond was the private part of the house with the peristyle, lined with columns and often embellished with statues, pools and fountains in the centre, surrounded by bedrooms, reception rooms, kitchen and dining-room. The family spent most of its time in the peristyle and sometimes took alfresco meals there from a stone dining-table. There might be a small garden here, but on larger properties the garden lay beyond.

All homes were fairly sparsely furnished – beds, tables, chairs, couches, candelabra and chests were still the basic pieces. The forms of the furniture were simple but in wealthy homes the decoration was often ornate. Rooms were enriched with wall paintings, often illustrating scenes from Greek mythology, and elaborate mosaic floors. Multi-coloured curtains, rich cushions and bed-spreads added to the general effect. A standard of solid comfort was achieved even in the provinces.

For family meals a small room, the *cenatio*, was used. The wealthy had a large formal dining-room, the *triclinium*, for parties. The dinner party was the main event of Roman social life. A Roman host would invite from three to nine guests. There were usually three capacious couches, each large enough to hold three reclining people; or there might be one semi-circular couch called a *sigma*, for a party of six, seven or eight. After removing their shoes, guests reclined on the couches on their left elbows, eating from movable round tables. Each guest had a servant to wash his hands, serve him and light him home after the meal. Bronze or silver candelabra, placed in strategic positions to light the dining-room, might be the only other furniture, or there might be a new type of table, the console table, which appeared during the Roman period. This was supported on three legs and placed against the wall. Another innovation was a bigger table consisting of a large slab of wood or marble supported on an elaborately carved marble base decorated with griffins and other fabulous beasts, used as a serving table. Metal tripods for supporting bowls or trays were popular.

Although the Greek style of couch was still used, by the end of the first century AD a characteristic Roman couch with a high back and sides and a thick mattress seat appeared. Low footstools were used with couches, chairs and stools. Roman

Roman interiors

Interior of Roman house; the atrium, looking through to the peristyle

Roman pavement mosaic

Ceiling of Roman tomb

Roman dining-room and seating plan, the place of honour is indicated by No.1, and that of the host by No.9

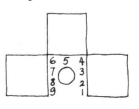

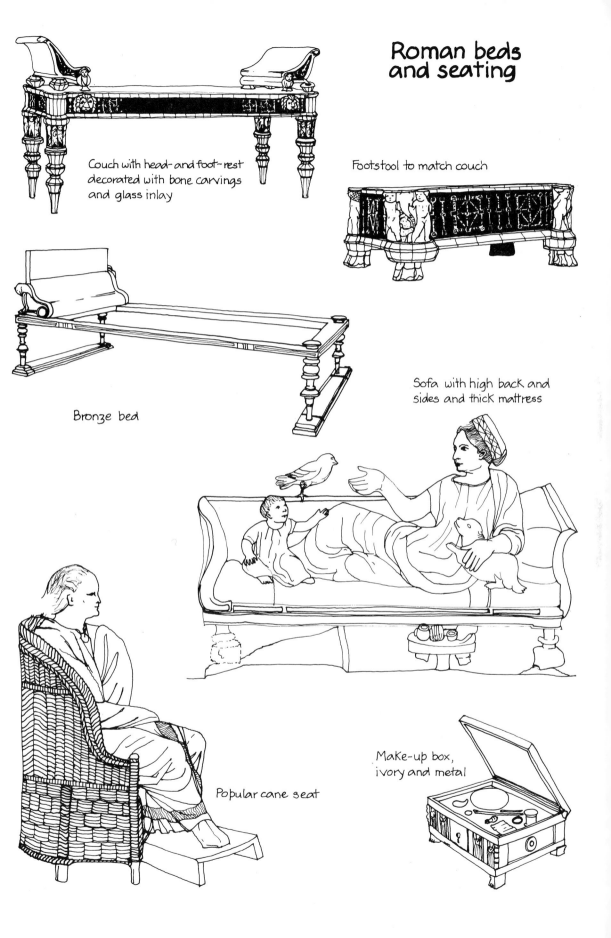

Roman beds and seating

Couch with head- and foot-rest decorated with bone carvings and glass inlay

Footstool to match couch

Bronze bed

Sofa with high back and sides and thick mattress

Popular cane seat

Make-up box, ivory and metal

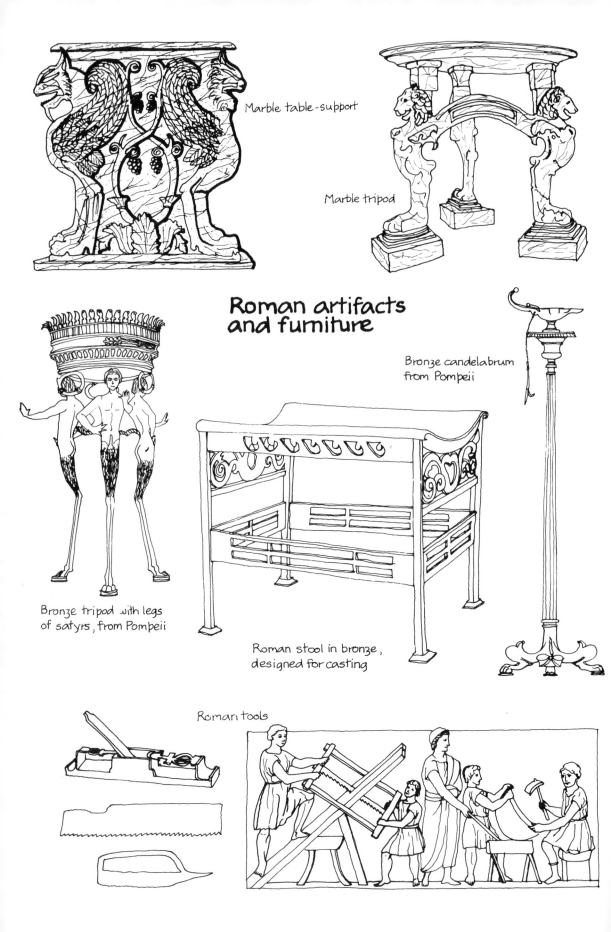

Marble table-support

Marble tripod

Roman artifacts and furniture

Bronze candelabrum from Pompeii

Bronze tripod with legs of satyrs, from Pompeii

Roman stool in bronze, designed for casting

Roman tools

seats and stools were based upon Greek prototypes. A wicker-work chair with a rounded back became a favourite with women, particularly when at their toilet. Some folding stools were made of brass or iron. The curule chair was a type of folding stool used by the higher magistrates; designed with curving legs and often inlaid with ivory, it could be folded up and carried by a servant or put in a chariot.

Furniture based on Roman patterns was made by craftsmen throughout the Empire. Roman metal folding stools have been found in graves in Britain and Belgium. Iron tools found in excavated sites are very similar to those in use today. The Romans introduced several innovations for saws, notably the setting of the teeth so that they were angled left and right alternately, enabling the saw to be pushed as well as pulled. The frame-saw was also developed in several sizes and planes were in general use.

In spite of its apparent prosperity, the Roman Empire spread its manpower and resources too thinly and no advances had been made in technology to remedy this. Social inequalities and high taxation to pay for the army, administrators and Rome's extravagant projects caused unrest. By 250 AD the Empire was already impoverished, 150 years before the arrival from the north of the barbarians who are usually said to have initiated its downfall and brought the Dark Ages to Europe.

Byzantium, early medieval and gothic Europe

In AD 330 Constantine transferred the capital of the Empire from Rome to Byzantium, a Greek city on the shore of the Bosphorus, which he re-named Constantinople. The name 'Byzantium' came to be used for the whole eastern section of the Roman Empire. Under Constantine's rule and that of his successors, Constantinople became a sophisticated successor to Rome. The city was a hybrid, situated midway between East and West – conceived as a new Rome with a Roman ruling class, yet with a mainly Greek-speaking population, many of them orientals, and with the new Christian faith as its religion. From this odd mixture grew a vital civilization and a unique art form.

At its height in the sixth century, Constantinople was the centre of a vast empire: North Africa, Egypt, Syria, Armenia, Asia Minor, Sicily, parts of Italy and Spain. Although the boundaries fluctuated, the art of this whole area remained essentially Byzantine in character for over a thousand years, and its influence stretched even further. As far north and west as Scotland and Ireland, Byzantine motifs can be found intermingling with Celtic motifs.

Situated at the hub of trade routes, Constantinople became the great trading, political and religious centre of its day. It was also the leading art centre, gathering to it and supporting the most skilful artists and craftsmen in all kinds of luxury trades. Most of the emperors were patrons and collectors of the arts and their palaces were superbly furnished. Factories and workshops for the craftsmen were situated within the walls of the Great Palace of the Emperors and were renowned for ivories, metal working, enamelling and embroidery. Here, too, were produced the famous silks used by the royal family and the rich for clothes and hangings.

The houses of the rich within the city were inward-looking, built around a central hall, the reception area for the men of the household. The principal rooms on the first floor were also used by the men. Women, children and maids lived on the floor above.

Unfortunately, no domestic furniture survives, and the only evidence we have is in pictorial records of the period – manuscript illuminations, ivories, murals, and mosaics. Mosaics, the great glory of Byzantine art, clothed the walls and

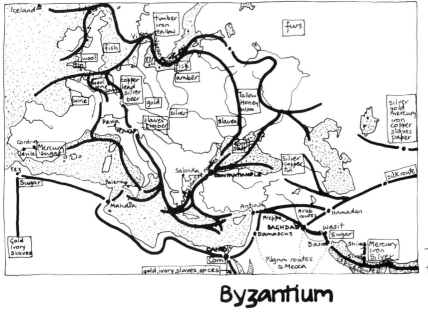

Trade routes and goods traded in 11c AD

Byzantium

Motif from Byzantine **woven** silk chasuble, 10c or 11c

From a mosaic excavated at the Emperor's Great Palace, Constantinople, depicting scenes from country life

Sarcophagus in church of S. Apollinare in Classe, Ravena. The monogram of Christ is combined with pagan motifs

floors of palaces, monasteries and churches, which were furnished with richness and comfort and with the lavish use of cushions, drapes and rich textile hangings. The mosaics show clearly the blend of the two traditions which formed the basis of Byzantine art – the graceful refinement of Hellenism joined to the solemn formalism of the East. Gradually classical naturalism gave way to static formalized figures and rich, colourful abstract patterns and symbolism became more important than perspective, proportion and a feeling of space. This fusion of styles is reflected in all the minor arts.

The elegant, subtle, curving forms associated with classical furniture were superseded by ponderous static shapes to suit the regal and formal splendour of the Byzantine palaces and houses. Furniture in the royal palace was particularly splendid. Records speak of tables of ivory and gold used for banquets. One dining hall housed a table made entirely of gold, large enough to accommodate thirty-six couches. At royal banquets guests reclined in the Roman manner and were served from gold plate. When alone, the royal family used chairs for meals – many households used stools and benches. The Byzantines set their tables with care, often using beautifully embroidered cloths. Knives, forks and spoons were common although many people ate with their fingers. Tables, usually of metal or stone, followed the Roman patterns; dining-tables were mostly round or D-shaped. Simple wooden rectangular tables were common in modest homes. Some elaborate cabinet-maker's pieces were of wood with fitted cupboards under the table top. Fortunately all the techniques and skills of the classical cabinet-makers were preserved in Byzantium.

The most frequently illustrated pieces of furniture are thrones and chairs. Thrones appear in the main to have been heavy constructions of wood, architectural in form, with painted decoration, usually set with a matching footstool on a dais with a canopy above. Some were very splendid – made of precious materials, decorated with jewels, draped with sumptuous and rare fabrics, and heaped with ornate cushions.

Emperor Theophilus commissioned a mechanical chair to impress his visitors with his imperial majesty. An envoy of the King of Italy has left a description of this seat, which it seems could be raised or lowered at will. It was flanked by two bronze or gilded lions which beat the ground with their tails, opened their mouths and roared with quivering tongues. A bronze tree with branches filled with birds of various species stood before the throne. As the envoy approached, the birds all uttered their particular calls.

Byzantium was renowned for its fine relief carvings in ivory. Ivory panels were incorporated into many articles – chests, caskets, reliquaries, even doors. A superb extant example is the chair known as the 'throne of Maximian', now kept in Ravenna. This has an unusual tub-shaped base and a curved back of Roman form. The main structural members are embellished with flowing carvings of foliage and fruit interspersed with birds and animals. The finely carved infilling panels illustrate scenes from the life of Christ, St John the Baptist and the Apostles.

The ever-popular classical folding or X-form chairs and stools, with slung

Ivory casket decorated with scenes from Old and New Testament; Hellenistic style. N. Italy, late 4c

Skilled craftsmanship

Ivory carving of Consul Flavius Anastasius, AD 517, seated on an official chair flanked by statuettes of Constantinople and Rome

Throne of Maximian, made up of a large number of ivory plaques carved by various artists in different styles; Ravenna, 6c

Heavy static throne of timber with thick cushioned seat, painted and jewelled decoration. From a mosaic, Ravenna, 6c

Scholar seated on a stool bench with square legs. The small table has turned legs and crossed stretchers and a fifth, central leg. Cupboard with panelled doors has a pediment top. (From 7c MS)

The Virgin's throne (from Byzantine triptych, 11-12c) has elegantly turned upright members and a simple footstool with arcaded sides

Later Byzantine

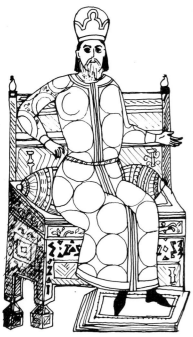

X-shaped chair of chased iron, damaskeened with gold. 12c

A large, decorated wooden throne with bolster and footrest

Box-type bed with panelled sides and curved head-rest. The tester is supported on twisted columns with carved capitals and elaborate bases. S. Mark's, Venice, 13c

leather seats, survived. Simple frame stools and benches, and stools with turned legs, were made; some of the turning was very elaborate. Footstools of many shapes and sizes to match the various chairs and thrones were popular.

There was an abundance of boxes for every purpose from the small jewelry casket to the large storage chest which could also serve as a seat, bed or table. Some were of primitive structure but others were of framed construction and panelled, painted or inlaid with fine wood, gold, silver or ivory, and some were plated with ivory. Although household goods and clothing were commonly stored in chests it is possible that some were placed on the shelves of the cupboards which appear in illustrations at this time. There were as yet no wardrobes or chests-of-drawers.

Bookcases housed the priceless manuscripts in monasteries and palaces. Many were elaborate cabinet-maker's pieces of architectural form with pediments and pilasters, or were embellished with decorative painting.

The profound respect for learning inherited by the Byzantines from the ancient world is reflected in the large number of lecterns and writing desks illustrated. These were of various forms: a favourite seems to have been a combination desk-cum-lectern. The desk portion often had a cupboard fitted with shelves on one side, and the lectern had a hinged arm which supported a book rest and adjusted to several positions. Free-standing lecterns also existed. Calligraphy was an art practised by many educated people and the work of scribes and illuminators was highly respected.

Simple beds followed classical forms but the graceful headrests disappeared. Some had elaborately turned supports, others were architectural in structure with testers and columns. The rich had elaborately embroidered bed-linen, blankets, quilts and bedspreads. From the odd assortment of household objects which survive – silver, cutlery, oil lamps and stands, balances and weights, candlesticks, dishes etc. – and from surviving inventories, we can assume that the rich and merchant classes achieved a high standard of living.

In contrast to the prosperity of the Eastern Empire, western Europe fell gradually into a state of decay. After Constantine's move to Byzantium, Rome became no more than a provincial town although still the seat of the 'Emperor of the West'. For over two hundred years the legions vainly attempted to hold back the barbarians. Eventually most centres of urban life, already impoverished and depopulated, were destroyed. Only where there was a religious centre or an ancient industry that managed to survive did a town continue to function. Throughout Europe German chiefs elected themselves kings or barons and the peasants worked for them in return for protection. Property was held by strength. Castles sprang up everywhere, towns were walled, houses and religious buildings were fortified. While the Empire decayed, the Church, gathering strength, spread throughout Europe and kept the old learning alive. Life for all was very hard and the household arts had slowly to develop again from primitive beginnings.

Three factors dictated the design of furniture in the Middle Ages: the nature of the houses in which people lived, the peripatetic life led by the upper and some of the middle classes, and the rules of precedence.

There was no plan common to all houses throughout medieval western Europe, yet all had one element in common – the hall, a main room used by all the inhabitants as a living-room. In many houses it was the only room, serving also as bedroom, workroom, kitchen and byre for the household animals. Aisled halls built like a church with nave and aisles, in order to span a large area, were common in early times. Smoke from the central fire drifted up and out through chinks in the roof. One aisle was used for storage and servants' quarters, the other was often used for stalling animals. This type of house was still in use in the fifteenth century.

Another type of home common in the eleventh and twelfth centuries was the bi-cellular or two-part house of two or three storeys. On each floor was a hall with an inner room. There were also many Norman tower-houses or keeps, three or four storeys high, which, although used as dwellings, were designed for defence and housed a garrison.

The medieval hall, with its central hearth and many people milling around inside, needed furniture which could be ranged against the wall or taken apart and stored away when not in use. This was also true of two-part houses and castles. Another factor that influenced the type of furniture required was the mobile life led by seigneurial households. In the early Middle Ages huge areas of Europe were uninhabited, and landowners had to be continually on the move to administer their scattered properties. Their houses might be as much as a hundred miles apart and stood almost empty while the owner was absent. Furniture had to be heavy, immovable and built into the walls to avoid theft, or free-standing and easy to dismantle and move to another house.

A large household might number over a hundred people. Many horses and carts and pack-horses were needed to transport the collection of chests stuffed with the rich tapestries, hangings, cushions and bedding which provided the main furnishings of castles and manors. The family plate, jewelry and clothes, folding furniture, even the glass from the windows had to be packed away. Anything delicate would be vulnerable, and this was a governing factor in design.

Meubles, the French word for furniture, is a relict of this time; originally it meant movables, anything transportable.

In the feudal societies of this period a lord's power had to be made known and supported by ceremonial display – a man's estate was proclaimed by visual means. The standing of every person at court was governed by rules of precedence. Everything about him – the clothes he wore, his furnishings, his code of behaviour, the food he ate – was determined by his rank or estate. This is a most important element in the development of furniture design in the later part of the Middle Ages. It dictated the materials, the shape, the decoration and the use of a particular piece of furniture by a particular individual. Chairs, especially, played their part in the rules of precedence. In his lord's house a man would sit on a stool, but in his own house with his own household around him, he would use a chair. Entertaining his king in his own house a nobleman would give up his chair to his lord and use a stool himself. He might possibly not even sit at the high table if others present took greater precedence.

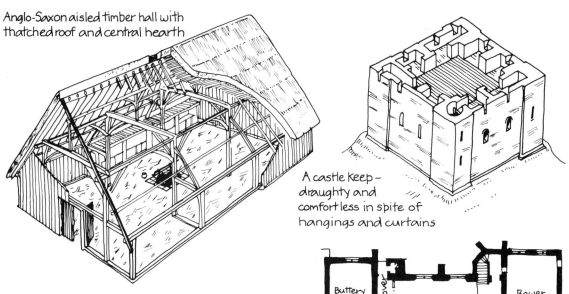

Anglo-Saxon aisled timber hall with thatched roof and central hearth

A castle keep – draughty and comfortless in spite of hangings and curtains

The medieval home

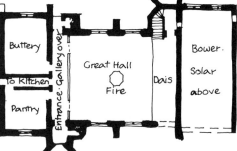

Buttery		Great Hall		Bower.
	Entrance. Gallery over	Fire	Dais	Solar above
Pantry				

← To Kitchen

Plan of medieval manor house as it evolved in England from earlier forms

Medieval dinner table. Note canopy, hangings, musicians' gallery and buffet

At a banquet there would be one important seat, the high chair, occupied by the man of greatest importance (the origin of our word 'chairman', who sits at a 'board', the medieval word for a table). This high chair was distinguished by a hanging behind it and a canopy above. The remainder of the company sat on stools or benches.

The canopy became a symbol of rank, often put up to honour a visitor of importance. Canopies were found above thrones, chairs, beds, and even above pieces of furniture, such as a buffet, not intended for the use of one particular person.

The buffet or *dressoir* was another adjunct of state. It was a simple stepped piece of furniture consisting of open shelves, the number of which denoted the owner's rank: a baron would have two steps, his immediate superior one more, and so on up to the royal *dressoir*. French ambassadors made Henry VIII of England a gift of a *dressoir* of twelve steps. The buffet was kept in the hall or chamber and was used for displaying the family plate and for serving wine to important visitors. None of them has survived from the Middle Ages, probably because of their size and rough carpentry – they were always draped with rich fabrics when in use. Since they were too cumbersome for everyday use a narrow buffet was produced. This was not draped but the exposed woodwork was carved with heavy ornament. It was a most useful piece for storage or display, and could be used as a sideboard.

In France the rules of precedence were carried to extremes. Life in the Burgundian court was most extravagant, and its influence was felt in England. From the time of the Norman invasion there was close contact between both sides of the channel, and the language and manners of the Courts were French. French and Burgundian fashions also spread to the Low Countries – the rich Flemish merchants carried home to Ghent, Brussels, Bruges and Ypres patterns of furniture which were translated eventually into the serene, elegant, domestic interiors of the bourgeois houses illustrated in the paintings of the van Eycks, Rogier van der Weyden and Robert Campin.

A house could quickly be transformed on the arrival of the owner by the use of textiles – rough tables and chairs were hidden beneath fabrics and cushions, armorial bearings were put in place, tapestries and other hangings provided warmth and colour. Fine fabrics and furs created an atmosphere of luxury and could be easily transported. In most inventories of this period fabrics came at the head of the list and were the most expensive items. Precious plate of gold and silver, whether for the table or the chapel, was equally important as a status symbol. A man's possessions reflected not his personal taste but his 'estate', his rank.

The part played by the hall in the life of households throughout western Europe was so important that often the name for hall was applied to the house itself – thus in medieval France *salle*, and in Italy *domus*, meant hall or house. In England today many a house of certain status is still called The Hall.

Within the hall the fixed table of honour, or high table, stood on a platform at one end facing the screens. Here, on the chair of estate, sat the master, with important members of his household and guests. For the rest of the household tables would be ranged down the hall at right-angles to the high table. These consisted of heavy boards resting on trestles, held in position by sheer weight; they would be taken down at the end of the meal and stored away. They were relatively narrow, so seats were placed on one side only for easy service.

The high table, if not the others, would first be covered with a fine woollen cloth, probably scarlet, with embroidered edges reaching to the floor. Over this would be laid two white cloths revealing the edge of the undercloth. Since the bread trenchers used in the early Middle Ages were absorbent, two white cloths were necessary to protect the undercloth; they also tended to serve as napkins, for fingers were used freely for eating. The principal 'salt' was the first article to be placed on the table and the last to be removed. Next the drinking vessels were taken from the *dressoir*. People carried and used their own knives – the use of the fork spread slowly across western Europe and it was the thirteenth or fourteenth century before it reached France and England. Against the walls of the hall were benches or chests, all covered with carpets and cushions in a well-kept noble household. Cheerfully patterned draperies excluded draughts and added colour.

A similar piece of furniture to the narrow *dressoir*, of rough utilitarian character, was used in the service part of the hall, near the screens. Hutches (long side tables with cupboards underneath) were used for storing or dressing food in the hall.

In a princely dwelling there would be two halls – a Great Hall for banquets and grand occasions with adjoining it the state bedroom where the king or duke held state. The state bed was splendidly accoutred but it was never slept in. It might, however, be sat upon instead of a chair of state, and a new royal baby would be placed on it on its baptism day. A lesser hall, connected to the private bedrooms, was used for everyday meals and lesser functions.

A lord's immediate subordinates or guards often had beds in his room, and maids might sleep in the lady's room. They would use straw mattresses or, if they were fortunate, a truckle bed which could be stored away under the big bed. In *The Merry Wives of Windsor*, Falstaff's room at the Garter Inn is described as containing 'his standing-bed and truckle bed . . .'. It was unusual to have a bed to oneself in a medieval household – servants slept together, brothers and sisters, even complete strangers. One would expect to share a bed with a stranger in an inn. There was no false modesty – everyone slept naked.

There was little variety in medieval bedrooms. Apart from the bed and hangings there would be a chest and probably a chair and a perch, a rod on which to hang clothes. There might even be two perches – one for the falcons to roost on! Comfort and colour were added to the sparsely furnished room by the addition of rich hangings, cushions, rugs, painted walls and painted furniture.

A bed or *lit* at this time referred to the mattress and bedding – only the fortunate had a bedstead, and it was common for servants to sleep on pallets until the nineteenth century. There are no surviving bedsteads of interest earlier than the fifteenth century; one must refer to paintings for a knowledge of earlier styles. A twelfth-century bedstead was supported by four posts which usually rose about a foot above the bedding and were decorated with carving or bobbin turning, terminated with ball finials. A low railing held the mattress and bedding in place.

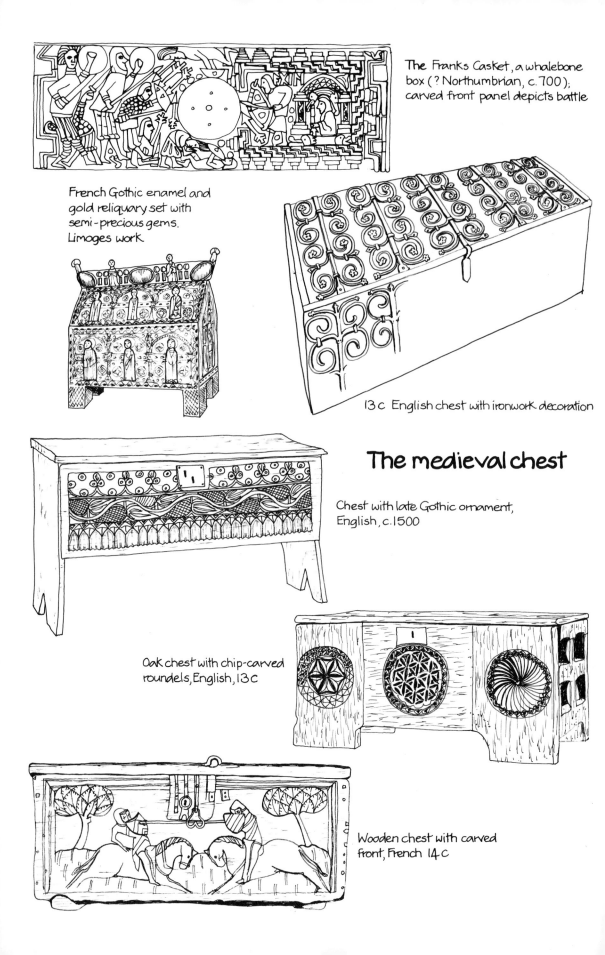

The Franks Casket, a whalebone box (? Northumbrian, c. 700); carved front panel depicts battle

French Gothic enamel and gold reliquary set with semi-precious gems. Limoges work

13c English chest with ironwork decoration

The medieval chest

Chest with late Gothic ornament, English, c.1500

Oak chest with chip-carved roundels, English, 13c

Wooden chest with carved front, French 14c

Curtains, slung on rails around the bed to form a private compartment in which the bed stood, were part of the bed-chamber, not the bed. In the thirteenth century the canopy or tester became an important part of the bedroom. At first it was slung from the ceiling and had no visual link with the bed. A half-canopy was used for persons of lesser rank. The quality of the bed-hangings and drapes and the kind of furs used could also denote rank. Even cradles could show the rank of the family – a noble baby would have two cradles, a cradle of estate for receiving visitors and a night cradle for the nursery.

The chest was the most common and most necessary piece of medieval furniture. In its most primitive form, apart from the hollowed-out log, it consisted of four vertical boards and a base, nailed or dowelled together, with a lid. This construction was improved by using two side uprights, into the upper part of which the front and back boards were housed, thus raising the base from the damp floor. Chests were used for storage and could also serve as seat, bed or table.

During the Romanesque period – the tenth to twelfth centuries – chip carving was a popular method of decorating chests. The most attractive were decorated with architectural motifs such as arcading. Chests were usually gaily painted. Iron parts, often needed to reinforce badly jointed structures or for added security, frequently became the primary decoration. In many cases the iron work was grander than the chest – the smiths turned their scrollwork into a work of art.

A simple box without projections was more convenient for travelling: this often had a domed lid to throw off water. Travelling chests had to stand up to very rough treatment packed on the backs of horses or slung under carts.

The *armoire* or aumbry was the medieval equivalent of the modern cupboard. It could be free-standing or might be part of the fabric of the building, constructed as the main body was built. It was basically a storage space, either shelved or unshelved, behind closed doors, usually monumental in style and decoration. Some had pigeon holes or drawers in place of shelves and some were fitted with perches to support vestments. One type with decoratively pierced doors was probably used for storing food. Of the very few that survive, most are found in religious buildings.

There were imposing thrones of stone, metal or wood, of architectural form, at this time, but the X-stool or fold-stool proved the most popular and indispensable form of seating in the Middle Ages. It was comfortable, light and easily trans- ported. A survival of the Roman curule used by magistrates, and still endowed with official dignity, it became the seat of kings, important laymen and ecclesi- astics. Added dignity was achieved by placing it on a dais with a footstool and comfortable cushions, probably with a canopy above. The misnamed 'Throne of Dagobert', which undoubtedly was the throne of one of the Carolingian rulers, was an imposing fold-stool of gilded bronze with claw feet and lions' heads at the top of the stretchers. In the twelfth century it was altered by Abbot Suger, who added a rigid back and arms. Thus adapted, with a fixed back and open arms and the addition of comfortable cushions, the fold-stool had evolved into an armchair.

Four-legged stools with turned or rectangular members were common, and forms and benches of similar construction were found in castles and merchants'

Rectangular bench throne with foot-rest; the high back, curved like a camel's hump with two heads, is elaborately draped (from MS at Trier, c.800)

Ceremonial seating

Throne chair of Emperor Otto III, in architectural style; late 10c

Bishop's throne, S. Italian Romanesque, late 11c, shows classical influence

Oak armchair carved with Gothic tracery, probably once part of a set of stalls. English, c.1250

Carolingian ruler's bronze folding-chair, so called Throne of Dagobert, early 9c; arms and back added in 12c

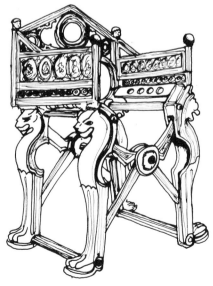

Decorated fold-stool from Styria, c.1200

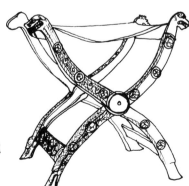

houses. The bench was considered superior to the stool or form, and was often used as a bed. Stone seats built into or against the wall were a common feature in religious buildings but were also found in domestic situations.

Improvements in carpentry technique came about very slowly in western Europe. Butt-joints and mortise and tenon joints secured by big nails were used until about 1200. As furniture making improved in the thirteenth century mortise and tenon joints secured by dowels became more common and dove-tail joints evolved. Iron reinforcements were no longer necessary in the Gothic period although iron trimmings survived to become an art form.

Oak was the most common wood throughout Europe; walnut was used to a lesser extent in Spain, Italy and France and softer woods in central Europe.

The invention of the saw-mill in Germany in 1320 contributed to the changes found in later medieval furniture, The hydraulic saw made it possible to saw boards, instead of splitting logs with an axe and adze. Craftsmen were now able to create lighter, more easily decorated furniture for which there was a growing demand. A technique, new to western Europe, was evolved in which thick hewn boards of great weight were replaced by rectangular frames made up of uprights and cross-rails, secured by mortise and tenon joints, into which thin panels were inserted. This type of framed construction could be adapted to any kind of furniture and also came to be widely used in northern Europe for covering interior walls, when it was known as wainscot.

Furniture reflected the changes that were taking place in medieval society in the fourteenth century. Peace had gradually been restored to Europe, and with growing trade, government became more centralized as it grew more complicated. Noblemen, like kings and princes, were moving around less and with fewer houses to support could concentrate their wealth upon those they retained. There was also growing taste for comfort among the wealthy merchants and bankers in the towns.

The hall, although still the most important room in the house, began to decline in importance as smaller rooms were added for specific uses. Furniture, no longer a fitting anchored to the wall, moved out into the room and acquired a new status. Fabrics and hangings became less important as the wood was increasingly revealed in furniture and wainscot covered the walls.

While these changes were taking place, the gothic style was gaining ground in western Europe. The word 'gothic' seems to have originated in Italy, applied as a term of abuse to the architecture of the Middle Ages, but by whom is not clear. It has been attributed to Raphael, Vasari and others. The style originated in twelfth-century France, spreading quickly across Europe, flourishing, particularly in the north, during the next four centuries. It reached its purest and most harmonious peak in France; in England it was simpler and less refined. The style never had much appeal for the Italians, particularly in the south. The classical tradition had never entirely disappeared in Italy, and the gothic style of architecture with its huge areas of glass was unsuited to the climate. Gothic design hardly affected Italian furniture – by the fifteenth century a revival of old influences was growing in Italy with the Renaissance.

Construction of medieval furniture

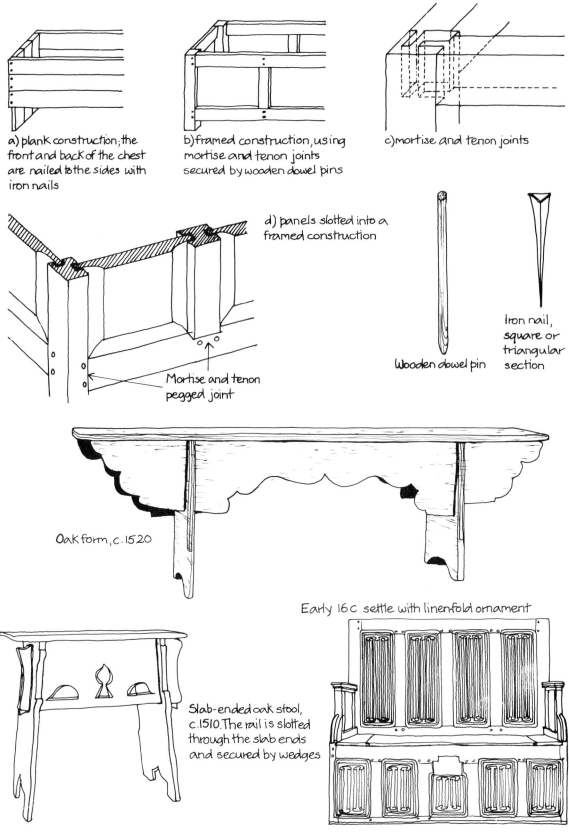

a) plank construction; the front and back of the chest are nailed to the sides with iron nails

b) framed construction, using mortise and tenon joints secured by wooden dowel pins

c) mortise and tenon joints

d) panels slotted into a framed construction

Mortise and tenon pegged joint

Wooden dowel pin

Iron nail, square or triangular section

Oak form, c.1520

Slab-ended oak stool, c.1510. The rail is slotted through the slab ends and secured by wedges

Early 16c settle with linenfold ornament

Monk seated on a folding stool with his writing slope resting on a table. Cupboards line the walls and rush mats the floor

Late medieval writing desk with ingenious mechanism for adjusting angle

Refinements in design

Typical 15c Flemish interior (from a painting attr. Robert Campin). Open-backed settle has back rail which can be swung over to the other side. Note x-form stool, and ewer and basin on cabinet

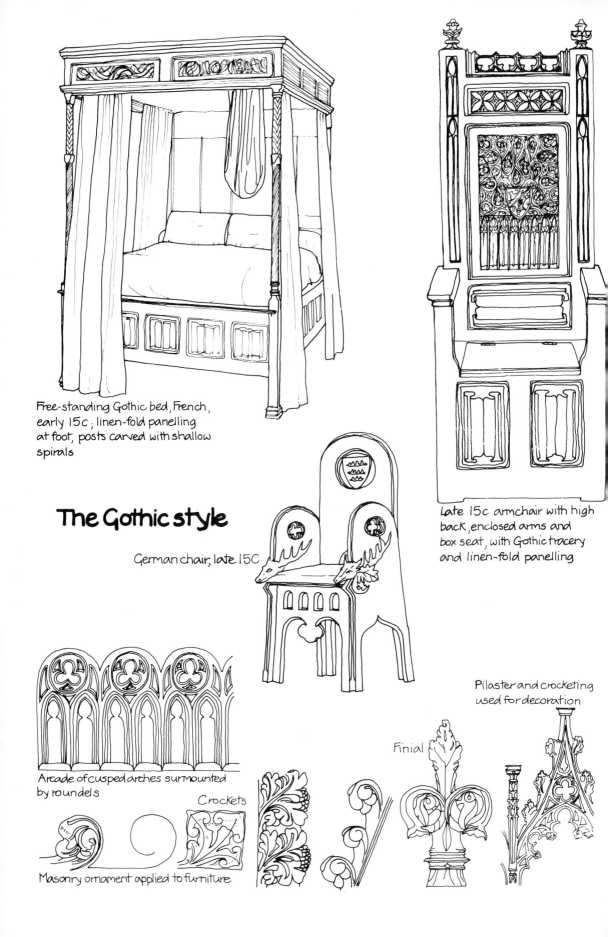

Free-standing Gothic bed, French, early 15c; linen-fold panelling at foot, posts carved with shallow spirals

The Gothic style

German chair, late 15C

Late 15c armchair with high back, enclosed arms and box seat, with Gothic tracery and linen-fold panelling

Arcade of cusped arches surmounted by roundels

Crockets

Masonry ornament applied to furniture

Pilaster and crocketing used for decoration

Finial

French throne chair,
late 15C

Elaborately carved
French dresser, c.1500

French Gothic chest in oak with fine iron lock-plate

15c English oak side table
supported on columns

A perch to hold clothes (early 16c)

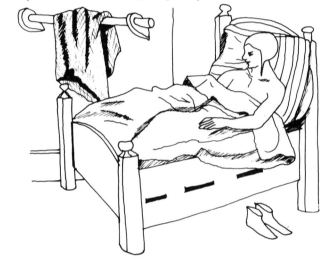

Stone sideboard or buffet
at Dirleton Castle, E.Lothian

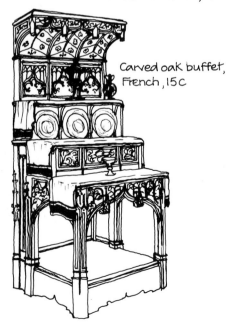

Carved oak buffet,
French, 15c

English livery or food
cupboard, c.1500

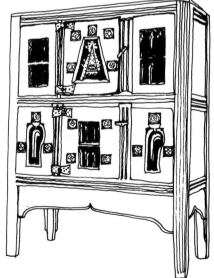

15c sleeping arrangements

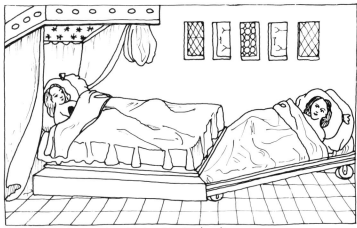

A valet slept on a truckle bed pulled out on wooden casters from under his master's bed

A settle used as a bed, and a small turned stool

Italian bedroom, from 'Hypnerotomachia Poliphili', shows classical influence. Note platform, and the chests ranged around the walls

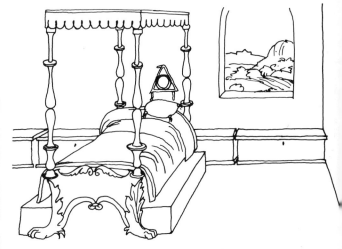

Royal bedroom enriched with hangings, 15c France; bed hangings tied up in bundles. The Queen sits on a day bed, her ladies on cushions

In the rest of Europe the development of gothic architecture was quickly echoed in furniture design. Since mason and carpenter worked side by side in the cathedrals and churches, there were many similarities between masonry and furniture. Wainscot was directly influenced by the mason, and all kinds of masonry decorations – cusping, crocketing, finials and pilasters – were adapted for furniture. Many pieces of furniture, particularly chests, had the appearance of miniature buildings. The infilling panels were elaborately carved with flamboyant tracery in the manner of soaring church windows. Linenfold panelling, introduced by Flemish craftsmen, became a most popular and easily adaptable motif for wainscot, chairs, benches and chests, both ecclesiastical and secular, and was produced cheaply and easily to satisfy the growing market.

Although master carvers were busily employed creating splendid choirstalls, screens and other woodwork in ecclesiastical buildings, the formation of guilds and the large number of specialist craftsmen during the gothic period indicate growing secular patronage. This in time led to a greater variety in the pieces of furniture made and the uses to which they were put. There was a wider choice of tables in varied sizes and shapes. A more elaborate buffet was developed with open shelves above, for displaying plate, a closed cupboard in the middle and a stand below; this was found not only in the hall but in the chamber, where important guests might now be entertained. Fold-stools, although still popular, were gradually giving way to chairs of estate – high-backed, panelled armchairs with box-like seats. The slab-ended stool made its appearance during the gothic period. It had a flat plank seat supported either side by slab-ends splaying outwards and was strengthened under the seat by a wide rail or stretcher which passed through slots cut in the ends and was secured by wedges. Long forms, virtually extended stools, were made in exactly the same way.

An early fifteenth-century innovation was the livery or food cupboard, with doors pierced in a tracery pattern for ventilation. One was often kept in the chamber for the relief of hunger during the night.

The bed became a free-standing piece of furniture rather than a fitting against the wall. The tester and curtains were supported by bedposts, now part of the bedstead, rather than suspended from the ceiling or wall. More attention was given to the wooden framework of the bedstead and exposed woodwork was decorated with carving. Since the chamber was used as a sitting-room, the bed came to be used as a couch from which to receive visitors. People of rank often received their guests in bed. The curtains at the foot of the bed were frequently looped up into pendant pear-shapes to allow more room during the day.

Even in the grander houses there was still no unity in the overall arrangement of a room – furniture seemed to be placed haphazardly with no precise location and with little concern for symmetry, even where wall decorations had been carefully considered.

The Renaissance

'The Renaissance' is the name given to a period in which the rediscovery of the ancient world was inextricably linked with the development of a new 'modern' society to replace medieval feudalism; a period of new ways of thinking, new values, new social and political habits and patterns of living which gradually spread throughout Europe. When Byzantium fell to the Turks in 1453, hundreds of Greek-speaking scholars fled to Italy bringing with them many old manuscripts and contributing to the revival of interest in classical art and culture which had begun in Italy early in the fifteenth century – in literature earlier than in the visual arts.

An added stimulus was the introduction of the printing press in the 1460s to Rome, Venice and Florence. Publication of the classics led to careful research of ancient texts; among Greek and Roman literature brought to light at this time was the manuscript of *De Architectura* by the Roman architect, Vitruvius. Printed first in Latin and then in Italian in 1521, it helped to spread a knowledge of Greek and Roman building methods. Every new investigation of classical remains fed the outburst of creative activity. The discovery of the stucco decoration of the Baths of Titus and the Golden House of Nero on the Esquiline Hill in Rome provided a whole new repertoire of ornament for the early sixteenth-century designers. The delightfully elegant human, animal, floral and grotesque motifs were not only used by mural artists but were seized upon by metal-smiths, potters, jewellers, and furniture and textile designers. The finest examples of the adaptation of this style for interior design are the painted stucco ornaments in the Loggie of the Vatican by Raphael and his students, and the interiors of the Villa Madama, Rome, by Giulio Romano and Giovanni da Udine.

Italy was advantageously situated at the heart of the greatest trading area of the Renaissance world. Ports like Venice and Genoa made the most of their trading opportunities, and inland towns such as Florence and Milan became prosperous as redistribution centres for goods from the ports and from northern Europe across the Alps.

The vast expansion of trade in the fifteenth century made merchants rich and powerful as never before. They built banks and exchanges and lent money for interest. Their patronage of the arts began to rival that of the Church. Having to some extent absorbed the old nobility and adopted their life-style, these new merchant princes had the money and the leisure to employ artists such as Michelangelo, Leonardo da Vinci, Raphael and Cellini. There was a new wave of building in the city states. Ambitious popes restored Rome's importance and drew families of standing to Rome to build new palaces within the city and villas without. The new patronage encouraged experiment and variety, fashions changed quickly, and display was lavish.

The new *palazzi* were grand, rather than domestic, in scale and design. The Italians did not need small rooms dominated by a fireplace as did their contemporaries in northern climes. They preferred lofty elegant spaces, and their artists were given free rein to create great houses which were to be the admiration of the world.

The early renaissance interior was often designed on the principle of a contrast between details of jewel-like quality (usually beautifully textured stone or stucco-work) and expanses of plain surface. Rooms were dignified and spacious with an aura of coolness. Classical detail was a delightful inspiration, not a model to be slavishly followed. After 1500, however, the designers' attitude became more academic. Italian furniture in the early fifteenth century was rich in detail and of large dimensions but rather sparsely distributed. The great families who employed the foremost artists of the day – architects, sculptors, fresco painters, smiths and jewellers – paid extraordinarily little attention to the design and positioning of their furniture. It was considered not as part of the over-all scheme but as something which might detract from the work of a great painter. It was mid-century before this attitude to furniture changed: only when classical rules of proportion and decoration were applied to its design was it considered part of the general decorative theme.

The most prestigious and elaborate piece of furniture of the Italian Renaissance was the *cassone*, the traditional marriage chest. Some of the most splendid came from Florentine workshops. By the beginning of the fifteenth century Florence, like most cities, was controlled by a small number of rich, influential families; a marriage was an occasion for great family display and *cassoni* played an important role as status symbols during the ceremonies. They were usually ordered in pairs and would often carry the armorial bearings of the intermarrying families, the bride's coat of arms on one *cassone*, the groom's on the other. Filled with the bride's trousseau and the portable part of her dowry, they were carried through the streets to the groom's *palazzo*. Since they played such a prominent and public role it was important that the design of these *cassoni* should be appropriately splendid.

The earlier *cassoni* were embellished with painted panels executed by the foremost painters of the day who were not embarrassed to use their talents for furniture decoration. Fifteenth-century painters and sculptors had not yet acquired the social status that a century later would make them consider such work beneath them. Botticelli, Uccello, Piero di Cosimo, Perugino and Donatello are all known to have painted *cassone* panels. The subject matter varied: scenes from

Decoration by Raphael in a Loggia of the
Vatican

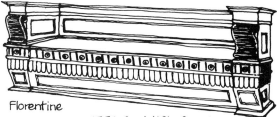

Florentine
cassapanca, c. 1550. Seat lifts for storage

The Nervi Cassone, Florentine,
late 15C, with painted panels

Carved walnut cassone 16C

Sgabelli: carved walnut
decorated with gilding,
Florentine c.1500

Savanarola chair, carved oak,
Florentine c.1550

Venetian centre table, carved and gilt

16c Italian carving
and inlay

Mirror frame, carved walnut,
late 16c

Inlaid marble table top on
carved and gilt base;
late 16c

the lives of Christian saints or from classical mythology (Piero di Cosimo's 'The Death of Procis' was one), battle scenes, tournaments, triumphal processions, and allegories representing the elements, seasons and virtues were common. Favourite subjects appear to have been those taken from popular vernacular literature such as the *Decameron*. Some *cassoni* had elaborately carved relief-work in gilt gesso with volutes and friezes of acanthus leaves, swags of fruit and flowers, putti and other classical decoration; others were decorated with intarsia, an elaborate kind of inlay.

During the sixteenth century the design of *cassoni* changed. A new type, of carved, polished wood without painting, gilding or inlay, came into fashion. This change was partly due to the growing importance of painters, who were no longer willing to paint furniture, and partly to changes in the layout of domestic interiors. *Palazzi* were growing increasingly splendid, their design and decoration were more carefully organized, and painters were occupied with the embellishment of walls and ceilings. The painted chest would have been eclipsed by this splendour – it had therefore to become a contrasting foil. It was also felt that painting would be out of place in the classical design of the new chests, many of which were modelled on ancient sarcophagi – classical both in form and decoration. In this elegant, more shapely form can be seen the prototype of the commode.

A *palazzo* would have a large number of more modest chests ranged around the walls, as well as in the traditional position at the foot of beds, for storing linen, clothes and household goods. They also made convenient seats.

The *cassapanca* was a development of the *cassone*. The addition of a back and arms converted the box seat into a primitive sofa. This prestigious piece of furniture was traditionally placed in the entrance hall; watched over by an armed guard, it held the owner's most precious possessions and served as a symbol of his wealth and status. It was the forerunner of the seventeenth-century sofa. Another piece developed from the *cassone* was the *armadio*, a small cupboard.

The cabinet made its first appearance in the sixteenth century. At first its outline and general design were suggested by Roman triumphal arches or temple architecture. This was later modified.

Chairs became more numerous as life became more sociable and intimate. Padded armchairs with high backs and knob terminals became common in larger houses. The lighter-weight, more easily movable chair was popular. The folding X-shaped chair had survived from the Middle Ages and now appeared in its most elegant and balanced form, called either a Savanarola or Dante chair in Italy, a Luther chair in Germany.

Another lightweight, mobile chair called a *sgabello* appeared towards the end of the sixteenth century. It was completely original in style, a stool with a deeply carved upright back; though rich and impressive, it was hardly designed for comfort. *Sgabelli* were clearly intended to accompany the very grand tables, closely modelled on ancient Roman patterns, which were becoming fashionable. Two or three heavy stone or wooden supports richly carved in animal or monster forms supported the table top, which in wealthier houses would be of finely inlaid marble. Wooden examples followed the Roman originals less closely; these were often in the Mannerist style, using flamboyant, rather contorted figures, half-animal, half-human, in agitated compositions.

Italian houses did not have separate dining-rooms until the nineteenth century – tables and light stools or chairs were set up wherever required. To replace the simple table draped with a cloth, carved wooden sideboards, usually monumental in scale and decorated with classical orders, came into fashion during the sixteenth century. Smaller hall tables were also made, supported on one central pillar, similar to the Roman stone tables.

The most magnificently designed room in the *palazzo* was the *studiolo*, or study – the master's 'inner sanctum', where he kept his collection of paintings, statuettes, books, manuscripts and other objects of vertù. The rich impression was, however, created by works of art rather than by the furniture, which probably consisted of only a Savanarola chair, a table and a candelabrum. There were no free-standing bookcases, and cupboards were built into the walls.

The mistress's haven was her bedroom. Here too the room was architecturally rich but sparsely furnished, probably with only a canopied four-poster bed on a raised platform, a chair and *cassoni*. Gay rugs enriched the marble tiled floor, and the walls were painted or covered with patterned leather or tapestry. Some beds were decorated with painted panels, but none have survived. By mid-sixteenth century, the Tuscan bed was more popular, particularly with the Florentines. It had an elaborately carved and gilded headboard and four twisted wooden columns topped by classical urns.

By the early sixteenth century the glass-makers of Murano had greatly improved the manufacture of mirror glass. Mirrors, hitherto very small, became much larger and more elaborately framed, and were ornamental and useful articles of furniture. Pictures, as distinct from frescos, were framed in a similarly rich manner.

Many new decorative techniques were introduced in Italy, particularly on more important pieces of furniture. Console tables, chairs and mirrors were often gilded – Venetian and Florentine gilders obtained an especially fine effect by laying the gold leaf on a red ground and highly burnishing the prominent parts. *Cassone* fronts were sometimes partly picked out in gold, which contrasted beautifully with the warm colour of the walnut or chestnut wood.

There was a revival of a type of decoration known as tarsia, intarsia or certosina, widely used for boxes and chests. It consisted of laying pieces of ivory or bone into an ebony or brown walnut surface in a geometric design. The name was supposedly derived from the Carthusians, who were very skilful at this work. The technique had developed into a minor industry towards the end of the fourteenth century, when makers of ornamental furniture began to copy the designs of marble mosaic work, forming similar patterns in coloured woods. Later craftsmen produced elaborate landscapes with houses, picturesque ruins, churches, figures and animals or still life pictures in this technique to decorate table tops, chests and the fronts of cupboards in the sixteenth century. With early intarsia work, the decoration was cut and laid into hollows gouged in the surface of the panel, piece

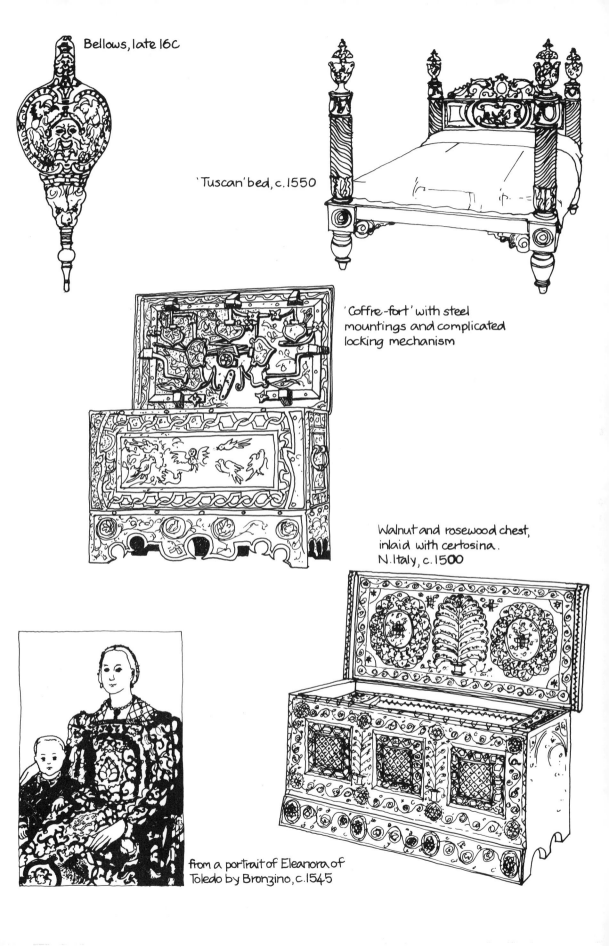

Bellows, late 16c

'Tuscan' bed, c. 1550

'Coffre-fort' with steel
mountings and complicated
locking mechanism

Walnut and rosewood chest,
inlaid with certosina.
N. Italy, c. 1500

from a portrait of Eleanora of
Toledo by Bronzino, c. 1545

by piece. As craftsmen became more skilful, veneers were applied. The lines left by the saw cuts were filled in with stained glue to give clarity to the design.

Pietre dure was another technique introduced into Italy in the sixteenth century. This was a form of inlay using highly polished marbles, pebbles, agate and lapis lazuli among other stones. As merchant princes vied with each other in increasing extravagance, all kinds of materials were employed for cabinets and chests. Carved ivory was used as a bas-relief; brass, silver, mother-of-pearl and tortoise-shell as inlay. Ivory was also used for inlay in elaborate arabesques.

The enrichment of chests with metal ornament reached a high peak in the sixteenth century. Beautiful mountings in iron, steel and brass were produced in both Italy and Germany. The decoration was bitten with acid to give the effect of being damascened. Highly complicated locks also helped to make these chests works of art.

To a visitor from anywhere else in Europe at this time, the Italian *palazzi* must have appeared overwhelmingly splendid, though to twentieth-century eyes they would seem sparsely furnished.

An interest in the Italian way of life and Italian ideas felt in France early in the fifteenth century was further stimulated when Charles VIII returned from his campaign against Naples in 1495. As well as a rich booty of paintings, fabrics and furniture, he brought back a team of architects, sculptors, scholars, interior decorators, goldsmiths, furniture-makers and gardeners with the idea of recreating the splendours of an Italian palace at Amboise. At first the impact of the Renaissance upon French design was superficial. Medieval pieces of furniture – the buffet, the chest and the throne-chair – were up-dated by the addition of classical motifs such as carved heads in medallions, grotesques and pilasters to the gothic form, often mixed with linenfold panelling and other gothic decoration. More decisive changes came about during the reign of François I (1515–47), who aspired to make his court an intellectual centre. Literature, architecture, painting, sculpture and the crafts were to flourish in the old medieval hunting lodge at Fontainebleau, which François decided to transform into a sumptuous palace. A great body of Italian and French artists, including Leonardo da Vinci, were drawn around him to contribute to the *château* and give birth to the famous School of Fontainebleau. Here, during the next three decades, a sophisticated decorative style developed in which forms were drawn out and contorted in the Mannerist idiom to achieve a dramatic effect, flouting the rules of the classical renaissance.

Two distinguished Italians, Rosso and Primaticcio, both of whom were architects, sculptors, painters and stuccoists, revolutionized interior design. Their frescos in the Italian manner for the walls of the royal apartments at Fontainebleau, framed and interspersed with large stucco decorations, created an entirely new concept of interior decoration. A whole new grammar of ornament was introduced – stylized scroll-work, garlands of flowers and fruit, draped and undraped figures, *putti*, chimeras, masks, etc. These motifs were eagerly adopted by the furniture makers.

Courtiers and nobles followed the king's lead, building and improving their *châteaux* and *hôtels* in the new Italianate style. This created a demand for luxurious, fashionable furniture, which in turn stimulated improvements in the technique of furniture making. The most important of these was the invention of the mitred joint (a corner joint made by cutting the two pieces of wood at an angle of 45°); because the joint could be concealed within the thickness of the wood, it became possible to cover large areas with continuous decoration without dividing the surface up into panels.

Carving became the most popular type of decoration for French renaissance furniture. Oak was replaced by walnut, a softer wood with a finer grain which was easier to carve. Its oiliness gave it a smoothness and a beautiful sheen similar to that of the renaissance bronzes so much admired in France. The importance of fabrics in interior design was now greatly reduced by the growing interest in carving.

It was Primaticcio who evolved a particularly French style of furniture. The full impact of his taste was felt about 1550, when the designer Jacques Androuet du Cerceau published a collection of engraved furniture designs. It is impossible to tell how much of his work was derived from furniture which he had seen in Italy, from the drawings and designs of other Frenchmen, or from his own imagination. His designs were certainly 'renaissance' with a vengeance – overloaded with antique ornament, acanthus scrolls, heavy swags, mythological creatures such as sphinxes, harpies, griffins, and long-limbed nymphs. It is hard to imagine that designs such as his cradle shaped like an angry griffin were ever built. Du Cerceau himself said he was only offering as many models as possible for craftsmen to interpret as they wished. Another book, *Livre contenant passement de moresques*, published in 1563, contained a selection of strap-work and arabesque designs. These pattern books helped to spread the court styles and must have been immensely useful for craftsmen in northern Europe whose clients demanded furniture in the new fashion.

A contemporary of du Cerceau, Hugues Sambin of Dijon, is usually recorded in furniture histories as the first French cabinet-maker. Although he was a woodcarver and an architect, and some buildings have been attributed to him, no single piece of furniture has been credited to him. His publication, *Oeuvre de la diversité des termes dont on use en architecture* consists of thirty-seven pages of fanciful term figures, all of very odd design. This is probably why a number of cabinets decorated with almost equally weird figures have been attributed to him (or to the Burgundian area) without any documentation.

In France the *dressoir* or buffet took pride of place, as the *cassone* did in Italy. In the late sixteenth century all the skill of the *menuisier* was lavished upon it. Its ancestor was the 'cup board' on which the drinking cups had been placed and the plate displayed in medieval times. It was used for a variety of purposes and was made in several versions. In the early part of the century the upper section was enclosed by two or more doors decorated with carved portrait heads in medallions, surrounded by wreaths of ornamental foliage. There were usually two drawers beneath. The whole was supported on columns or pilasters or an enclosed base, also with doors. From the reign of Henry II (1547–59), the *dressoir* became much

French Renaissance

Design for a cradle
or bed by du Cerceau,
c.1550

Design for a bed
by du Cerceau, c.1550

High-backed state chair
with semi-circular
pediment, Gothic and
classical motifs;
early 16C

Design for a table, du Cerceau

more architectural in design. Many examples appear to have been strongly influenced by the designs of du Cerceau and Sambin. There is some confusion of names at this time – this piece is often referred to as an *armoire*. The junction of the upper and lower parts was emphasized by a frieze in which one or two drawers were fitted. Gradually the *dressoir* became fully enclosed and made in two stages, and was sometimes called an *armoire à deux corps*. The upper part was smaller than the lower and was stepped back to emphasize the two-stage construction. In the seventeenth century, the upper part became as wide as the lower section and the piece became a full-length wardrobe.

The late-sixteenth-century *armoire* was richly carved with classical decoration in the Mannerist style, sometimes further enriched by inlaid panels of marble, precious woods or ivory. The verticals consisted of pilasters or carved human figures. The upper part was often surmounted by a broken pediment, with a figure in the centre.

The cabinet was a highly sophisticated version of the *dressoir* – only a few were found in France, as in Italy, in the sixteenth century.

The increasing taste for luxury in the sixteenth century led to the general adoption of the *table à l'italienne*, a monumental piece richly decorated with carving. The pattern books show various examples. The rectangular top rested at either end on massive supports carved in the form of mythological animals or human figures, fanning out from base to top and resting on scrolled bases linked by a stretcher. The space between stretcher and top was usually linked by additional carved decoration or arcaded columns. This very handsome piece was prominently placed in the centre of the room.

The draw-leaf table appeared at this time. Probably invented in the Netherlands, it became popular also in France and Britain. It was ideally suited for the less formal domestic scene. Capable of extension to twice its length, it fitted easily into the fashionable smaller dining-rooms. It had a framed construction of four turned legs linked by stretchers at the bottom and a frieze above. The table-top rested on this frame but was unattached. Underneath it at either end a leaf was concealed which could be drawn out, resting on sliding bearers. When both leaves were pulled out to their full extent the main table top dropped into position between them. This simple, easy mechanism proved so successful and popular that it is still in use today. The *table à l'italienne* was also sometimes fitted with extending leaves.

As tables became heavier, chairs on the whole became lighter. The heavier, immovable throne-chair still survived, updated with grotesques and pilasters, and the ever-useful X-chair was still popular, but new forms were making an appearance. With time on their hands for conversation, card games, music and other pastimes, the upper classes needed a lighter, easily-moved chair. The *chaise à bras* filled this need. Its seat rested on four columns joined together at the base by stretchers. The lowered back and arms were opened up, making the whole structure much lighter. The arms, often terminating in carved rams' heads, were gently curved to support the sitter's elbows.

Among chairs specifically designed for women (a sure sign of their rising status

Table à l'Italienne-top has extending leaves

French
Renaissance

Design for female term
figure-Hugues Sambin

Stucco and fresco by Primaticcio,
Palace of Fontainebleau

16C walnut buffet with carved ornament

Caquetoire or
gossip chair, late 16C

Carved oak cabinet, Henri II

'Armoire à deux corps',
carved in typical Mannerist
style, mid 16C

Death of Henri II, from a 16C engraving. Note carved
headboard and graceful caryatids supporting canopy

in society) was the *caquetoire*, more commonly called the conversation or gossip chair. It had a high narrow back, an unusual trapezoid seat, and wide curving arms designed to accommodate the wide skirts of the period. Though French in origin, it was much used in the Netherlands and, to a lesser extent, in Britain. Another seat modified for ladies' dresses was the back stool, a padded stool fitted with a low padded back, which later became known as the farthingale chair. At this time a seat without arms was considered a stool, not a chair.

The basic form of the bed remained that of the fifteenth century; it still consisted of a wooden frame with four posts at the corners supporting a canopy from which curtains were suspended. Costly fabrics were its main embellishment until mid-sixteenth century, when the structure of the bed itself became increasingly ornate. This was encouraged by the habit, adopted in polite society by perfectly healthy people, of receiving guests while lying in bed. Life at the French Court revolved around the King's bed rather than his throne. The bedposts became outrageously elaborate or were replaced by carved caryatids or Sambin terms; headboards became important features, covered in elaborate carving. The day bed was equally rich in appearance. Unfortunately few beds survive but engravings and paintings testify to their lavishness.

The Renaissance in France brought about outstanding changes in interior decoration, and in the form, decoration and use of furniture, but towards the end of the century the flame of inventiveness was burning low. It was not until the reign of Louis XIV that it was fanned to radiant life again.

In Germany it was the *Kleinmeisters*, the designers of ornament, rather than the architects or painters, who had the greatest influence on interior decoration and furniture. They followed eagerly the example of Italian artists and discarded gothic motifs in favour of those of antiquity. Their designs, either cut in wood or engraved in steel, provided patterns for smiths, wood-carvers, masons and furniture makers. There was an unprecedented demand for fine furniture as not only noblemen and courtiers but rich merchants and tradesmen took advantage of the more peaceful and prosperous times to build themselves splendid palaces or fine houses, both for prestige and for comfort. Furniture makers acquired a new status in society as furniture became a symbol of wealth. They practised a high standard of craftsmanship, employing fine woods, both indigenous and imported, precious metals, ivory and semi-precious stones.

Not all the work of this period in Germany is anonymous – some authenticated pieces have survived together with their creators' names. One designer, Peter Flötner of Nuremberg who was also a sculptor and carver, had been to Italy and was one of the first to introduce renaissance designs. His woodcuts, intended as patterns to guide builders and craftsmen, showed ornamental fillings for panels and architectural designs such as mouldings and doorways. Another artist and cabinet-maker is known only by his initials, 'H.S.'. Twenty-five of his woodcuts survive, showing designs for beds, cupboards and wall-panelling, all architectural in style and making use of columns and pilasters.

There is a marked difference between the renaissance furniture of north and south Germany. Northern furniture resembled that of the Low Countries, northern France and England; in the south it was similar to that of northern Italy. The difference lies mainly in the use of materials. Hardwoods, mainly oak, predominated in the north. Oak lent itself to sturdy construction and to deep carving in the manner of the stone masons. Craftsmen tended to work in an architectural manner, treating the framework of a piece of furniture in a way that emphasized its structural quality. The non-structural infilling panels were considered suitable areas for carved decoration. Romayne work – carved heads in profile within medallions, in the Italian manner – was a popular form of decoration in north European countries. In the south softwoods such as pine and larch were common, and inlaid or painted surfaces were favoured. Any carved decoration was very shallow and it was customary to cover the structural uprights and cross pieces with flat carving of interlacing vine leaves or twisted ribbons, and to leave most of the panel surfaces plain.

By mid-sixteenth century both north and south Germany had evolved a 'classical' style, German craftsmen were becoming renowned for their technical skill and the quality of their products, and a large market abroad was opening up for smaller pieces which could be easily exported. German cabinets and small writing desks for the newly-educated were in demand. The misnamed 'Nonsuch' chests so popular in England originated in Germany at the end of the century. At one time these architectural compositions of fanciful, pavilion-like buildings topped with towers and pinnacles, carried out in various coloured woods, were believed to illustrate Henry VIII's Nonsuch Palace at Cheam and to have been made in England. The pattern was applied directly to the body of the chest.

By the end of the century a particular type of cabinet, made solely as a prestige piece and commissioned for many foreign palaces, was produced in southern Germany. These cabinets became works of art rather than ordinary pieces of furniture, involving the skills not only of cabinet-makers and turners, but of gold- and silversmiths, ivory carvers, sculptors and jewellers. They were used for housing small curios, scientific instruments, writing materials, cutlery, jewelry, etc.

Although the Netherlands and Spain were closely linked by their Hapsburg rulers and both came under renaissance influence in the sixteenth century, their interiors and furniture differed greatly in style. Spanish décor was grimly austere but enlivened by furniture made of lavishly rich material, whereas the interiors and furniture of the Netherlands blended to create an intimate, friendly atmosphere.

The homes of the rich citizens of the Low Lands shown in contemporary paintings have shining tiled floors and furniture of panelled construction designed to harmonize with the wall panelling. The popular closet or cupboard-bed, built into a corner of the room, was an important feature. Its decorative treatment echoed that of the panelling on the walls. There was obviously a high standard of comfort, but interiors appear modest in comparison with the splendours of Italian domestic settings. The gothic style lasted well into the second half of the sixteenth century; the distance from Italy and the bitter religious struggles which split the country meant that the transition to new styles was very gradual. Several

Decoration from pattern book of Wendel Dietterlin

The Renaissance in Germany

Cupboard design by H.S. c.1530-40

16C metal coffer

Design for a bed by Peter Flötner, c.1530

Design for inlay, Peter Flötner, 1533

Strap-work

Portrait medallion of type
Known as 'Romayne work'.
N. European style

Romayne work

The 'Erasmus' chest, said to
have been made in his memory;
his portrait is on the left.
Basle, c.1539

Shallow carving

Softwood cupboard with
shallow carving. S. Germany

Ebony cabinet with silver-
gilt mounts. S. Germany,
c. 1600

Designs for cabinet, tables and chair from 'Verscheyden Schrynwerck' by Paulus Vredeman de Vries, 1630

Flemish design

from engravings by Crispin de Passe

Flemish cabinet carved in ebony, late 16C

publications helped to spread the new ideas. Lucas van Leyden produced sheets of engravings of renaissance ornament for craftsmen in the 1520s. A Flemish translation of the Italian architect Serlio's *Fourth Book of Architecture*, published in the thirties, encouraged the notable designer, architect and painter Johannes Vredeman de Vries to produce several publications: the first, relating to classical architecture, was followed by designs for ornamental motifs and his own furniture designs in 1580. His son and collaborator Paulus published two similar books, incorporating many of his father's designs, in 1630. These were to be a major influence on the furniture makers of the Netherlands until well into the seventeenth century. Johannes has been criticized for his over-elaborate ornament – he had a tendency to leave no area undecorated, but his designs for everyday furniture were sparsely decorated in the Mannerist style.

Lighter chairs of open construction were introduced from France, among them the *caquetoire*. Under the influence of French styles in the latter half of the sixteenth century a more sculptural treatment was introduced for better-quality furniture. Walnut began to replace oak for finely carved pieces. The French designer Hugues Sambin's florid designs appealed to Dutch taste, and monumental two-stage cabinets with elaborate grotesque figures became fashionable. Towards the end of the century, however, the excessively fussy decoration of all types of furniture began to lose favour, foreshadowing the more restrained taste of the seventeenth century.

Spanish furniture of the Renaissance period had a distinctive style; certain pieces of furniture and forms of decoration are so uniquely Spanish that they are usually referred to by their Spanish names. *Mudéjar* work was a typical form of Spanish decoration named after the Mudéjares, Moorish people who had remained in Spain after the fall of Granada at the end of the fifteenth century, who were highly skilled at decorating furniture with elaborate and often very small geometric designs executed in marquetry of coloured woods and ivory or bone. *Mudéjar* work was a favourite method of decorating the ever-popular chests and the new cabinets which were coming into vogue. Another form of ornament, particularly applied to cabinets, was plateresque marquetry, a type of inlaid decoration of very fine scrolls of flowers and leaves with small vases in the classical manner, also used by silversmiths – hence the name 'plateresque'.

Relief-work of wrought or pierced iron, or occasionally silver, laid on to a red velvet ground, was another distinctive Spanish embellishment. Sometimes carved boxwood ornament would be backed by velvet in a similar fashion. Spain also produced the finest leatherwork in Europe at this time, known as *guadamecil*. Originally a Moorish speciality, it was elaborately tooled and often coloured, a rich material for upholstery. It was unique to Spain and highly prized in all European countries.

A unique piece of Spanish furniture was the *vargueño*, a chest with a fall front which opened to reveal a number of small drawers, the faces of which were richly decorated. The fall front rested on pull-out supports and could be used as a writing surface. A stout loop handle of iron, decoratively treated, was housed at either side for carrying. The *vargueño* was frequently used as a travelling chest for

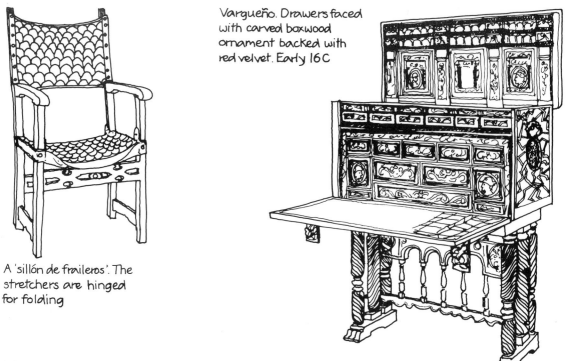

Vargueño. Drawers faced
with carved boxwood
ornament backed with
red velvet. Early 16C

A 'sillón de fraileros'. The
stretchers are hinged
for folding

Unique Spanish pieces, 16-17CC

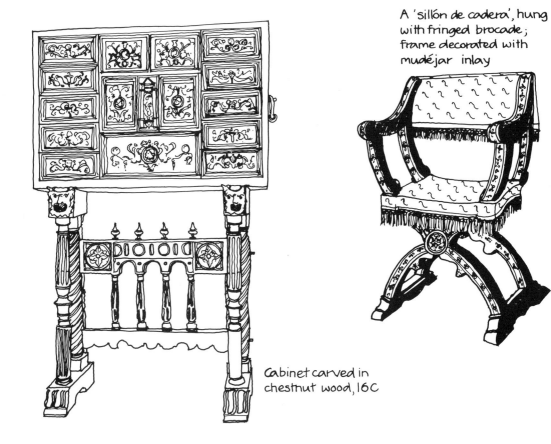

A 'sillón de cadera', hung
with fringed brocade;
frame decorated with
mudéjar inlay

Cabinet carved in
chestnut wood, 16C

small valuables and as a mobile writing desk. It rested either on a *pie de puente* (a trestle stand) or a *taquillón* (a chest of four drawers). Occasionally a side table was used as a support. Draw-tables also appeared in Spain; most had a distinctive Spanish look, the table tops resting on *pie de puente* supports.

Some distinctive Spanish chairs were developed at this time. A sophisticated version of the X-chair or hip-joint chair, the *sillón de cadera*, usually decorated with *mudéjar* inlay, was introduced early in the sixteenth century. The most characteristic Spanish chair appeared in mid-century, a new type of armchair known as the monk's chair or *sillón de fraileros*. It was plain, strong, and of open construction for lightness and mobility. The seat and back were covered with hide fixed by large decorative nails or with a textile with fringed borders. The fabric was the main decorative feature, but the deep front stretcher was fretted or carved. A similar chair was made without arms for the use of women when large hooped skirts came into fashion.

The Renaissance came later to England, on the cultural fringe of northern Europe, than to countries nearer Italy. It pleased Henry VIII to pose as an enlightened renaissance prince and patron of the arts: Holbein and John of Padua were encouraged to come to England and many Italian and Flemish craftsmen were employed on the King's and Wolsey's palaces. But the Italian influence was transient – Henry's break with Rome in 1535 severed direct contact with Italian classicism. It was from the Protestant Low Countries and Germany that future cultural contacts were to come. There were strong religious and commercial ties between England and the Netherlands during the late sixteenth and early seventeenth centuries. The persecution of the Protestants brought thousands of refugees to England. Many houses in the south-east, within easy reach of London, were decorated by Flemish craftsmen. Furniture was imported and, probably far more important, the pattern books of men like de Vries of the Low Countries and Wendel Dietterlin of Germany were brought into the country.

During the Tudor period Italian ornament had been applied to a gothic framework – the basic method of furniture construction was still 'frame and panel'. The new repertoire of ornament consisting of Romayne work, scrolling or arabesque work, and the vase and the dolphin motifs, was used in combination with gothic decoration such as the linenfold panel and Tudor roses. Romayne work was very popular – the medallion heads either represented gods and goddesses or sometimes the owner and his wife, shown in profile surrounded by wreaths. They were often grotesquely rendered. The motifs became merged into a native style but the true classical spirit was not assimilated.

The rich and florid Flemish Renaissance design which followed was admirably suited to Elizabethan taste for ostentatious display. Characteristic of Anglo-Flemish work was the over-elaboration of ornament which left few undecorated areas on any piece of furniture. The most distinctive kinds of decoration were strapwork (a pattern of interlacing strap-like bands and scrolls which developed in the Netherlands and was used extensively on sixteenth- and seventeeth-century furniture in northern Europe) and running and formal flower patterns;

Spanish splendour

Silver table, late 16-early 17C

Charles V's sedan chair, probably made in the Netherlands. Movable back and uprights form canopy if required

English Renaissance

Cabinet in classical architectural style, like a miniature gateway

Carved oak panelling from a 16C house, with 'Romayne' medallion heads

inlay work; and bulbous ornamentation on the legs of tables, cupboards and bed supports. These bulbous forms also appeared on Dutch and German furniture but they were less gross and were undecorated. The cup-and-cover variation, so called because it was shaped like a fat vase with a lid, was unique to England. It was usually carved with foliage and surmounted by a crude Ionic column, and the bulb was often so big that it could not be cut from a single piece of wood. Terminal caryatid figures were another feature of this style, very crudely carved in comparison with their Flemish counterparts.

The great new houses of Elizabethan England and the more modest manor houses with large, lofty well-lit rooms, are evidence of the country's growing prosperity. This new domestic comfort was not limited to one class: William Harrison in his *Description of England* (1577–87) remarks that even farmers were able 'to live wealthie, keep good houses and travell to get riches' and to 'garnish their cupboards with plate, their joyned beds with tapestries and silk hangings, their tables with carpets.'

As the size of great households gradually decreased in number, the layout of the English house changed considerably. The hall declined in importance as it ceased to be the main meeting place of the house and became a reception area. The family ate in a smaller dining parlour, the servants in their own hall. The dining-table moved to a permanent position in the middle of the room and became more elaborately embellished in accordance with its new status. Since a smaller table was needed most of the time, the draw-table with pull-out leaves was popular. With the table no longer against the wall, benches became inconvenient and were gradually discarded in favour of chairs.

The main reception rooms moved to the first floor and with plenty of space available for entertaining, relaxing and exercising in the new Great Chamber and Long Gallery, furniture no longer had to be ranged against the wall or moved from room to room. There was a growing demand for a wider variety of furniture – small tables, many chairs, court cupboards, etc.

After the Spanish conquests in Mexico and Peru, a steady flow of silver (acquired legally or by piracy) into England led to a greater use of silver plate, which was displayed on court cupboards in the Parlours, Hall and Long Gallery. In the Elizabethan household the prestigious position held by the *cassone* in Italy and the *dressoir* in France was given to the court cupboard, a piece unique to England, consisting of two or three open shelves designed to hold the family plate. The supports were either shaped like heraldic beasts, or were of bulbous form. Drawers were often fitted into the upper and lower friezes. One version had an enclosed compartment with either straight or angled sides between the top and middle shelves. Court cupboards were usually very ornate pieces, often inlaid. The origin of the name is a little uncertain – it may have derived from the French for 'short' since they were rarely more than four feet high. It was the end of the century before the cupboard in its modern form, enclosed by doors, appeared.

The Great Bed of Ware, celebrated for its gigantic proportions, is also a fine example of the lavishly carved decoration liked by the Elizabethans. The wooden tester had by this time become very heavy and was often supported on two large

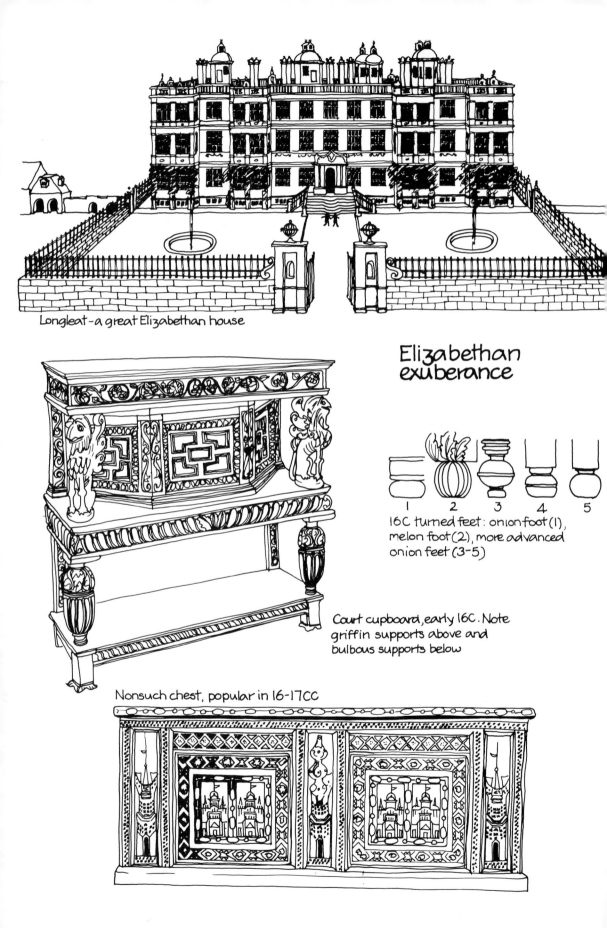

Longleat - a great Elizabethan house

Elizabethan
exuberance

16C turned feet: onion foot (1),
melon foot (2), more advanced
onion feet (3-5)

Court cupboard, early 16C. Note
griffin supports above and
bulbous supports below

Nonsuch chest, popular in 16-17CC

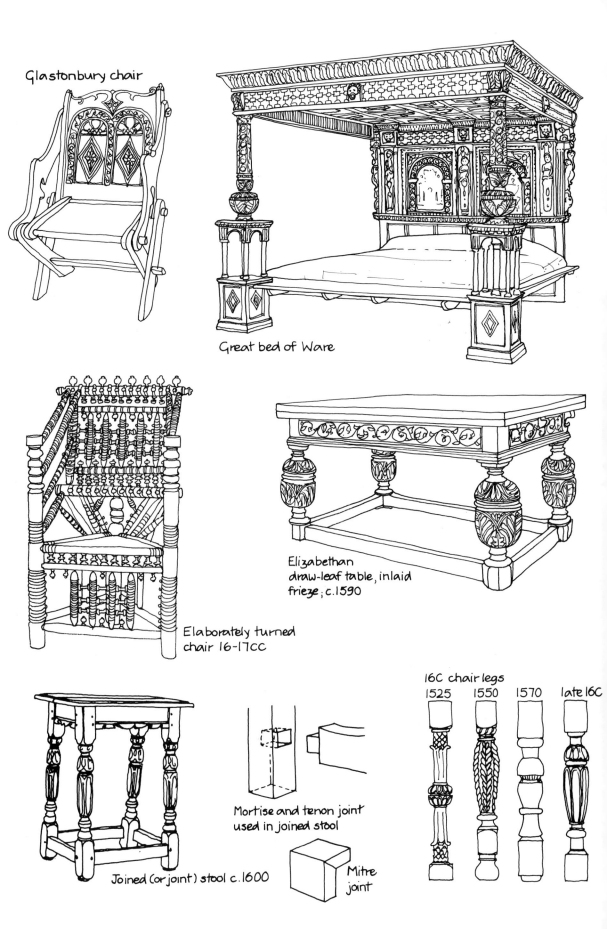

Glastonbury chair

Great bed of Ware

Elaborately turned chair 16-17CC

Elizabethan draw-leaf table, inlaid frieze; c.1590

Joined (or joint) stool c.1600

Mortise and tenon joint used in joined stool

Mitre joint

16C chair legs

1525   1550   1570   late 16C

posts which stood clear of the bed frame at the foot. At the head it rested on an elaborately carved headboard, eliminating the need for posts. Inlay was also a favourite form of decoration for headboards. Not all beds of this period were canopied. A simpler bed was made with a panelled headboard and turned balusters and rails at the foot, closely following an earlier type.

Following the continental pattern, the traditional panel-back chair took on a new look – the panels were removed from below the seat and arms to make a lighter structure, and the back was raked for comfort. When chairs and stools were constructed with an open framework, joiners employed turners to decorate the legs of these pieces. The four-legged joined stool replaced the early type with solid end supports during the latter part of the sixteenth century. Matching sets were housed under the dining table when not in use. Turners were also responsible for the turned or 'thrown' chairs used in farmhouses and smaller homes, and in the kitchens of large houses; these grew increasingly elaborate – some were 'turned all over'. Ladies favoured the French *caquetoire* and the back stool introduced from the Low Countries.

By the end of Elizabeth's reign richly upholstered chairs were becoming plentiful. Few have survived since they were made of beech, a perishable wood. Chairs of X-form were common. Their frames were completely covered with silk or velvet trimmed with fringes, glued down and secured by ornamental gilt pins. The seats consisted of loose cushions supported on webbing strung between the side rails. A new form of X-chair was also developed, known as the Glastonbury chair because it was mistakenly supposed that the prototype belonged to an Abbot of Glastonbury executed in the reign of Henry VIII.

The Elizabethans appreciated rich upholstery, tapestries and carpets. Carpets from India and Persia were hung on the walls, laid across tables, buffets and chests, but only put on the ground for very special occasions such as a royal visit. A carpet placed on furniture was called a 'borde' carpet; one on the floor was a 'ffote' carpet. Rush matting was the usual floor covering. A favourite material for upholstery and carpeting, which appears to have been made only in Britain, was Turkey work. Strands of wool were drawn through a linen backing to form a pile, in an attempt to imitate the carpeting imported from the Middle East.

Baroque grandeur

Italian supremacy in furniture design lasted well into the seventeenth century. With the introduction of the baroque style, and the increasing search for comfort linked to a desire for lavish display, furniture became sumptuously ostentatious.

'Baroque', a term now used to describe the arts of the seventeenth century in general and those of Italy in particular, was originally a derogatory expression derived from 'barroco', a misshapen pearl, implying decadence and over-exuberance.

Baroque architecture, although still based upon the classical orders, interpreted them far more freely than before. Its characteristic features were curving plans, flowing surface forms, and interiors in which naturalistic painting and sculpture were cleverly blended with the architectural forms to suggest infinitely grander, more celestial spaces. Its character is deeply rooted in the society which created it. The Roman church felt the need for splendid buildings to counter the threat of the Reformation – the nepotistic Popes of the seventeenth century were cultured, vigorous men with a love of the arts and a passion for building. In the secular field building was encouraged by a number of emergent, extremely wealthy, families – some owing their riches to papal patronage, others to trade. The spirit of competition engendered among old and new families expressed itself in the increasing splendour of their palaces and the churches to which they gave their patronage, and the baroque style was admirably suited to a pretentious display of wealth and power. This is clearly evident in the state apartments of their *palazzi* where the *saloni*, suites of reception rooms on a grand scale, were given over to display. The gallery, formerly found only in the palaces of ruling princes, became the most splendid room. Here under frescoed ceilings were arranged the family collection of paintings and antique sculpture amid furniture designed for display rather than use – fine cabinets of precious materials and heavy marble console tables. Other major rooms contained similar furniture together with great gilded throne-like chairs, many of them masterpieces of wood-carving with legs in the form of human figures holding up the elaborately scrolled arms. Grotesque masks and playful cherubs, intertwined with foliage and drapery, formed the under-framing and the cresting. Though not specifically designed as a part of the over-

Italian baroque

The nuptial chamber at La Rocca, Soragna, showing typical palace furniture

Bed in alcove of nuptial chamber, La Rocca, has appliquéed velvet hangings and gilt canopy

Mirror with glass frame decorated with wheel engraving

Side table with stone top and carved,
gilt caryatid mermaid legs; early 17C

Technical skill in the 17C

Candlestand of carved and
gilt wood, c.124 cm. Florentine
c.1685

Cabinet in veneered ebony with inlaid
'pietre dure', made by Domenico Cucci
at Gobelins

17C console table, gilded wood
base, mosaic top

all decorative scheme, furniture was made with the scale of these rooms in mind. Out of context its massive size and elaborate decoration look absurdly pretentious, but under lofty painted ceilings and against walls covered with gilded leather, luxurious silk from Lucca or cut velvets from Genoa, it fulfilled its function. Lavish hangings and upholstery contributed to the total splendour.

The Italian bed now depended upon fabrics for its luxurious appearance. The four-poster went out of fashion and was replaced, in grander houses, by the half-tester covered in silk with appliqué decoration. The structure of the bed was completely hidden beneath fabrics – if any woodwork showed it was gilded.

The genre paintings of Pietro Longhi show how everyday life was led in the smaller, more modest rooms on the floors above the grand *saloni*, and the simpler traditional furniture made for daily use.

Of the grander furniture, the console or side table was the most distinctive innovation. A top of rare and brilliantly coloured marble rested on a massive, elaborately carved and gilded base. Favourite motifs for these supports were fat, wriggling cherubs, mermaids, tritons, negro slaves, shells and dolphins, eagles, luxuriant foliage and hook-like scrolls. The total effect was monumental and restless. The carving was executed in great depth and almost became sculpture; indeed, the greatest furniture makers of this *métier* were well-known sculptors. The most renowned, Andrea Brustolon, carved sets of chairs, tables and *guéridons* or candle-stands for the richest patrician families. His best-known work, the 'negro suite' executed for the Vernier family, still survives in Venice; the arms and legs of the chairs are made of curved tree branches wreathed with creeper, supported by small negro boys with lacquered heads. Matching *guéridons* are held by muscular negro slaves with chains around their necks, each standing on three Chinese dragons.

The console table was a prestige piece with little functional use. Linked with a large mirror, another innovation of this period, it helped to create a more completely integrated style of interior design. The glass makers of Venice, Murano and Altare produced mirrors well suited to the baroque style, usually with two frames – an inner one of coloured glass which followed the rectilinear shape of the mirror, and either a cresting or an entire outer frame of elaborately pierced and flowing decoration.

Large mirrors had a practical as well as a decorative value. During the day they brightened rooms by reflecting light from the windows; at night they magnified the light power of candles and lamps. The reflected area gave an impression of added space and multiple reflections from several mirrors produced a feeling of unity. Inspired by these effects, designers began to integrate furniture and interior decoration in a way never attempted before.

The high cost of good-quality mirrors made them prestige pieces in the great houses of Europe, and their lavish use in Italian *palazzi* inspired, among other mirrored rooms, the Galerie des Glaces at Versailles.

By now, Italian workshops were famed throughout Europe for their marble inlay work. The Grand Duke of Tuscany had set up a state workshop in Florence, the Opificio delle Pietre Dure, which conducted a flourishing export trade in

17C chairs

Part of a suite made for
Pietro Vernier by Andrea
Brustolon. Carved boxwood,
partly lacquered; tapestry
seat and back

Less ostentatious
chair of type used
in middle class
houses

17C chair legs: farthingale,
knobturning, spiral twist,
baluster

Type of chair used
in the smaller rooms
of grand palaces

Carved and gilt throne
chair

coloured inlay table tops, mainly to France where supporting wooden table frames were made. *Pietre dure* panels of marble and semi-precious stones, sold in large quantities for making up into cabinets, were 'collectors' pieces' for rich travellers on the Grand Tour. The English diarist John Evelyn, on such a journey, purchased nineteen which were made up into a cabinet on his return. Transport problems made it a common practice to move panels unassembled. Although most panels had a flat surface some were made in relief, usually depicting rounded fruits in various colours, sometimes garlands of flowers, and occasionally cherubs' heads. A cheaper, but very effective, substitute for *pietre dure* was *scagliola*. In this process powdered marbles were used as tempera to paint designs into marble or composition slabs.

Table tops mounted on carved and gilded wooden supports were produced in both *scagliola* and *pietre dure* for palace reception rooms. The gilt supports of tables, cabinets and chairs, all of boldly carved sculptural form, show a strong family likeness. Even smaller objects such as candle-stands were elaborately carved.

During the seventeenth century the cabinet replaced the buffet as the major prestige piece, and became a fashionable and highly prized article in every country, designed specifically for display. It consisted of a rectangular upper stage, made up of many small drawers which were sometimes hidden behind doors, mounted on a stand, and the most precious materials and most up-to-date techniques and innovations were lavished upon it. In the seventeenth-century craze for collecting, cabinets made useful repositories for some of the objects amassed by their owners – precious stones, shells, geological specimens, manu-scripts, coins, medals, memorabilia and – a particularly feminine passion – oriental china. The splendour of the cabinets rivalled their contents in value.

The growth of trade with distant lands proved to be the greatest incentive for change in the seventeenth-century interior: not only pieces of furniture but also a wide variety of exotic woods were imported, which stimulated innovations in design. The re-introduction of ebony into Europe at this time gave furniture makers a new problem: besides being expensive, ebony was also a hard, brittle wood unsuitable for use in the solid; before it could be employed successfully, it was necessary to rediscover the technique of veneering. Once this had been solved the much prized cabinet was the obvious piece to embellish with veneers of ebony and other exotic woods. Woodworkers who used this specialist technique became known as cabinet-makers, whether they applied it to cabinets or to other fine pieces; in France they were called *ébénistes*, an indication of the popularity of ebony.

The veneer panel perfected by cabinet-makers was based on the use of glue prepared from horses' hooves. When set hard this glue is still slightly elastic and will give a little when subjected to strain. The cabinet-makers' panel was made up of strips of a soft straight-grained wood such as lime, $\frac{3}{4}$in. (20mm) thick by $\frac{3}{8}$in. (10mm) wide, glued together along their length to make up a board or core $\frac{3}{4}$in. (20mm) thick. This was planed on each side with a toothed plane to provide a 'key' for the glue. A fairly thick veneer was then glued to either side with its grain running across the strips. The surface of these veneers was also planed with the toothed plane so that a thinner finishing veneer could be glued to each, with its grain running in the same direction as the softwood strips. The completed panel was just over an inch (c.30mm) thick. There would be no movement in such a panel if the damp were kept out by polishing, which also brought out the grain and the colour of the wood. Polishing had not become a common practice until painted furniture went out of fashion in the sixteenth century. It was probably the accidental result of efforts to protect the wood by rubbing with nut, poppyseed or linseed oil or beeswax (which gave oak a beautiful golden tone). Walnut was polished with its own oil.

A later advance in cabinet-making technique made possible a panel curved in one direction like a cylinder: the core strips were cut slightly wedge-shaped in section so that when glued together side by side they formed a curved board. The veneers were cut thin enough to bend easily and the glue held the assembled board in shape when it had set. The next problem was to make a board that curved in two directions like the section of a globe. The core strips were cut into short pieces with ends as well as sides slightly wedge-shaped. These were glued together in a brickwork arrangement so that no join appeared above another. Curved panels gave the cabinet-maker much greater freedom of design. He was able to get away from rectangular shapes and employ flowing forms.

Veneering made it possible to use irregularly grained woods selected for beauty rather than strength. The veneer need not be laid on in a single sheet – woods of different colours, even ivory or mother-of-pearl, could be cut into irregular pieces and fitted together like a jig-saw puzzle to build up a pictorial design: this kind of decorative veneering is called marquetry. All kinds of ornament were incorporated into the delightful floral marquetry of the late seventeenth century – vases of flowers standing on little tables, vines, birds, butterflies, acanthus leaf scrolls, ribbons and bows. Arabesque marquetry, which came a little later, consisted of fine tendril-like scrolls arranged symmetrically, often called 'seaweed' marquetry.

Parquetry is a type of veneer made up of geometric patterns by laying small squares of contrasting woods side by side in the manner of a parquet floor. By careful contrast of grain and colour a very convincing three-dimensional effect can be built up.

Especially popular was oyster veneering, using the grain pattern of smaller branches of timber; walnut and laburnum gave particularly beautiful patterns. Transverse saw cuts produced 'roundels', and slices cut at an angle provided an oval pattern similar to an oyster shell; both cuts showed the 'fan' of the grain to the best advantage ('faneer' was the earlier word for veneer). 'Roundels' and 'oysters' were arranged in radiating circles and geometric patterns. Rich 'burr' or 'burl' veneers, with a tightly curled grain, were obtained from walnut and elm by cutting across the grain from the root area of the tree or from the junction of a branch and the trunk.

Cross-banding – a veneering band of a contrasting colour used as a border to the ground veneer, with the grain running outwards towards the edge – was a simple but effective way of adding interest to a large area of plain veneer. The two veneers were usually separated by a fine inlaid line of light-coloured, or

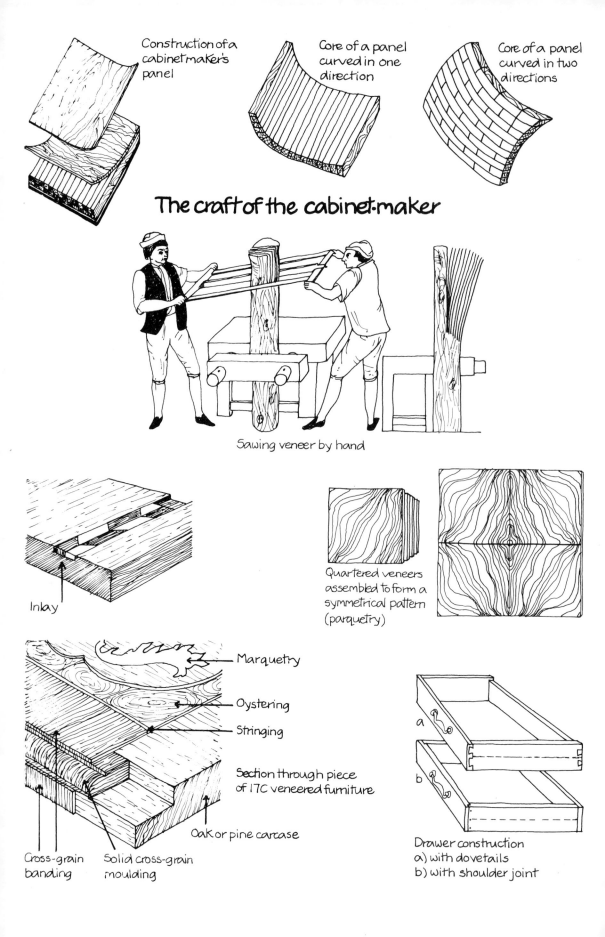

Construction of a cabinetmaker's panel

Core of a panel curved in one direction

Core of a panel curved in two directions

The craft of the cabinet-maker

Sawing veneer by hand

Inlay

Quartered veneers assembled to form a symmetrical pattern (parquetry)

Marquetry

Oystering

Stringing

Section through piece of 17C veneered furniture

Oak or pine carcase

Cross-grain banding

Solid cross-grain moulding

Drawer construction
a) with dovetails
b) with shoulder joint

occasionally black, wood called stringing. Cross-banding was often used as a frame for more decorative marquetry panels. Bandings were sometimes cut and arranged to create a feather pattern known as feather or herring-bone banding.

Furniture imported from India introduced European craftsmen to the use of cane for the backs and seats of chairs. This proved very popular – it was lighter, cheaper and more durable than other available materials. Its lightness made chairs portable and its resilience provided greater comfort. The upper classes tended to despise caned chairs because of their cheapness, but their usefulness eventually found them a place in the greatest apartments.

Other imports such as Indian painted hangings and needlework and hand-painted wallpapers from China inspired imitation – usually on a less professional level. Women in many English country houses produced delightful embroidered Chinoiserie designs, of Indian winding-tree patterns, exotic birds and dragons, mixed with very English flowers, for bed-hangings and spreads and curtains. They were even tempted to try their hand at lacquering (japanning) in the oriental manner, encouraged by a pattern book, *A Treatise of Japanning and Varnishing* by Stalker and Parker, published in 1688. Japanning was considered a social accomplishment suitable for young ladies.

The introduction of lacquerware, imported in the form of chests, cabinets and panels for screens, had an enormous impact upon European furniture design. Panels were usually cut up and adapted to make tables, chests, cabinets and mirror frames. There was hardly a great house in Italy, France, England, Germany or the Netherlands without at least one piece of lacquer work. Some rooms, it was said, were 'overlaid with varnish more glossy and reflecting than polisht marble'.

The oriental cabinet was similar in form to the European type, having a number of drawers enclosed behind doors, the whole covered in lacquer. Cabinets arrived without bases and were usually mounted on ponderous gilt or silver baroque stands with which they had little stylistic sympathy but which neverthe-less contributed to the splendid decor of the rooms in which they stood.

Since the oriental cabinet-makers did not satisfy all the furniture needs of a European house, certain enterprising merchants sent out furniture patterns to be copied in the East. Unfortunately eastern cabinet-makers were less skilled than those of Europe. Occasionally unpainted furniture was shipped out to be lacquered, but this costly practice died out as soon as European lacquerers perfected their skills and could satisfy their discerning patrons. Lacquering soon became a profitable industry with centres in London, Venice, Berlin, Spa near Liège, and the Gobelins factory. Since it was impossible to import the resin from which the true oriental lac was made, European craftsmen laid numerous coats of a varnish made of shell-lac or gum-lac upon a prepared ground of whitening and size. The decorations were outlined in gold size, built up with a composition of gum arabic and sawdust, then coloured, polished and gilded with metal dust. The surface was later burnished. The finished product was not as hard and glittering as the oriental but European lacquer has surprisingly stood the test of time better than its model.

The fashion for lacquer provided European craftsmen with a new repertoire of fanciful designs which introduced a lighter touch to baroque rooms, helping to pave the way for the rococo style which followed. Its influence can be noted particularly in the work of some of the French designers.

The long period of civil and religious upheaval in France caused an unproductive period for the creative arts at the end of the sixteenth century. Henry IV (1589–1610) initiated a revival of craftsmanship by bringing to the Louvre, in 1608, Flemish craftsmen skilled in Italian techniques and familiar with veneering, intarsia and inlay. Marie de Médicis employed Italian workers to provide her with the luxuries of her native land and introduced ebony furniture to France. Court fashions were thus infused with the taste of baroque Italy, and until the establishment of the Gobelins factory in 1662 there was a constant infiltration of foreign craftsmen.

When Cardinal Mazarin died in 1661, Louis XIV, who had reached his majority two years before, took over the goverment of France. He sought a way to encourage the arts and French industries and at the same time provide himself with a suitably magnificent setting to impress the rest of Europe with France's power and civilization. Colbert was responsible for establishing in 1662 the *Manufacture Royale des Meubles de la Couronne* at Gobelins, to be devoted to the manufacture of all the luxury arts, but its success was entirely due to its first brilliant director, Charles le Brun. He brought together all the best foreign and native talent in the country to create new standards of taste and craftsmanship in an entirely new French style. The setting up of this establishment was a major event in the history of the French decorative arts. A cohesive style was developed under Le Brun's guidance – nothing was undertaken at Gobelins without his approval. He provided designs for most of the decorative arts produced there – furniture, sculpture, architectural decoration, tapestries, door-furniture, goldsmithing, etc. He was probably the last great artist who did not consider it beneath him to spend the major part of his time designing for the industrial arts.

Le Brun was able to impose a restrained and classical style of symmetrical form on the productions of Gobelins – no mean accomplishment considering that many of the craftsmen had been trained in the restless baroque manner of Italy and elsewhere. The first formidable task that awaited the *Manufacture* after its foundation was the interior decoration and furnishing of the new Palace of Versailles. It was to be a palace of unrivalled splendour, regardless of cost (which proved to be unparalleled in history). Unfortunately only a fraction of the original productions of the *Manufacture* survive. However, some idea of the range of the Gobelins output and the superb quality of its products can be gained by studying the famous tapestry (in the *Mobilier National* museum in Paris) which shows the King visiting the factory in 1667. Workers are depicted displaying their mosaic and 'Boulle' tables, unveiling a superb cabinet, staggering under the weight of great silver vases and plate, and unrolling carpets for his inspection.

Charles le Brun, aptly named *Premier Peintre du Roy*, successfully created a national style which provided a suitable décor for the royal palaces and the King's majesty – a style emulated and disseminated throughout Europe. The

Italian influence in France

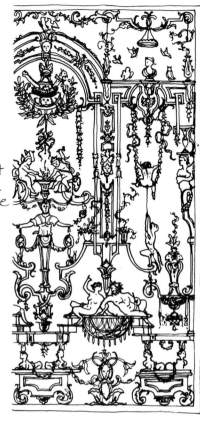

from a sheet of designs by court
'ornemaniste', Jean Bérain père.
Monkey shows oriental influence

Cabinet given by Louis XIV to Charles II of
England. Marquetry of coloured woods with
painted perspective view of Versailles in centre

Designs for sideboards, urns
and a candelabra by J. Bérain

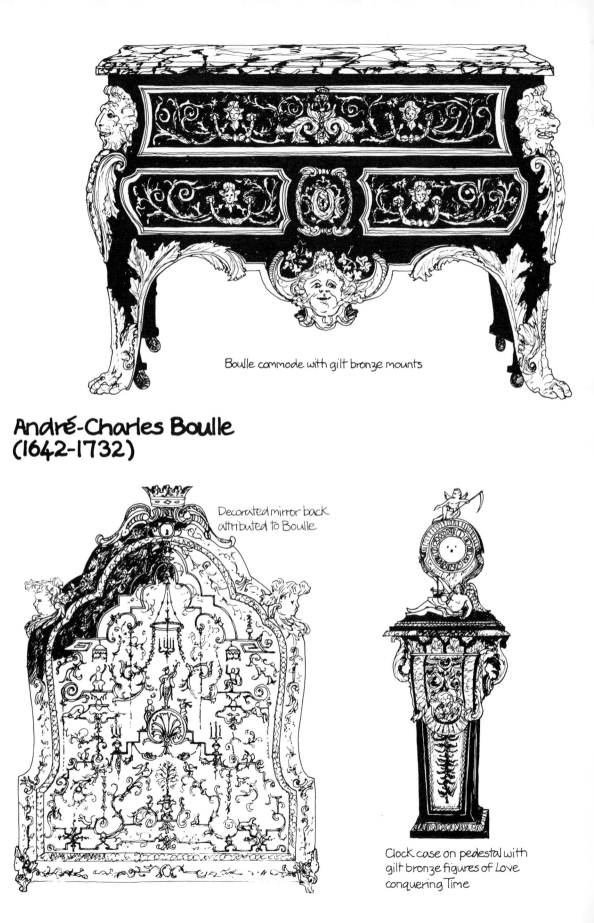

Boulle commode with gilt bronze mounts

André-Charles Boulle
(1642-1732)

Decorated mirror back
attributed to Boulle

Clock case on pedestal with
gilt bronze figures of Love
conquering Time

'integrated interior' which designers had been working towards in the Italian *palazzi* was perfected by Le Brun. The painted ceiling, the mouldings, the panelling, the hangings, the furniture and *objets d'art* were all considered as parts of a unit, each designed to blend with or complement the rest. Large mirrors played their part. A mirror factory established by Colbert invented in 1688 a method of casting large sheets of glass which made possible the glittering extravagance of the Galerie des Glaces at Versailles.

Le Brun designed a number of motifs which he combined with renaissance motifs. Each new motif was a reference to France or the King; the fleur-de-lys, the cock, the two interlacing Ls, the sun-burst and the Apollo's head symbolizing the Sun God. Louis's martial victories were commemorated with stuccoed trophies and painted ceilings – Versailles was a symbol of his power.

After the death of Le Brun in 1690 a new architect and designer, Jean Bérain, came to the fore. He introduced a lighter, gayer style of linear arabesques, combining the grotesques of antiquity as used by Primaticcio at Fontainebleau and Raphael at the Vatican with all sorts of oddities – chinoiseries, Chinamen, monkeys. These charming designs, which heralded the rococo style, spread through the field of decorative art and in particular influenced the first great French cabinet-maker, André Charles Boulle (1642–1732), who gave French furniture a national character. Until Boulle, French furniture had no distinctive style – it was a mixture of Italian and Dutch ideas.

Boulle is famed for the brass and tortoiseshell marquetry to which he gave his name. These materials had been used by Italian craftsmen since the sixteenth century but Boulle used them in an highly intricate and original way. His decorative panels were prepared by gluing together thin sheets of tortoiseshell and brass. A paper pattern was pasted to the top surface and the design was cut out through both layers with a fretsaw. The layers were then separated and the pieces combined to provide one panel of tortoiseshell ground inlaid with brass, called *première-partie*, and one of brass inlaid with tortoiseshell known as *contre-partie*. These designs were then glued with great care on to plain carcases. Pairs of wardrobes, cabinets or commodes might be decorated, one with *première-partie*, the other with *contre-partie* marquetry; or first-part and counterpart panels might be used for the outside and inside of doors. Those parts of the furniture not covered in marquetry were veneered with ebony. The colour was sometimes enriched by laying red foil under the tortoiseshell, the metal was often engraved. Silver, pewter, horn, ivory and mother-of-pearl were introduced into some pieces. The drawback to this technique was the difficulty of keeping the expensive materials firmly fixed to the carcase. Each reacted differently to atmospheric change and there was a tendency for them to lift. To counteract this and to protect vulnerable corners Boulle attached elaborate gilt bronze mounts (ormolu) which, with gilt handles and hinges, also enriched the pieces. So superb was Boulle's craftsmanship that he could model, cast, chase and gild his own mounts, thus assuring that the products of his workshop were of the highest standard.

Boulle's style is probably seen at its best in his wardrobes, which were new and favoured articles of furniture at this time. They are of severe architectural form in

91

State bed-end of
Louis XIV's reign

French splendour and comfort

Early 18C wardrobe-ebony
with Boulle marquetry;
probably from Boulle
workshops

Simple gilt wood chair
enriched with
upholstered Utrecht
velvet

Late 17C dress with long,
lean look and baroque
gentleman's dress, c. 1660

Comfortable wing chair
'en confessional';
walnut with velvet
upholstery, after 1673

the manner of Le Brun. The dark ebony and shell are a marvellous foil for the bright brass inlay and gilt bronze mounts. They must have glowed splendidly against the white and gold panelling and the marble walls of the royal palaces.

Boulle received commissions for bookcases with glazed doors, cabinets for medals and coins, and various versions of the bureau, writing table and desk, an indication that the pursuit of learning and the collection of antiquities and books was once more considered a worthy occupation for the nobility. The bureau had appeared at the beginning of the seventeenth century as a table fitted with narrow drawers; by mid-century it had become an eight-legged desk with a narrow central drawer and three drawers each side. Boulle also developed the commode, which began to replace the cabinet. His first step was a version of the bureau, with only two long drawers; his next, to satisfy the new fashion for less severity, was modelled on the elegant curved form of the ancient sarcophagus, and named a *commode-tombeau*. The final version heralded the form that was to become fashionable in the eighteenth century.

Boulle's decorative marquetry was applied at times to floors and even to walls. Contemporary sources describe floors inlaid with tortoiseshell and brass at the Louvre and at Versailles.

The most extravagant Gobelins furniture was that made of silver, a luxury without precedent in Europe. A detailed description of the contents of the Palace of Versailles appeared in the *Mercure Galant* in May 1682, shortly after the Court had moved in. Almost all the furniture in the Galerie des Glaces, the Salon de la Guerre and the King's bedchamber was of silver, as was much of the furniture of the other state rooms. Even mundane objects such as ewers, braziers, firedogs and irons, wall-lights and tubs for orange trees were cast in this valuable material. Seven years later Louis's military campaigns brought France to the verge of bankruptcy and most of the silver furniture was melted down. Ironically, some survives in other countries whose rulers modelled their courts upon Versailles.

At this time there was not only a move towards unified rooms and purpose-planned furniture, but a rationalization of the uses of different rooms – libraries, dining-rooms, etc. – varying according to the stratum of society involved. Court life was dominated by etiquette. Life in the palaces and grand houses of Europe followed the pattern established at Versailles, where people lived in apartments consisting of a suite of rooms, each room leading into the next until the last and principal room, the bedrom, was reached. The bedroom, with its Great Bed, still dominated social life at Court and it was still customary to receive visitors in bed. Throughout the seventeenth century the bed remained a most imposing piece of furniture, sumptuously upholstered and draped with hangings which completely concealed the structural framework.

The use of chairs at the French Court was still dictated by etiquette and was the cause of much discontent. Well-upholstered chairs with ample, low seats, higher backs and curved arm rests provided greater comfort than hitherto. A new winged armchair, which hid the occupant's face and became known as *en confessional*, was a forerunner of the eighteenth-century *bergère*.

The development of the Northern Netherlands during the seventeenth century was an extraordinary phenomenon. With Spanish domination at last destroyed, the Republic of the United Netherlands, an exceptional form of government for this time, was established. Mastery of the sea made Holland a wealthy country and this period of prosperity led to a flowering of the arts – the 'great century' of Franz Hals, Rembrandt and their school. A strongly indigenous style of domestic architecture developed; quietly elegant, comfortable houses sprang up in the Hague and along the canals of Amsterdam and Utrecht – pleasant settings for the prosperous merchants. Power was in the hands of the merchant class, into which a successful trader or artisan could move, and which dominated taste and fashion. The interiors of Vermeer and De Hooch were typical: chequered marble floors, plain walls with a few paintings, tall latticed windows, plain beamed ceilings, and beautiful furniture – unostentatious and orderly, yet rich.

Dutch furniture makers developed the use of veneers and excelled in marquetry using exotic woods, tortoiseshell and mother-of-pearl brought back from the East by enterprising Dutch merchants. They initiated French and English craftsmen in these techniques – many Dutch cabinet-makers were working in both countries. Towards the end of the century, however, the Dutch, inspired like the rest of Europe by the splendours of Versailles, accepted the French as arbiters of taste.

When the revocation of the Edict of Nantes in 1685 legalized the persecution of Protestants, many French Huguenots fled to the Protestant states of Germany, Switzerland, Holland and England. Most important among the emigré designers was Daniel Marot, who became architect and designer to the Stadtholder of Holland, William of Orange, later to become William III of England. Marot developed into an impressive designer of the domestic arts. William and Mary employed him, both in Holland and in England, mainly for interior decoration; in England he designed rooms and furniture for Hampton Court Palace. Following precedent, he published a collection of engraved sheets of ornament and furniture designs which influenced English craftsmen. A particular style of chair, with a high arched back elaborately fretted and carved and a distinctive leg of the inverted cup type, bears his name. However, it is probably in the area of upholstered beds that his influence in Holland and England was strongest. He realized that a stunning effect of opulence could be achieved (at comparatively little expense) with upholstered bedheads and an abundance of drapery. He excelled in the use of flounces, tassels, fringes and elaborate pelmets on canopies that soared up to the ceiling, topped by clusters of ostrich feathers.

The baroque style had been slow to make an impact on English furniture. It had begun to replace renaissance design during the first half of the century, but the disturbances of the Civil War, followed by Cromwell's Protectorate, hindered progress. Shortage of money and the Puritan dislike of ostentation kept furniture simple. During the first years of the century the arts prospered. The Mortlake tapestry works had been established in 1619 on James I's recommendation, and Charles I made them a gift of the famous Raphael cartoons, now housed in the Victoria & Albert Museum, London. Charles, a great patron and collector of the arts who employed Rubens and van Dyck, had gathered together some fine

From 'At the linen closet' by Pieter de Hooch –
a typical Dutch middle class home, mid 17C

17C table legs

Middle class styles

Oak gate-leg table with
egg-and-cusp turning.
English, mid-17C

Table settle with unusual
under-framing; back
folds over to form table top

Simple form of bedstead,
1700, follows an earlier
pattern

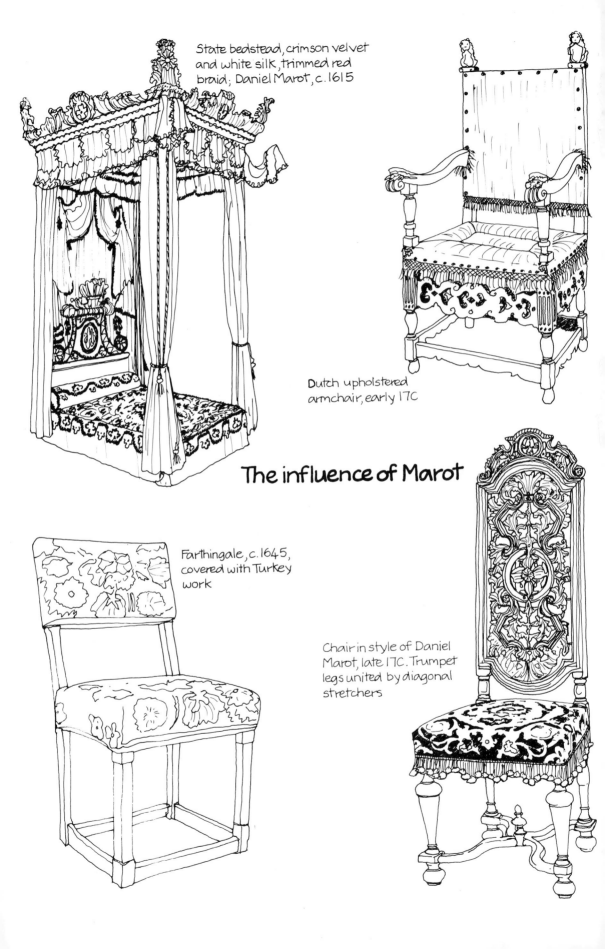

State bedstead, crimson velvet and white silk, trimmed red braid; Daniel Marot, c. 1615

Dutch upholstered armchair, early 17C

The influence of Marot

Farthingale, c. 1645, covered with Turkey work

Chair in style of Daniel Marot, late 17C. Trumpet legs united by diagonal stretchers

furniture, probably imported from the Continent. Normal items of furniture were made in England but luxuries such as cabinets and mirrors were imported. Apart from minor details, domestic furniture was still Elizabethan in character, though the detailing was a little finer, the carving less exuberant. Supporting members, for example, continued to be bulbous in form but the turning was fined down and carving omitted, until simpler baluster forms evolved.

The panel-back armchair survived, sometimes with a cresting at the top and decorative ear pieces each side; but more comfortable upholstered furniture was gaining favour. Many farthingale chairs and X-shaped armchairs with matching footstools were made, completely covered in fabric with decorative fringes attached by gilt nails.

One of the first fully-upholstered settees with a padded seat and back appeared at Knole c.1620. It had hinged, cushioned headrests attached to each arm, the angle of which could be adjusted by a ratchet to adapt the settee to a day-bed. It is not a particularly comfortable piece by today's standards, but for its time it was a luxury. A modern version of this, known as the Knole settee, is still made today.

Although the typical Jacobean bedstead continued to follow the Elizabethan pattern, the completely upholstered bed had arrived in the grandest households. Matching sets of stools and chairs were often made in the same expensive fabrics.

Coffers or travelling chests were used also for domestic storage within the house. They were usually of pine, covered with leather and studded with brass-headed nails in an intricate pattern, which not only strengthened the chest but made it an attractive piece to have in a living room. Coffers and traditional chests often had a small lidded box at one side, to hold articles such as gloves or sweet-smelling herbs. But the chest was an inconvenient method of storage – to reach something at the bottom the entire contents had to be disturbed or taken out. It became customary to arrange articles in tills or boxes within the larger chests, though it was still inconvenient to take something from one of the bottom boxes. Eventually the front of the chest was removed so that the boxes could be pulled out along grooves; handles were fitted to the boxes to facilitate this and the 'chest-with-drawers', later to be known as the chest-of-drawers, had arrived. The chest then began to decline in popularity. An intermediate step was a chest combining a box above with one long or two smaller drawers below known, because of its hybrid character, as a 'mule' chest – today it is usually called a dower chest.

The construction of drawers was at first fairly crude: the front was joined to the sides by a shouldered joint and held by nails. On better quality furniture dovetail joints were in use well before the eighteenth century in most countries. The drawer sides were grooved to slide on runners until the 1690s when the runners were set below the drawers.

With the restoration of the monarchy, new ideas were injected into the domestic arts. Charles II had acquired a taste for luxury and comfort during his exile in France and Holland. On his return to England the richness of the baroque style went with him and was eagerly adopted and to a certain extent tamed by English designers. His Portuguese wife Catherine of Braganza, and later William of Orange, reinforced the continental influence. The Restoration

James II oyster walnut and
floral marquetry chest of drawers,
cross-banded. c.1685

Lacquer cabinet with stand
and crestings of carved gilt wood,
c.1680

The 'Golden Age'

Long-case clock with
marquetry case made by
Edward East, London, c.1675

Veneered cupboard decorated
with three tones of walnut
oystered parquetry in floral
sunburst pattern. Netherlands,
c.1675-1700

Door of English long-case
'grandfather' clock c.1685.
Walnut ground decorated with
'seaweed' marquetry

English comfort

Cane arm-chair, carved with 'boyes and crowne' device of Restoration period

Settee in carved walnut and cross stitch needlework, English, c.1690

Carved wood truss by Grinling Gibbons

English 'sleeping chair' with adjustable back, c.1675

Knole sofa, with hinged and cushioned headrest attached to each arm; early 17C

was a period of rising national prosperity induced by growing trade and colonization and the flamboyant taste of Charles and his luxury-loving Court were eagerly adopted by aristocrats, rich landowners and wealthy merchants as an inevitable reaction to Puritan austerity.

The Great Fire of London in 1666 gave fresh impetus to the furniture industry. A vast quantity of replacement furniture was needed, and the development of new styles and the use of different materials were stimulated by the new building patterns for well-proportioned houses of brick and stone with large sash windows and light, airy rooms. The old oak furniture was too heavy and large for the elegant interiors of painted pine panelling and white moulded plaster ceilings. Oak went out of fashion, to be replaced mainly by walnut. Joiners gave way to cabinet-makers as veneering, marquetry and parquetry became popular. The cabinet was the important prestige piece in Restoration England. It was generally based on French and Dutch models but one feature, the introduction of a shallow drawer with a convex front into the frieze under the cornice, was an English innovation.

The exuberant spirit of the time is seen in the design of chairs. They were usually of elaborately carved walnut. 'Barley-sugar twist' turning was popular for the uprights, and the front legs, whether turned or scroll-shaped (another innovation), usually had a slim carved stretcher between them which matched the elaborate cresting rail. The device of a crown supported by cherubs often found on the cresting rail and stretcher was said to celebrate the restoration of the monarchy – but it was also popular in Holland. Although not applied to furniture design, the work of the great wood-carver Grinling Gibbons greatly stimulated English carving and raised the craft to a high standard.

Chair backs and seats were usually of cane mesh. Day-beds with cane platforms and adjustable backs were often designed to match sets of chairs. Upholsterers complained bitterly against the use of cane for chairs, although richly upholstered chairs were a feature of late Stuart furniture. Some were fitted with wings to repel draughts and some had ratchets for adjusting the back.

The chair back had grown gradually higher since the ruff was no longer worn, early in the century. The William and Mary period saw the production of some of the highest chairs ever made in England, echoing the exaggerated height of the wigs and headdresses of the period. The backs were sometimes as much as two and a half times the height from seat to floor. In spite of such exaggerations, a new feeling of restraint entered into the furniture of this period. Cabinets and mirrors also had a tall, lean look but the decoration was more restrained. Marquetry designs became quieter, less elaborate, using one or two muted shades.

The gate-leg table was a popular and useful item of furniture from the early seventeenth century. The fold-over gate-leg, forming a half-round table when closed, opening to a full circle with the leaf supported by a swinging gate, was common in France, Britain and the Low Countries. By mid-century it was superseded by the conventional gate-leg with two drop leaves. The draw-leaf table was equally popular.

To overcome the shortage of wood after the Great Fire, timber was imported from Norway, at that time tied politically to Denmark. To pay for the timber the English exported furniture to Denmark where it was much admired, particularly the chairs, and English design continued to influence Scandinavia until the early nineteenth century.

American furniture, from the early days of colonization, had a remarkably distinctive quality, although it followed the changing styles of Britain. Because it was necessarily functional it had a consistent simplicity. Out of this grew pleasing proportions and clean lines. The early settlers in the 1620s brought little with them. Once their small stock of provisions was used up they survived on what they could wrest from a wild unexplored territory and the sea. They had to hew their land for cultivation and their timber for houses and for most of their furniture from a dense, primeval forest. A chest to hold clothes and other personal belongings was probably the early colonists' only piece of furniture. A bed would have been a pallet of dried grasses and a heap of skins on the floor. Other basic pieces would have been knocked up when time allowed. None of this early furniture has survived – the earliest pieces made in America date from the second half of the century.

Colonization had been encouraged to promote trade – to acquire new materials and a market for manufactured goods. But it proved impractical for settlers to rely on goods from home. Before the end of the seventeenth century, in spite of regulations laid down by companies and nations, local craftsmen were making furniture, pewter and silver goods of quality.

The early furniture which survives was based on English Jacobean models of Anglo-Flemish renaissance form and decoration and of middle class taste. Most settlers came from provincial homes and would have been unaware of smart London fashions. It often took a decade or more for the styles of the capital to filter through to the English provinces, so it was little wonder that fashions might be popular in New England several decades after they had first evolved in London. Nevertheless, since the large colonial towns were sited near the ocean and had direct access to London, they were constantly exposed to ideas coming from the capital and other fashionable centres of Europe.

By the late seventeenth century there were substantial houses in New England built in the English medieval manner, very different from the wigwams and wattle-and-daub cabins of the first settlers. The Keeping Room illustrated on page 102 is typical of the early colonial parlour-cum-dining-room, dominated by the fireplace, with low-beamed ceiling and small windows with small panes of glass or semi-opaque oiled paper. There were few furniture forms. Chests and cupboards for storage were the only large case pieces and had the most distinctive appearance of all New England furniture, unlikely to be confused with similar pieces from any other country. One kind of decoration consisted of strips of moulding applied to the front of the chest, dividing it up into panels in shapes such as a modified cross or hexagon. Split turned wooden spindles and bosses were often applied to the spaces between the panels. A number of these chests are thought to have been made by the joiner Thomas Dennis, working in Ipswich, Massachusetts.

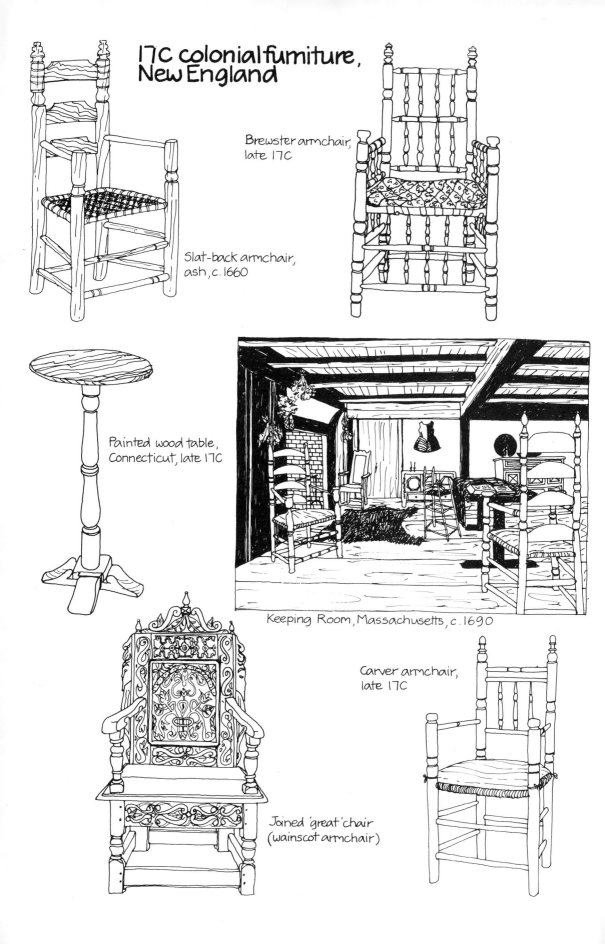

17C colonial furniture, New England

Brewster armchair, late 17C

Slat-back armchair, ash, c.1660

Painted wood table, Connecticut, late 17C

Keeping Room, Massachusetts, c.1690

Carver armchair, late 17C

Joined 'great'chair (wainscot armchair)

Early American 'sunflower' chest attributed to Peter Blin, Wethersfield, c.1675-1700, with distinctive flat carving

Buffet, c.1695

New England chests

American gate-leg table with Spanish or Braganza feet. Type popular in England, Holland and America 1650-1720

Carved and painted wood chest-of-drawers, probably by Thomas Dennis

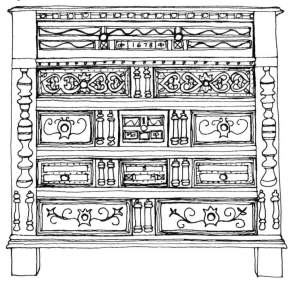

A Hadley chest ('mule' chest with one drawer) with chip carved design

A variation of this style associated with Connecticut is known as the Hartford or 'sunflower' chest, thought to be by Peter Blin of Wetherfield, Connecticut, and distinguished by very flat carving of stylized sunflowers and tulips on the three front panels. It was often decorated with split baluster turnings and oval wooden knobs known as 'turtlebacks'. Another group, identified as Hadley chests after a town in Massachusetts, is distinguished by the carved decoration of entwined tulip-like flowers and leaves in shallow chip-carved relief of looser design than that on the 'sunflower' chests. The carving covers the whole chest and in style is reminiscent of the decoration on Celtic manuscripts. Painting and staining in red, blue, green and black was a fairly common method of emphasizing the flat carving and mouldings on these chests. Small boxes for toilet articles or for storing books were common. Bible boxes had slanting lids to support a book or to provide a writing surface.

There were several varieties of chair: the wainscot chair of the type fashionable in Elizabethan England, the farthingale chair which closely resembled its European counterpart, and the chair with turned posts and spindles or slats, which can be grouped into three categories, the Carver, the Brewster and the slat-back. The Carver and the Brewster were named after two Pilgrim Fathers who used them: William Brewster who sailed on the Mayflower in 1620 and later became the elder and teacher at Plymouth, and John Carver who was the first Governor of the colony. Both were simple country chairs with solid seats and 'stick' backs of turned spindles. The Carver had one row of spindles in the back; the Brewster had two, with additional spindles under the arms and sometimes below the seat. The mushroom-shaped knobs at the top of some arm supports show a Dutch influence. The third version of this chair, the slat-back, had flat horizontal strips of wood in the place of the back turning. A similar chair in England was known as a ladder-back.

American tables followed European patterns, although some of the larger ones had movable tops for stacking. Although the early homes must have been fairly austere, table covers, cushions and curtains added colour and gaiety. By the turn of the century the population was expanding rapidly, towns were of a fair size and the standard of living was catching up with that of Europe.

Rococo and Palladian elegance

By 1699 even Louis XIV had grown a little tired of the grandeur with which he had surrounded himself. For the redecoration of the small Château de la Menagerie to receive the thirteen-year-old future Duchess of Burgundy, the King proposed a youthful theme throughout: 'there must be an air of childhood everywhere.' A young designer was employed to create this setting, which proved to be the first chink in the baroque armour. A little later the ante-room to the King's bedroom at Versailles was redecorated in a more light-hearted manner, with a group of dancing children bearing garlands of flowers set against a trellis-work background.

Life at Court, however, continued to be dull and stultifying. Courtiers had long since tired of the pompous and public life style, and towards the end of Louis's life were beginning to slip away from Versailles to open up and redecorate their Paris houses. On Louis's death in 1715 the Regent, Philippe Duc d'Orléans, moved the court to his own Parisian home, the Palais Royal, and established the five-year-old Louis XV in the Tuileries. In the relaxed, sophisticated atmosphere and more intimate style set by Philippe, a new zest and enthusiasm permeated court life.

Women played a dominant role in eighteenth-century Parisian society and their salons were centres for artistic and political as well as philosophical discussion. Entertaining became more domestic in scale, and smaller, more intimate rooms replaced the grand suites of linked rooms which had provided the long, impressive *enfilades* of the seventeenth century. A combination of increasing informality at Court and the growing influence of a new rich middle class steered fashion along new lines towards a taste for elegance and comfort. French genre paintings and prints of this period show people relaxing in low padded arm-chairs in easy, lounging attitudes as they gossip, read, flirt and play cards. The eighteenth-century notion of comfort came closer to twentieth-century ideals than that of any previous age. Familiarity with many pieces of eighteenth-century furniture still in use today can, however, give us a false idea of eighteenth-century manners and life-style.

French and English inventories of the period show that certain principles governed the placing of furniture. Some English conversation pieces give a truer picture of the accepted conventions of the time than French paintings do. They show rooms sparsely furnished, with the furniture arranged round the walls to enhance the architecture and chairs often placed close together in rows. The centre of the floor was usually kept clear of furniture and might not even have been carpeted; large areas of well-polished boards were common. This sparsity of furniture is a legacy from the previous century when people put a great deal of their wealth upon their backs and the vast and splendid baroque reception rooms were stages upon which they displayed themselves. In most of the grander eighteenth-century reception rooms throughout Europe the shapes of sofa and chair backs echoed and fitted into similar shapes in the wall panelling; window stools fitted the window embrasures, console tables or commodes with pier glasses above flanked the windows, which faced a chimney-piece with glass above, in turn flanked by a pair of sofas. *Torchères* stood in the corners. Seating was uniformly upholstered to form a band of colour around the room. Even at the height of the rococo period of flowing, asymmetrical forms, furniture was placed symmetrically. Servants brought tea tables or work tables into the room when they were needed. If furniture should be moved away from the walls for convenience there were servants in the background to tidy the room when vacated – which may explain why the position of Groom of the Chambers was held in such high regard in a large household. The charming scenes of disarray shown in French eighteenth-century paintings would soon have been put to rights.

In France, seating placed permanently against the wall and designed to match the panelling behind was known as *sièges meublants*. For entertaining, comfortable well-upholstered *sièges courants* would be placed in the centre of the room, and could be moved into groups for conversation and card-playing. These side chairs and elbow chairs would probably have been removed at the end of the evening. In high society the *sièges meublants* were reserved for the nobility.

Although these conventions were accepted, people became increasingly aware of the discomforts involved. Those who could afford it had duplicate suites of private rooms for family living located above the state rooms on the main floor, or, as in some of the great English country houses, a separate wing for private comfort. At Holkham Hall in Norfolk, for example, the family were housed in one wing while the *piano nobile* in the main block was given over entirely to grand rooms for entertaining and displaying works of art, and to the state rooms for an important guest. As the century progressed and the sophisticated villa became more fashionable in England, people began to consider the traditional state apartment a little old fashioned. The hidden *petits appartements* at Versailles allowed Louis XV and Madame de Pompadour to lead a comfortable private life on a small scale but in the height of luxury. Here they entertained a few intimate friends away from the public eye.

Although the Régence in France lasted only eight years (1715–23) it gave its name to the freer, more tolerant and more comfortable life-style which developed during the first thirty years of the eighteenth century. In design it spanned the transition from the formal baroque grandeur of Louis XIV to the full flowering

Clock case by Cressent, c.1747

Bureau plat, mid 18C

Le Style Régence – the evolution of rococo

Commode by Charles Cressent, with four drawers, in pairs, c.1730, veneered in kingwood. The scrolls of the gilt mounts are still symmetrical

Two-drawer commode by Antoine Gaudreau, designed by the Slodtz brothers, with asymmetrical gilt bronze mounts by Jacques Caffieri, c.1739

from a design for a salon in Palace of Pulawy by J.A.Meissonnier, carried out in 1730s

in the 1730s of the elegant flowing rococo style of Louis XV. The light, airy, ornamental designs of arabesques and grotesques developed by Jean Bérain in the late seventeenth century were a foretaste of rococo. Boulle had adapted these designs for his cabinet work and had introduced curved lines into his furniture, but it remained majestic in feeling. It was his friend and pupil Charles Cressent (1685–1768), the major cabinet-maker of this period, and the architect Gilles-Marie Oppenord (1672–1742) who precipitated the change in style. Both were employed by the Regent. Oppenord designed the interior of the Palais Royal and probably provided furniture designs for Cressent. The full curves of Cressent's furniture echoed the curving lines of Oppenord's richly gilt panelling. They shared a naturalistic use of flowers, leaf fronds and branches as decorative motifs. Cressent, however, was a designer in his own right. His early work as a sculptor probably accounts for the lively organic form of his furniture and the superb quality of his bronze mounts which he designed and cast himself. Some of his commodes seem to have been conceived as pieces of sculpture rather than as chests-of-drawers. Their curved shapes are overlaid with sinuous mounts representing trails of foliage which flow unbroken over joints and disguise the division of drawers. A leaf or an animal's tail is curved forward to form a handle.

Representative of this period was the large *bureau plat*, a writing table with three shallow drawers, which replaced the seventeenth-century bureau with eight legs. The finest, with costly veneers and fine mounts, came from Cressent's workshop. Some choice pieces have been attributed to another designer, Antoine Gaudreau, but Cressent's work overshadowed that of other *ébénistes* of the period. His designs were hybrid in character, retaining some of the monumentality of the Louis XIV style while creating the more elegant, light-hearted furniture his clients were looking for. His forms were fully developed during the reign of Louis XV.

The rococo style had very little effect upon the exteriors of buildings but was all-embracing within. Pale, fresh colour schemes were introduced. Panelling was predominantly white, filled with fanciful chinoiserie decoration – woodland scenes, exotic birds, monkeys, mandarins – painted with a light graceful touch in the manner of the decoration on a porcelain cup.

As the style, often known as 'Louis Quinze', progressed, classical orders and entablatures disappeared and swirling designs pushed their way up into coved ceilings, blurred the structure of rooms and mingled with the decoration of ceilings. The use of large mirrors gave an added feeling of spaciousness to smaller rooms: great play was made with mirrors to lose further the architectural features and unify the decorations. All the separate elements of a room – *boiseries* (panelling), furniture, fabrics, sculpture – shared a family likeness.

Asymmetry is the most notable feature of the rococo style. Although a few asymmetric motifs appeared in some of Bérain's designs, it was not until the design books of the ornamentalist and goldsmith J. A. Meissonnier (1695–1750) and of Nicolas Pineau (1684–1754) were published that asymmetry became a marked feature. Their motifs included all the baroque repertoire – leaf fronds, flowers, fruit, shells and waves. Some were derived from the grottoes which were a favourite feature of landscape gardens – jets of water, waterfalls, fanciful arrangements of rocks, shells, icicles, etc. These were such common elements that the style became known as *rocaille* and is still so called in France – 'rococo' is the Italian name for it. Flowers were usually arranged in the form of C- and S-shaped scrolls, often making an asymmetric cartouche-shaped ornament. Strange animals and masks mingled with these swirling forms.

The carved decoration of console tables, pier glasses, corner cupboards and *sièges meublants* was usually designed to match the mouldings of the panelling. Chairs not tied to the walls had little elaborately carved decoration: their distinctive features were lightness and elegant flowing lines. Their slender serpentine 'cabriole' legs had an air of movement. The cabriole leg is sometimes said to have been derived from a dance movement and sometimes from the shape of an animal's leg; the earlier form ended in an animal foot but this soon disappeared.

Chairs were the responsibility of the *menuisier*, or joiner, who was concerned with working solid wood: cutting, shaping, joining, carving and moulding, and waxing and polishing beds, chairs and other furniture made from plain or carved wood. He engaged the carver to add relief decoration and the upholsterer to provide the furnishings of seats and beds.

Once the hierarchical role of the chair was finally disposed of in the relaxed atmosphere of Louis XV's reign, several new designs for seating appeared. The elegant *fauteuil en cabriolet*, an upholstered armchair with a concave-shaped back for comfort and short, often padded arms curved outwards to accommodate the hooped dresses of the period, depended for effect upon its beautiful line and fine moulding. The ladies' favourite chair was probably the *bergère*, a large, comfortable low armchair well-suited to their proportions and clothes – its back and sides were closed either with upholstery or cane and its seat was fitted with a large loose cushion. There was also a winged version of the *bergère*. Another type of chair, with a sloping back and a very deep seat, designed for lounging, was named after the writer Voltaire. The *fauteuil à coiffer* was designed expressly for the lengthy process of dressing hair in the elaborate styles of the day: the top rail dipped down in the centre, allowing the hairdresser to reach the hair easily while the sitter rested in comfort. A fascination with mechanical devices led to the design of special chairs with swivel seats for use at the dressing table.

A special *bergère* with a wide padded top rail was developed for gambling, a passion of many people in society: while one person sat at the gaming table, a spectator could lean comfortably on the back. This was aptly named the *bergère voyeuse*. Another, the *voyelle*, was similar to the English library chair – the spectator straddled the seat, facing the back and resting his elbows on the top rail.

The *marquise*, a sofa shaped like a wider, deeper *bergère*, just large enough for two, was sometimes called a *tête-à-tête* or *confidante*. An up-dated *chaise longue* called a *duchesse* was made up of two or three sections, each well upholstered; the head end had a back and sides like a *bergère*, the second part was a low stool of the same height and the third piece, if included, was made like a low *bergère* to form a foot.

Both the Middle and Far East inspired rococo designers. Oval sofas known

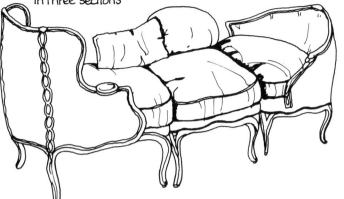

Duchesse or chaise-longue, in three sections

Bergère, 1720s

Elegance with comfort - Louis XV.
The art of the menuisier

Side chair, 1720s

from 'Le Petit Dejeuner' by F. Boucher, 1739 - domestic comfort

Fauteuil en cabriolet upholstered with Beauvais tapestries

Duchesse in two sections with winged back

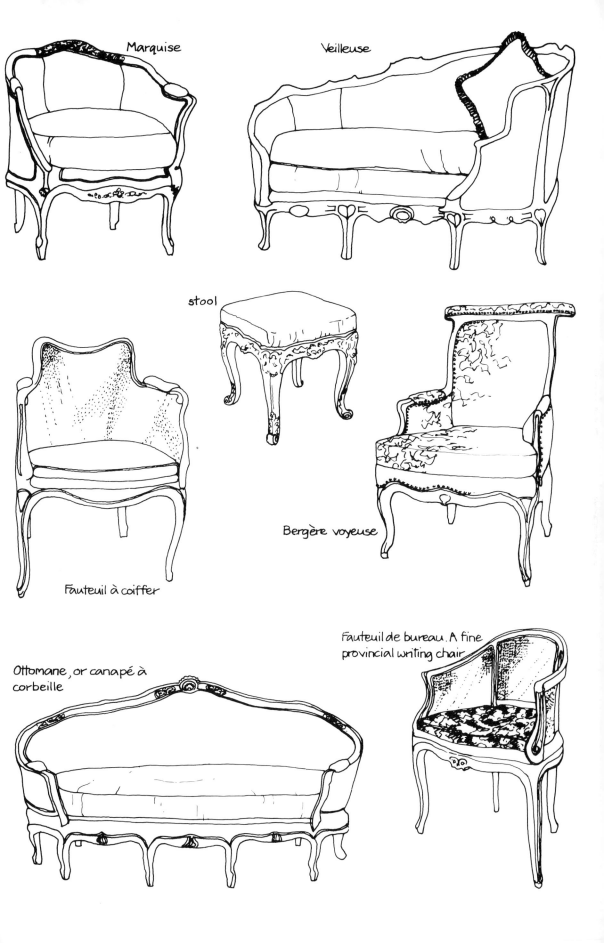

Marquise

Veilleuse

stool

Bergère voyeuse

Fauteuil à coiffer

Ottomane, or canapé à corbeille

Fauteuil de bureau. A fine provincial writing chair

as *ottomanes* were fashionable for boudoirs – a *lit à la turque* was a low couch with the outer ends scrolled and a draped canopy above. Another boudoir sofa, the *paphose*, named after the birthplace of Venus, had a kidney-shaped seat. The sultana was a sofa with two rolled-over ends.

All these chairs and sofas were richly upholstered in fabrics matching or blending with the hangings. The upholstery was the most expensive and prized part of the seating. It was changed seasonally – precious damasks and velvets for winter, printed cottons and silks for summer. Tapestry covers were popular and were specially commissioned to fit the shapes of the frames; many were designed by the painter Boucher. A method of attaching fabrics with screws and clamps was developed to facilitate the frequent changes of covering. The woodwork was either gilded, left natural and waxed, or painted with coloured varnishes. Favourite colour combinations were green, blue or pink and white, silver and yellow, pale green and pink.

Included always in sets of seating were firescreens and folding screens to exclude draughts, carved and upholstered to match seats and beds.

The traditional bed surmounted by a canopy continued to be used but also popular was the more secluded *lit à la polonaise* (illustrated on page 139). It was placed with one side against the wall with a canopy above, or sideways in an alcove which took the place of a canopy.

Now the wealthy Parisian bourgeoisie as well as the Court were prepared to pay exorbitant prices for fine pieces of furniture. Though many and varied, to satisfy every whim and activity of a critical clientele, these were mainly smaller, lighter, more movable pieces to match the smaller rooms, and of exquisite workmanship.

Furniture making in France was a very specialized business at this time, divided among guilds of craftsmen in a highly organized guild system. In spite of continual demarcation disputes among the various guilds, a high level of craftsmanship was sustained. French craftsmen were required to stamp their goods with their names unless excused by royal patronage. The middlemen, the *marchands-merciers*, now coming to the fore helped to bind the system together and to guide the taste of the cabinet-makers, suggesting new techniques and fresh combinations of materials to attract their customers. The Court employed craftsmen directly, but the rapidly growing class of bourgeois patrons went to these furniture dealers who could show them designs to be made up by the various craftsmen. The *marchards-merciers* were probably as influential in guiding the taste of the *ébénistes* as were the *ornemanistes*, design specialists like Meissonnier, the Slodtz brothers and Pineau.

The commode remained the most important piece of furniture and the best French and foreign cabinet-makers were employed in its decoration. The serpentine form introduced by Cressent, curving laterally as well as vertically, developed into the full *bombé* shape. The curve continued down the legs, which became longer and were often emphasized by mounts. A new type of commode, the corner cupboard or *encoignure*, as lavishly decorated as the commodes, was usually bought in pairs. Many varied and richly coloured woods were used on Louis XV furniture. Unfortunately many of the colours have faded so that we have little idea of their original brilliance. Popular woods were tulipwood, kingwood, purplewood, rosewood, satinwood and indigenous woods such as holly, maple, cherry, etc.

Pictorial marquetry featured a variety of subjects apart from the usual bird and flower motifs – musical instruments and scores, writing instruments, gardening tools, for example. Geometric parquetry of squares, chequered patterns, triangles and basket-work made full use of the tonal range of the woods. Some pieces were painted with *fêtes galantes* in the style of Boucher and Watteau, using a special varnish called *vernis Martin* after the four brothers who invented and patented it – a glossy pseudo-lacquer built up of as many as forty layers of varnish, available in many colours. Whatever method of decoration was used on case furniture, it was combined with elaborate gilt bronze mounts.

The sophisticated creations of Bernard van Riesenburgh (*c*.1700–65), a Fleming who settled in Paris, are among the finest Louis XV luxury furniture. Most of his work has a delicate, easy grace. It is small in scale, designed for boudoirs or bedrooms. The most mundane objects such as Madame de Pompadour's bidet and the cupboard to hold her *vase de nuit* were turned into elegant pieces of furniture by him. He is the first *ébéniste* known to have incorporated porcelain plaques from the Sèvres factory into his furniture.

Jean François Oeben (*c*.1720–63), one of several German *ébénistes* drawn to Paris, was another cabinet-maker patronized by Madame de Pompadour. He was particularly interested in mechanical devices which released hidden drawers and converted furniture to other uses. His renowned *table à la Bourgogne* included several such devices: from what was apparently just a chest with six drawers, a little bookcase could be made to rise out of the top, and when certain levers were released the bookcase opened up to reveal semi-circular recesses designed to hold a variety of objects. Craftsmen in Germany had been renowned for mechanical gadgetry, particularly clocks and automata, for many years. Oeben also excelled at another speciality of German craftsmen – elaborate floral marquetry, carried out in a very personal style, and geometrical patterning in cubes, rosettes and lozenges.

Although Oeben's pieces have a satisfying fullness of form the rococo curves are restrained – the beginning of a reaction to rococo excesses. He was the inventor of the roll-top desk, *le bureau à cylindre*, which became fashionable around 1760. He was working on the Bureau du Roi Louis XV at the time of his death. This, probably the most elaborate and famous piece of eighteenth-century furniture, took nine years to complete. It was finished by one of his pupils, J. H. Riesener, and bears his signature. Oeben and his workshop dominated the transitional period which lasted well into the 1770s.

All the sophisticated courts of Europe looked to Paris for the lead in fashion – the charming rococo style spread swiftly across Europe as far east as Russia, north to Sweden and south to Italy. Germany at that time was divided into many states owing allegiance in varying degrees to the Hapsburg Emperor whose official residence was in Vienna. The style was eagerly adopted in Germany, but since

Cartonnier for filing papers in style of Van Riesenburgh

Side table by Bernard van Riesenburgh, decorated with Japanese lacquer, European japanning and gilt bronze mounts

Cabinet-making, mid 18C – the art of the ébéniste

Commode by van Riesenburgh, lacquered with 'vernis Martin'

Drop-front secrétaire by Jean-François Dubot

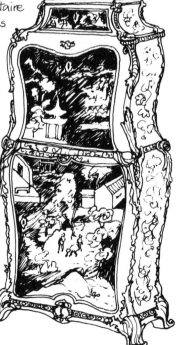

Writing table by van Riesenburgh; veneered tulip-wood, inlaid mother-of-pearl, horn, various woods

Console table, c.1740; marble top
on unusual iron stand

Transitional furniture

Small roll-top desk with
delicate floral marquetry
by J. F. Oeben, c.1760

Marquetry top of a
writing table by J. F. Oeben

'Bureau du Roi Louis XV' by
J. F. Oeben, completed by
J. H. Riesener, 1760-9. Marquetry
with bronze mounts

Combination writing and toilet table
with floral marquetry top and sides
by J. F. Oeben and Roger Vandercruse
for Madame de Pompadour

each prince sought to impose his own taste upon his Court there were many variations. Cultural life was stimulated by the constant rivalry and striving for prestige among ambitious princes. The two most clearly defined styles are Bavarian and Frederican (or Potsdam) rococo.

The most brilliant designer in the south was François Cuvilliés (1698–1768) who had started life at the Bavarian Court as the court dwarf. The Elector recognized his ability as a designer and sent him to Paris to study. On his return he worked with the old court designer Joseph Effner (also Paris trained) whose furniture showed the influence of Boulle and Cressent. Upon the accession of Charles Albert as Elector, Cuvilliés was appointed to re-design the interiors and furnishings of a suite of rooms in the Elector's Palace in Munich. His finest work is at the Nymphenburg Palace where he created the delightful Amalienburg Pavilion. This small pleasure house is a work of great elegance and delicacy with subtle colour schemes of two tones of yellow with silver stucco work in the bedroom, and white, pale grey and pale ice-blue with silver stucco in the Hall of Mirrors where large mirrors enhance and reflect the tracery, an unusual feature on such a small scale. By overseeing every detail of furniture and decoration Cuvilliés achieved a remarkable harmony between the two. His method of covering pastel coloured walls with a gold or silver filigree, which he carried over to the faces of his painted commodes, helped to integrate his interiors. His furniture shapes echoed those of the *boiseries* and mirrors. The whole had a stylized, dream-world quality about it. A sense of balance and sophistication was achieved by the use of straight vertical and horizontal lines contrasted with flourishes and gentle curves.

Rococo reached the north of Germany a decade later with the accession of Frederick II of Prussia in 1740. Frederican rococo flourished from the 1740s to the 1760s. A talented group of craftsmen was employed to transform the palaces of Berlin and Potsdam, the greatest of whom was Johann August Nahl, designer and carver. His interiors had an element of fantasy and sophistication which rivalled those of Bavaria – palm trees, chinoiseries and dragons were depicted in a strange flickering style. His furniture, although rather heavy and uncomfortable, with over-deep seats, had a unique exuberance.

The brothers Hoppenhaupt, both fine designers, concentrated on the use of plain veneers either alone or contrasted with marquetry and bronze decoration. The designs of Johann Michael Hoppenhaupt published between 1751 and 1755 were charmingly light-hearted. Most of his pieces have a buoyant quality – the bulbous forms with tiny feet appear barely to touch the ground.

The Swiss Johann Melchior Kambli made superb, elaborate gilt bronze mounts of chains of flowers, curling acanthus leaves, trellis work and cherubs, set off by rich tortoiseshell veneers. He supplied mounts for the Spindler brothers – Johann Friederich and Heinrich Wilhelm. Their ambitious and dazzling marquetry, including silver, mother-of-pearl, ivory and tortoiseshell, if slightly overpowering, was of faultless craftsmanship.

The rococo style in Italy had an air of melodrama about it, particularly evident in the furniture of Venice – that mysterious, theatrical city which for the

Corner cupboard by
J.A. Nahl, Berlin, 1745

Design for chest-of-drawers by
Johann Michael Hoppenhaupt,
c.1751

German rococo

Commode by Heinrich Spindler, c.1765,
veneered in tortoiseshell. Elaborate
mounts probably by Johann Melchior
Kambli

Stucco work in the Hall of Mirrors,
Amalienburg Palace, by Cuvilliés

Commode designed by
François Cuvilliés, Munich, 1761.
Carved gilt wood on white
painted ground

Italian rococo
Venetian

Commode, yellow lacquer, gilded and painted with flowers

Small painted commode, one of a pair

Sofa, one of a set of four for a large reception room

Two cut-outs for 'lacca contraffatta' decoration

Corner of the Porcelain Room in the Royal Palace, Portici. Most of the wall surfaces were covered in Capo di Monte porcelain

Piedmontese - a distinctive style

Writing desk by Pietro Piffetti, 1741, inlaid with precious woods and ivory

Grand Tourist of the eighteenth century was a dazzling centre of opera and theatre, masquerades, carnivals and gambling. Italian craftsmen on the whole exaggerated the features of French rococo – the elegant *bombé* shape was expanded to give a top-heavy, full-busted appearance above tiny feet. Sofas were drawn out to ridiculous lengths, particularly those in the formal reception rooms or *porteghi* which ran from front to back of Venetian palaces. They were made in sets of varying sizes – some could seat up to ten people. They often incorporated multiple chair backs linked by a serpentine top rail.

Once the *cassone* ceased to be fashionable, Italian craftsmen transferred their interest to the commode. The Venetians in particular produced some charming but rather absurd creations, painted with flowers in lively colours on ivory, blue and green grounds. Unfortunately, fine craftsmanship was sacrificed to effect – many pieces were very shoddily made.

Venice was a centre for lacquered furniture in the eighteenth century. The work was less fine than that of the north and even further removed from the oriental originals, but it had a charm of its own. A cheaper substitute known as *lacca contrafatta* was made by gluing coloured cut-out prints, often designed by well-known artists, on to a gesso ground and varnishing them.

The fussy, over-elaborate furniture of the brilliant craftsman Pietro Piffetti epitomizes the Piedmontese style. The general design of his work was sacrificed to the display of inlaid panels of precious materials.

English society, by the beginning of the eighteenth century, had already adopted a relaxed and informal way of life fairly independent of the Court. It was the informality of the country house, however, rather than of the boudoir. The English aristocracy were not town dwellers by choice. They would desert their town houses in London when not attending Parliament or entertaining during the 'season'. Their interests and lives revolved around their country estates; country mansions grew more imposing as their owners' standard of living steadily improved throughout the century. The patrons of the day were men of learning and culture; many had made the Grand Tour and were familiar with European taste. They had a broad understanding of the arts, particularly architecture, and some were amateur architects and designers themselves. The role of the architect became increasingly important in house design as, for the first time, he became concerned with interior design and furniture design.

During the reign of Queen Anne (1702–14) a very English style of furniture emerged, from which the Georgian style was to evolve. It was marked by a preference for simplicity; for beauty of line rather than ornament. The elaborate marquetry and parquetry fashionable since the Restoration gave way to all-over veneers, usually of warm-toned walnut, carefully selected for the beauty of their figuring. Of the earlier decorative features, only cross and feather banding were retained to define the boundaries of each drawer or door panel.

These simpler pieces were curvilinear in style with the cabriole leg, used as a support for all kinds of tables and chairs, developing easier, more elegant lines than in its earlier form. The most important element of Queen Anne furniture was the elongated S-shaped curve, what Hogarth called 'the line of beauty'. The cabriole leg was cut from one piece of timber, square in section. It was very strong, and as craftsmen were now able to cut good, firm joints that did not move, it was possible to eliminate the stretchers which interrupted the flow of the curves.

The beautiful hooped-back chair, the product of the specialist chair maker, is the most distinctive piece of Queen Anne furniture. The solid splat-back curved to fit the occupant's spine, the comfortable 'drop-in' upholstered seat with its rounded front rail and the easy, elegant lines of the cabriole legs all contributed to a most satisfying form. The legs terminated in pad, claw and ball, hoof or lion's-paw feet. Carving, if introduced, was applied with restraint to the knees of the front legs, often in the form of scallop shells, lions' masks, cartouches or husk ornaments. A shell might also be applied to the seat rail and there might be a slight decoration on the back. This new chair, known also as a bended-back, was a most comfortable and pleasing seat. Armchairs followed a similar pattern with the arms resting on supports set back on the seat rail, rather than on an extension of the front legs which would have been incompatible with the new cabriole shapes. Sometimes the arms were of the scrolled type known as shepherd's crook, sometimes they terminated in lions' or more commonly eagles' heads; they were circular in section, flattening out where the occupant's elbows rested. The double-chair settee followed the same pattern. Day-beds, which remained in fashion, also had hoop backs and cabriole legs, linked by much simplified stretchers. The winged armchair survived with modifications to the leg design.

With the decline in marquetry and parquetry, textiles provided the main areas of decoration. The growing demand for upholstered furniture stimulated the production of embroidery of a very high standard, both amateur and professional. Designs in wool and fine silk were of a charming hybrid nature combining Indian and Chinese motifs with indigenous ones such as strawberries and roses. The richest embroideries included silver and gold thread and were intended for matching sets of bed-covers and cushions.

Among the new pieces of furniture introduced at this time was the bureau with a sloping top which opened to form a writing surface and reveal a nest of tiny drawers and pigeonholes. It was sometimes surmounted by a two-door cabinet and sometimes by a bookcase. The upper portion had either a double-hooded cornice or a broken swan-necked pediment with a cartouche in the middle. The equally elegant chest-on-chest or tallboy was also fashionable. It provided plenty of storage space, with a set of three long drawers surmounted by three short narrow drawers in a row in the top half, and three long drawers in the lower portion, with a pull-out brushing slide between the two sets. Its height, often as much as six feet, made the upper drawers a little inaccessible, but its beauty surely compensated for this. These composite pieces are among the finest articles of furniture ever made in England. Among other new articles was a very useful small kneehole dressing table, which could also be used as a writing desk. A toilet mirror, pivoted between two uprights supported on a stand with drawers, was also introduced.

The gambling craze, as strong in English society as in French, produced a variety of folding card tables, sone of very ingenious construction. Some were dished to support candle stands by each player's elbow and had sunken recesses for counters. The inner sides of the top were usually lined with fabric. The earlier circular tables had a folding top which rested, when open, on two legs which swung out in gate-leg fashion. A square table with rounded ends supported the flap on one leg. A later ingenious improvement moved the two back legs out on a folding framework, concertina-fashion, to support the flap, hence the name concertina table. Pairs of round card tables folded into semi-circles served as useful console tables against the wall. Queen Anne furniture had an elegant, unassuming, rational grace.

During the early Georgian period in England there are two distinct lines of development. Walnut and walnut-veneered furniture continued to be made in the domestic style of Queen Anne with minor changes until mid-century; for example, the decoration on the knee of the cabriole leg became more complex, rising up into the seat rail. From the 1720s carving generally became more elaborate with the increased use of mahogany. A shortage of walnut in France forced English craftsmen to turn to other woods, and in 1721 the government passed an act abolishing the heavy import duty on most timbers from the British colonies of North America and the West Indies. This stimulated trade in mahogany which gained favour rapidly with craftsmen and clients. It had a beautiful patina which improved with use, great strength, a large range of colours and figures, very wide boards suitable for tables, wardrobes, etc., and a strong resistance to decay. Its hardness and closeness of grain made it suitable for crisp, detailed carving.

Another small table, introduced in the 1730s, was the round tripod tea table; the top was supported on a central column with three cabriole legs ending in claw and ball, club or paw feet. It had become a fashionable ritual to take tea or coffee after dinner. The hostess with her lady guests would retire to the drawing-room or a special tea-room to make the beverages herself, and the gentlemen would then join them. (A gradual extension of this brief separation of the sexes may account for the development of the English custom, considered barbaric by other nationalities, of the men sitting for hours over their port while the women gossiped in the drawing-room.) From this time the drawing-room became larger and its furnishing more feminine.

Most tripod tables had hinged tops which allowed them to be used as firescreens and made it easier to store them out of the way. These handy tables were put to many uses. A larger version made a useful supper table and was usually dished to hold up to eight plates. A tripod base was also used for a pole firescreen.

The second type of early Georgian furniture, associated with William Kent (1685–1748), is distinctly Italian in style. Kent was one of the circle gathered around the rich young Lord Burlington, a talented amateur architect eager to establish Palladian architecture in England. With Kent, his friend and protégé, Burlington designed a villa for himself at Chiswick, closely modelled on the Italian architect Palladio's Villa Capra at Vicenza. Kent was responsible for the landscape gardening, the interior decoration and the furniture. In his work one sees the first fully-integrated interiors in England.

England –
Queen Anne and
early Georgian

Wanstead House c.1715 by
Colen Campbell – model for
the English Palladian house

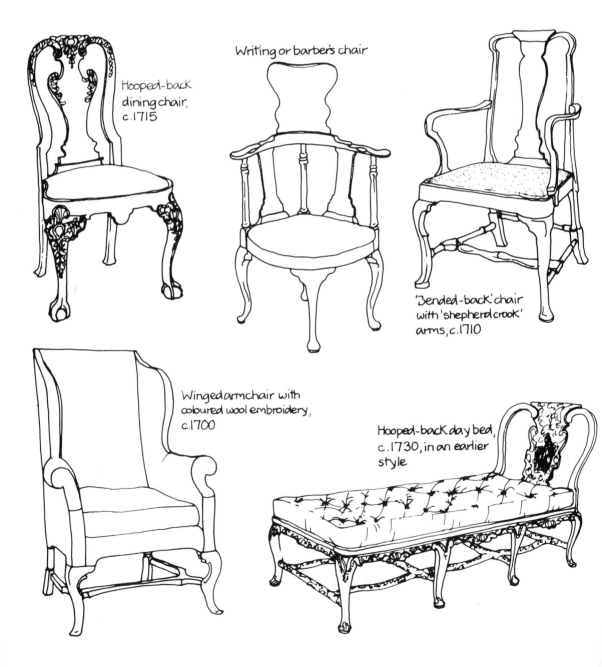

Hooped-back
dining chair,
c.1715

Writing or barber's chair

'Bended-back' chair
with 'shepherd crook'
arms, c.1710

Winged armchair with
coloured wool embroidery,
c.1700

Hooped-back day bed,
c.1730, in an earlier
style

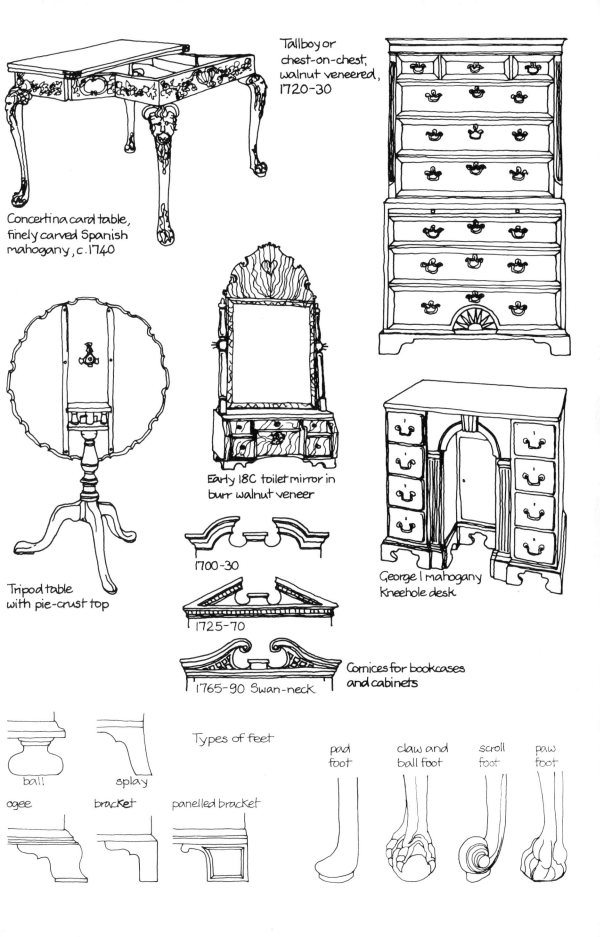

Concertina card table,
finely carved Spanish
mahogany, c.1740

Tallboy or
chest-on-chest,
walnut veneered,
1720-30

Tripod table
with pie-crust top

Early 18C toilet mirror in
burr walnut veneer

1700-30

1725-70

1765-90 Swan-neck

Cornices for bookcases
and cabinets

George I mahogany
kneehole desk

Types of feet

ball

splay

ogee

bracket

panelled bracket

pad
foot

claw and
ball foot

scroll
foot

paw
foot

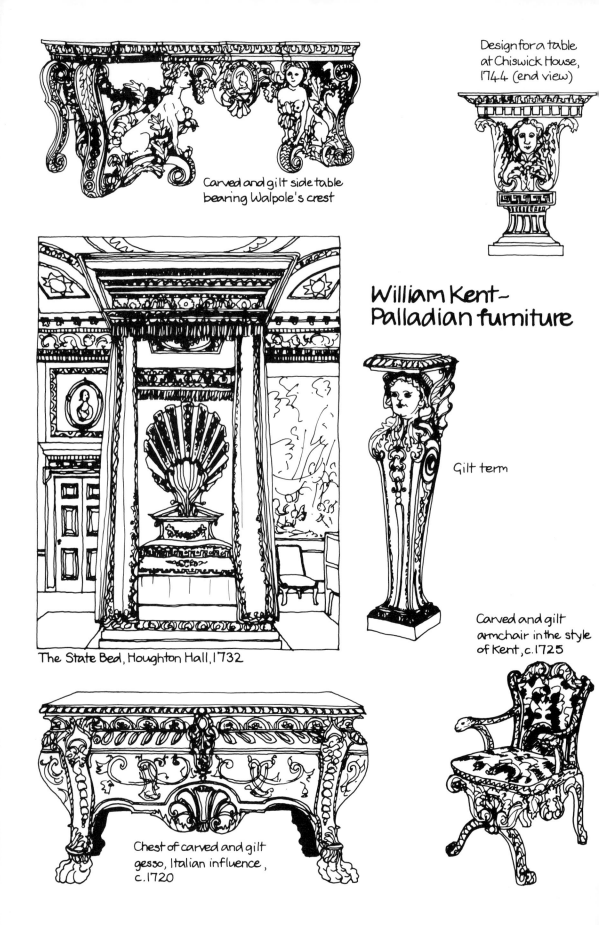

Carved and gilt side table
bearing Walpole's crest

Design for a table
at Chiswick House,
1744 (end view)

William Kent –
Palladian furniture

Gilt term

The State Bed, Houghton Hall, 1732

Carved and gilt
armchair in the style
of Kent, c.1725

Chest of carved and gilt
gesso, Italian influence,
c.1720

Although there were many design precedents for the Palladian houses now being built by enlightened noblemen, there was little precedent for Palladian furniture. Kent disliked the French taste of Louis XIV and wanted to return to a purer classical style; but he gave his classical motifs and mouldings such flamboyance and verve that his furniture became truly baroque in character. These exuberant pieces in their settings of magnificent splendour were in direct contrast to the austere exteriors of the houses – Palladian theories were left at the front door.

Kent's rooms were designed like stage sets – each room having its focal points to which the eye was drawn in turn. Only the grandest furniture could stand up to the heavy stuccoed and gilt ceilings, walls hung with rich damasks, tapestries and velvets, rich coloured marbles, and elaborate doors and overmantels.

Kent was obviously strongly influenced by the interiors of Venetian palaces. His monumental furniture, like its Italian prototypes, was designed for display rather than comfort. His massive side tables, usually accompanied by pier glasses, were extensions of the interior decoration. Large slabs of Italian marble were often supported on heavy, scrolled legs connected by a central motif made up of festoons of foliage and birds, animals, cherubs, shells, or sphinxes, often with armorial bearings. Sometimes the whole structure stood on a moulded plinth which emphasized its sculptural and architectural quality. Favourite supports for his console tables were linked dolphins or eagles with outstretched wings. Some supports were painted to suggest white marble but fine gilding was usually preferred. Kent's various seat forms are prestigious rather than comfortable – reminiscent of the throne-chairs of Italian *palazzi*.

The State Bedroom at Houghton, Kent's *tour de force*, is dominated by an enormous bed in the manner of Marot. One hundred yards of green velvet, the rarest colour in velvet, were used to upholster it. The upholstered bed head is surmounted by a towering double shell, the spines picked out in braid, which stretches upwards almost to the canopy. The architectural character of the canopy is emphasized by gold braiding, suggesting the gilded ornament on a classical entablature.

Palladian furniture of a simpler form than Kent's but showing his influence became fairly common for the 'show' rooms of grand houses in the 1730s and '40s.

It was mid-century before the influence of the rococo style became perceptible in the stucco decoration and furniture design in houses of consequence, although Huguenot goldsmiths working in England had been using it since the 1730s. Most cabinet-makers continued to produce serviceable, unpretentious, pleasing furniture in the style established earlier in the century. Rococo was in the main a style for the fashion-conscious. It did, however, mark a swing away from the more ponderous Kentian style to a lighter vein. Whereas it took thirty years to develop in France, it was but a passing, though charming, fancy in England; it was the more frenzied characteristics of *rocaille* that the English designers adopted, though often with little understanding.

Probably the most prominent exponent of the English rococo style was a carver, Matthias Lock, who produced several collections of drawings – the most

Rococo and other fantasies

Design for a girandole by Matthias Lock, c.1750

Girandole by Thomas Johnson from his 'Collection of Designs' 1758

Design for a garden chair made of roots, Edwards & Darby 1754

Dressing table design, William Ince c.1760

Night table in the 'Gothick' style

successful, *A New Book of Ornaments*, was published with H. Copland in 1752. His most memorable designs are those for mirrors or girandoles in which he successfully blended chinoiserie motifs – mandarins, dragons, monkeys, exotic birds, icicles, etc. – with *rocaille* work and rustic scenes of shepherds and shepherdesses or characters from Aesop. These are highly individual and very English in character. They were designed as separate pieces rather than as part of a larger decorative scheme.

The carver Thomas Johnson represents the more bizarre type of English rococo. The creatures of his imagination inhabit a strange, spiky world – hunters and fishermen, nymphs and shepherds, dogs, foxes, dragons, long-tailed birds, mandarins and sea-creatures balance precariously on strange organic structures, part coral reef, part swirling plant, part tree, part rock or dripping icicle. These strange fantasies, translated into girandoles, chimney-pieces, looking-glasses, *torchères*, console tables, have an irrational charm. Johnson also published pattern books: *Twelve Girandoles* (1755) and *One Hundred and Fifty New Designs* (1761), the latter first issued in instalments.

As well as using Chinese motifs for decoration, English designers also attempted to reproduce Chinese furniture. Since few models were available, the English pieces bore little likeness to the authentic furniture, but the introduction of certain features, however misapplied, did enrich British design – lattice-work patterns in chair backs and glazing bars of bookcases, pagoda roofs, Chinese railings in miniature as an edging to tea tables, and so on.

A new interest in England's medieval past produced another kind of fantasy in the 1750s – the 'gothick' style. Although the furniture had no true likeness to medieval pieces, gothic ornament such as ogee arches, quatrefoils, cusping and crocketing was introduced into the decoration of chair backs, bookcases, cabinets and other items. Sometimes 'gothick' and 'Chinese' motifs were combined in the same piece.

All these fanciful styles are incorporated in the repertoire of Thomas Chippendale (1718–79), the most renowned name among English furniture designers. His life and that of his son Thomas the Younger span over one hundred years, so it is little wonder that the name is synonymous with eighteenth-century design. Little is known of his early career, but by 1753 he had a prosperous business, the Cabinet and Upholstery Warehouse, in St Martin's Lane. In the following year he published his famous book of designs, *The Gentleman and Cabinet-Maker's Director*. Devoted entirely to furniture, it contained the most comprehensive collection of furniture designs to be found in the workshops of leading London cabinet-makers of the day. Chippendale intended it as both an advertising brochure to beguile his customers and a pattern book for other tradesmen – an ambitious innovation. His project was so successful that his influence spread not only to provincial craftsmen but to those of North America and other British colonies. Copies of the third edition were published in French. His business acumen shows in his readiness to supply alternative ideas – all the current styles rub shoulders without embarrassment, and a choice of decoration is shown on some of his illustrations.

Thomas Chippendale

Chinese bed from 'The Director'

Ribband-back settee in manner of Chippendale

Construction of Chippendale-type chair

cresting rail

stile

splat

seat rail

shoe brace

bracket

leg

stretchers

open fret

Chippendale 'Gothic' chair

Chippendale 'Chinese' chair from 'The Gentleman and Cabinet Maker's Director', 1754

'Chinese' railing, 1754

'Gothic' frets, 1754

Mahogany commode based on Chippendale design, of bombé shape rarely attempted in England or America

It is uncertain to what extent Chippendale was responsible for the *Director*'s contents. It is believed that Matthias Lock, who worked for him in the fifties and sixties and who taught him to handle the rococo style, may have contributed many of the designs. Chippendale appears to have been primarily a business man employing specialist craftsmen and designers. In 1754 he entered into partnership with James Rennie who, it is thought, attended to the interior decoration and upholstery side of the business while Chippendale ran the cabinet-making side. The firm supplied every kind of furniture, elaborate or simple, expensive or cheap; they hung wallpapers, made and draped curtains, laid carpets.

With the growth of the middle class, more and more people were buying good furniture. Provincial towns had excellent cabinet-makers who supplied goods to all classes, although it was rare for the upper classes to patronize local craftsmen. London held supreme in matters of taste, particularly as regards house furnishings. Many rich families employed London agents to shop for them, to send them news of the city, newspapers, and illustrations of the latest fashions.

The lesser gentry and middle classes usually found local sources of supply adequate – good, carefully made furniture which reflected the latest London fashions with only a brief time-lag. The ordinary townsfolk were served by less skilled craftsmen whose solid furniture was often made in out-dated styles. In a seaport or on a waterway, cheaper furniture shipped from London as part of the coastal trade could often be bought.

The quality of village furniture varied. In remote areas it might be very scarce and basic; on the other hand, some cottages had good furniture handed down from the local halls and manor-houses when it went out of fashion.

Transport remained a problem as roads were often very treacherous. A revealing entry in Parson Woodforde's diary in April 1793 describes how some furniture bought in Norwich was delivered to his parsonage some ten miles away: 'About 2 o'clock this Afternoon two men of Sudbury's at Norwich came with my Side-Board and a large New Mahogany Celleret bought of Sudbury, brought on the men's shoulders all the way and very safe.'

Eighteenth-century life in the major cities of America – New York, Boston, Newport, Philadelphia – followed much the same pattern as in England. A steady flow of emigrant English and Dutch craftsmen throughout the century brought with them the latest fashions from Europe. The Queen Anne style was adopted in the 1720s, after her death, and remained popular until *c.*1760. The Chippendale period lasted from *c.*1760 until nearly the end of the century. In spite of the War of Independence, the *Director* remained a bible for furniture makers.

American furniture was rather more restrained in character than its models, in keeping with the less extravagant life of the New World. Craftsmen achieved beauty through simplicity of form rather than elaborate carving or gilding. With the exception of the Chinese-Chippendale looking-glass frame, the light-hearted, frivolous rococo style of Lock and Johnson rarely caught on. There was some slight mixing of styles – chairs of Chippendale form might well retain Queen Anne back-splats or kidney-shaped seats. The cabriole leg, usually with claw and

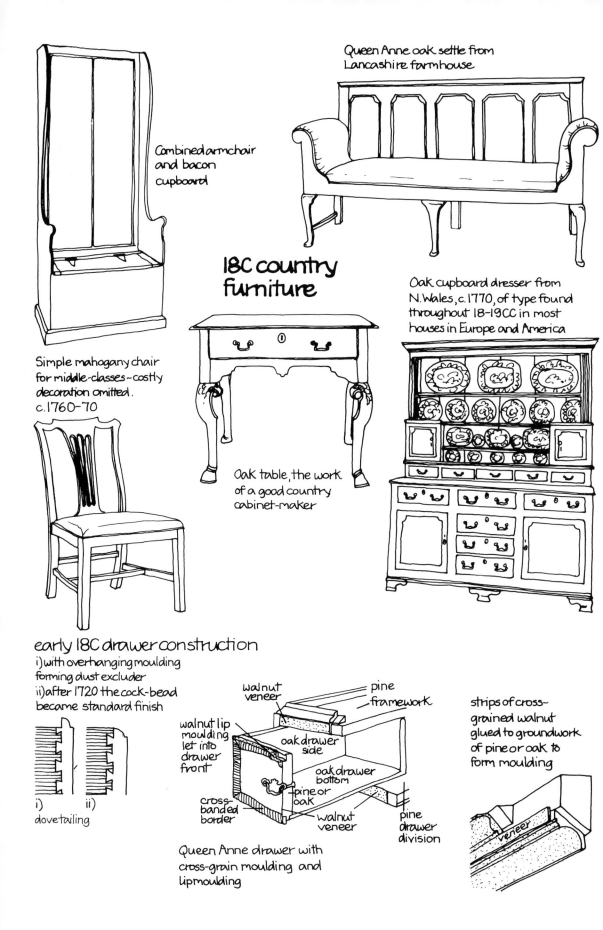

Combined armchair
and bacon
cupboard

Queen Anne oak settle from
Lancashire farmhouse

18C country
furniture

Oak cupboard dresser from
N. Wales, c.1770, of type found
throughout 18-19CC in most
houses in Europe and America

Simple mahogany chair
for middle-classes - costly
decoration omitted.
c.1760-70

Oak table, the work
of a good country
cabinet-maker

early 18C drawer construction

i) with overhanging moulding
forming dust excluder
ii) after 1720 the cock-bead
became standard finish

i)   ii)
dovetailing

walnut lip
moulding
let into
drawer
front

oak drawer side

cross-
banded
border

walnut
veneer

walnut
veneer

pine
framework

oak drawer
bottom

pine or
oak

pine
drawer
division

Queen Anne drawer with
cross-grain moulding and
lipmoulding

strips of cross-
grained walnut
glued to groundwork
of pine or oak to
form moulding

veneer

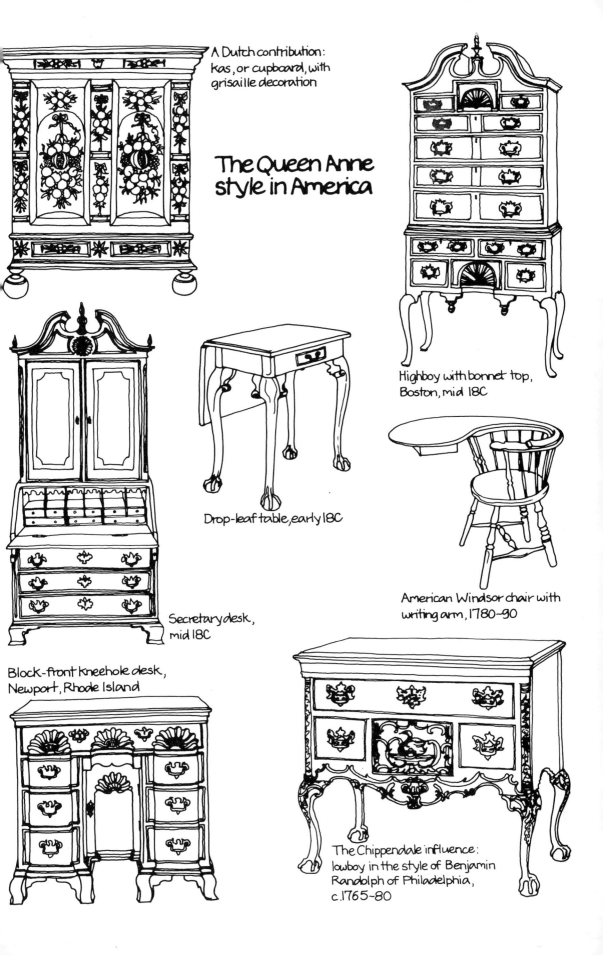

A Dutch contribution: kas, or cupboard, with grisaille decoration

The Queen Anne style in America

Highboy with bonnet top, Boston, mid 18C

Drop-leaf table, early 18C

American Windsor chair with writing arm, 1780–90

Secretary desk, mid 18C

Block-front kneehole desk, Newport, Rhode Island

The Chippendale influence: lowboy in the style of Benjamin Randolph of Philadelphia, c.1765–80

ball foot, remained popular until well into the nineteenth century. Mahogany was as favoured for fine pieces in America as in England, but was rarely used before mid-century. Popular local woods were black walnut from Pennsylvania, pine, maple, and fruit woods such as cherry, pear and apple.

Unique in North America was the block front carcase furniture in which the centre front section of the piece is recessed slightly in a shallow concave curve while the area on either side is projected forward in a convex form. This blocking was used in conjunction with large carved scallop shells, more deeply and crisply cut (since the block front provided a greater thickness of wood) than similar carving in England where wood was scarcer and dearer. Block fronting was a favourite feature for the bureau and bureau-bookcase and occasionally appeared on another favourite piece of American furniture, the highboy. The highboy was supported on high cabriole legs (unlike the tallboy in England which was a chest-on-chest) and was usually surmounted by a swan-necked broken pediment or a 'bonnet-top'. The lowboy, another popular piece, was in effect the lower part of a tallboy, usually richly carved.

The English Windsor chair, a country chair made of turned members with a saddle-shaped seat, was taken to America in the early 1700s and became enormously popular. An unusual Windsor writing chair with a distinctive low back, introduced around 1780, had the right arm extended to form an oval writing surface with a drawer beneath for writing materials. In some versions the arm was pivoted to swing towards the sitter. The Windsor chair was also made as a 'rocker', which became a great favourite in the nineteenth century. The rocking chair seems to have been an American invention – it did not appear in Europe until it had become well established in America.

Neo-classicism

By the middle of the eighteenth century sophisticated society had begun to tire of rococo fussiness and was ready for a change. Although her name is synonymous with the rococo style, the Marquise de Pompadour, a distinguished patron of the arts, gave active support to the neo-classical movement which began during the last few years of her life. Under her influence her brother, the Marquis de Marigny, was appointed Director of Buildings in 1751. He had visited Italy to study its antiquities with the architect Jacques Soufflot and the writer and engraver Nicolas Cochin, who both became leaders in the revolt against rococo. The archaeological discoveries at Herculaneum and Pompeii and the Greek temples of Athens and Paestum revealed to the eighteenth-century world that the decorative arts of the Greeks and Romans had a richness very different from what had previously been assumed from the grand exteriors of their buildings. The time was ripe for a renewed appreciation of classical art, architecture and institutions. As archaeologists went even further afield, designers added Egyptian and Syrian motifs to their vocabulary. This eclecticism was to lead at its worst to an uneducated mixture of ornament from different cultures but at its best to the evolution of a completely new style.

Public imagination was stirred by publications on ancient Greece and Rome. The Comte de Caylus, in a number of volumes published 1752–7 under the title *Recueil d'antiquités Egyptiennes, Etrusques, Grecques, Romaines et Gauloises*, provided designers and artists with a whole new repertoire of decorative motifs. Nicolas Cochin's *Antiquities of Herculaneum* (1758), and Abbé Johann Wincklemann's *Geschichte der Kunst des Altertums* (1764) which established him as the most distinguished art historian of his era, also helped to promote the new style. Piranesi's evocative engravings of imperial Rome did much to stimulate a romantic interest in that city. He also published a book which included designs for furniture in what he imagined was the ancient Roman manner. Further investigations at a later date in the Naples area were to prove that his concepts came very close to the truth.

French and British designers led the neo-classical movement. They evolved their own individual styles, influenced each other and later were to influence

Italy which had hitherto been more interested in Roman sculpture than in its decorative arts. Known in France as *le style Louis Seize* (although it began at least ten years before his accession in 1774) and in England as the Adam style, neo-classicism spread steadily to the rest of Europe and to America.

The first Parisian house to be decorated in the new style, in the 1750s, was that of the classical scholar Lalive de Jully. The architect Barreau transformed it in the Greek style with urns, decorative garlands and laurel wreaths and matching furniture. At Court, the first example of neo-classicism was the Pavillon de Louveciennes, built in 1771 for Madame du Barry, Madame de Pompadour's successor as royal mistress. The architect C. N. Ledoux modelled it on a Greek temple and decorated and furnished it throughout in the neo-classical manner including, for the first time, chairs with horse-shoe-shaped backs.

French craftsmanship reached its zenith at this time – rarely before had such a profusion of rich materials been used with such consummate skill. No new types of furniture were invented, however; the forms of the previous period were simply updated. During the transitional period of the 1760s, rococo curves still mingled with the straight lines of neo-classicism on many pieces. Lines gradually became more severe, classical proportions and classical decorations were gradually adopted. Straight legs, tapering to the feet, replaced cabriole legs. Some were square in section, others round, with a turned moulding at the top and a small moulding at the foot. The straightness was sometimes emphasized by vertical flutings or spirals. By the 1770s outlines had become rectangular, forms sym-metrical and the rococo S-curve had given way to the circle or the arc. Greek motifs such as the key pattern, egg and dart, paterae and wave bands were used increasingly for furniture decoration. Ormolu (gilt bronze), still a popular decorative material, was usually confined to bands and rectangles.

Seating followed the basic types – the *bergère*, *fauteuil* and *canapé* or sofa – established during the rococo period. A variety of new shapes came into use for the backs of *fauteuils*. Oval or medallion backs often had a carving of a small floral wreath and two sprays tied with a ribbon, or just a ribbon bow, in the centre of the cresting rail. Rectangular backs could be long or almost square with a plain cresting rail. A cresting rail arched in the middle like the handle of a basket was known as an *anse de panier*; if cut away in concave curves at its junctions with the uprights it was called *en chapeau*. The uprights of the later type were often carried up to form finials in the shape of fir cones or feathers. Arm posts were no longer set back on the side rails of the seats but grew out of the top of the straight legs. They were curved inwards until ladies' panniers went out of fashion. A cube decorated with rosettes was usually placed above each leg as part of the seat rail, which was often curved. The carving of all structural parts was elegant and delicate.

Comfortable *bergères* remained in fashion, following the shapes of the *fauteuils*, apart from one version which had a gondola-shaped back with a continuous curve from the end of one arm through the back to the end of the other. Among the more fanciful chairs introduced during this period were those with backs shaped like balloons to commemorate the first flight of the Montgolfier brothers in 1783.

French neo-classicism 1

Bergère with bow-fronted seat and straight legs, and 'chapeau de gendarme' back

Fauteuil in the manner of Jean Baptiste Sené with distinctive thin spirals around the tapering legs

Filing cabinet. One of the first neo-classical pieces commissioned by Lalive de Jully; made by Louis Joseph de Lorrain c.1756

Chair back designed in the shape of the Montgolfiers' balloon

Mahogany chair in 'Etruscan' style - painted back inspired by decorations on Etruscan vases. Georges Jacob

Gilded 'fauteuil de cabinet' with console legs by Georges Jacob, 1787

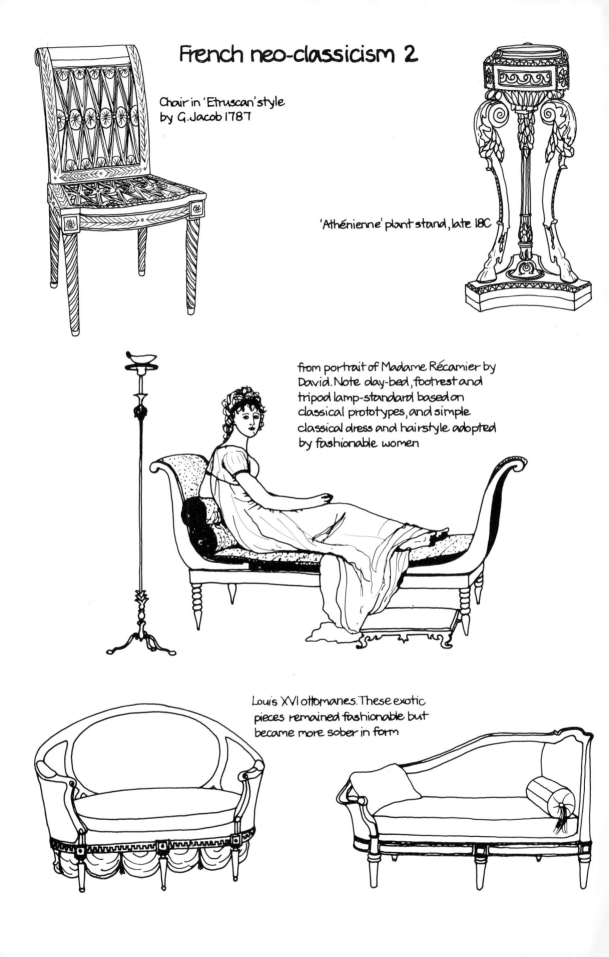

French neo-classicism 2

Chair in 'Etruscan' style
by G. Jacob 1787

'Athénienne' plant stand, late 18C

from portrait of Madame Récamier by
David. Note day-bed, footrest and
tripod lamp-standard based on
classical prototypes, and simple
classical dress and hairstyle adopted
by fashionable women

Louis XVI ottomanes. These exotic
pieces remained fashionable but
became more sober in form

Sofas and day-beds were still popular with ladies who liked an easy lounging position, but the curves were more restrained and symmetry in the main prevailed. The exotic ottoman also remained – one version had only one side, with the back curved round in a controlled manner to form the other side.

The exceptional *menuisiers* of this period were Jean-Baptiste Sené (1740–1803) and Georges Jacob (1739–1814), the greatest eighteenth-century carver. In chair-making Jacob surpassed all others and was constantly introducing new forms and ideas. He was the first to use solid mahogany for chairs in France – a fashion adopted from England. So strongly was he influenced by Chippendale that his chairs in the Chinese taste are very close to *Director* designs. Among Jacob's many innovations were chairs with round seats, console feet and backs with carved, pierced splats in the English manner known as *chaises à l'anglaise*. He introduced the lyre shape to furniture, particularly for chair backs, and was the first to use the sabre-legged chair, anticipating the Empire style.

The greatest among a glittering constellation of *ébénistes* was J. H. Riesener (1734–1806), a German like many other cabinet-makers drawn to Paris to cater for the extravagant tastes of the Court and Parisian society. Riesener, who made a fortune during the good years, was ruined by the Revolution like many other craftsmen. His work displays immense variety. Probably his most exuberant and imposing piece is the commode made for Louis XVI's *petits appartements* at Versailles: its full shape, flanked by four ormolu statues, supports a thick marble slab top, and the central trapezoid shape, a characteristic motif of Riesener, is decorated with floral marquetry and framed with more elaborate ormolu mounts. His best furniture was made after 1780. A roll-top desk and work table made for Marie Antoinette's boudoir at Fontainebleau, combining marquetry of unusual materials – polished steel, mother-of-pearl and ormolu – show Riesener's work at its most delicate and intricate. At the same time he was producing sober pieces of plain veneers enriched with delicate gilt bronze mounts.

Martin Carlin, a compatriot of Riesener, worked almost entirely for the great Parisian *marchands-merciers*, not for private clients. These merchants specialized in the lightweight pieces required for the extravagant yet intimate domestic settings of the rich. Painted Sèvres plaques and lacquer panels favoured in the rococo period continued to be popular until the Revolution, as part of the vogue for highly coloured furniture. Carlin and another German, Adam Weisweiler, both excelled at the prevailing Parisian taste. Their more delicate pieces resemble jewelry rather than furniture. Distinctive features of Weisweiler's work are charming feet like spinning tops and unusual interlacing stretchers on tables, desks, worktables etc.

Pietre dure was again in vogue. Some of the outdated cabinets of Louis XIV's reign were dismantled so that their mosaic panels might be remounted in contemporary pieces.

Imitations of the English potter Josiah Wedgwood's jasperware plaques were inset into furniture – another instance of French anglomania in the 1780s. England now set the fashion in many ways – English gardens were admired and copied, men favoured the comfortable clothes of the English country gentleman,

Neo-classical Ébénistes

Commode made for Louis XVI by J.H. Riesener, enriched with marquetry and opulent ormolu mounts. 1775

Doorway of Marie Antoinette's boudoir at Fontainebleau. The room was decorated by Rousseau in 1785

Roll-top desk and work table by Riesener for Marie-Antoinette's boudoir; veneered with mother-of-pearl, with gilt, steel and silver-gilt mounts

Secrétaire by Martin Carlin decorated with porcelain plaques. 1773

Bed 'à la polonaise' c.1785.
Canopy and upholstery in
the same silk, curtains
draped over classical poles

Writing table by Adam Weisweiler,
decorated with bronzes and with
plaques of Chinese lacquer and
ebony. 1784

Commode by Jean-François Leleu
exemplifies more restrained
masculine side of neo-classicism.
c.1772

Secrétaire by Weisweiler
veneered with thuya wood,
with Sèvres porcelain plaques
and ormolu mounts

young men about town adopted an English accent, English wallpapers were popular.

The work of J. F. Leleu represents a more severe and masculine approach to neo-classical design. Although he used marquetry, his furniture is of massive, simple forms with plain veneers decorated with classical motifs such as pilasters and key patterns, the whole often supported on enormous lion's paws.

Undoubtedly the most commercially successful eighteenth-century *ébéniste* was the German, David Roentgen. His main workshops were in Neuwied, but he was given the post of *Ebéniste-Méchanicien du Roi et de la Reine* – probably because Louis XVI, himself a talented locksmith, was impressed by Roentgen's mechanical genius. Both Roentgen and his father Abraham designed many pieces, particularly writing desks, with complex locks, secret drawers and ingenious machinery to raise and lower various parts and alter the function of the pieces. Their business became the first great international firm. In 1779 Roentgen opened a branch in Paris, the major market of the day where fortunes were spent annually on furniture. By then the clientele was expanding beyond the confines of the Court and Parisian high society – the rich bourgeoisie, other European courts, the English aristocracy were all eager buyers. To meet the demands of a growing European market, subsidiary workshops were set up in Berlin, St Petersburg and Brussels. Probably the secret of Roentgen's success was his ability to satisfy the individual tastes of his eminent clients. As the century waned his early taste for skilful, intricate marquetry gave way to plain, finely marked veneers on more severe neo-classical forms.

The Directoire period takes its name from the government of the Directors which spanned the four years 1795–9, between the Terror and Napoleon's coming to power. It was too short a period for a distinctive style to develop. Like the Régence, it was a transitional period during which ideas germinating for several years before the Revolution were consolidated. During Louis XVI's last years designers were adopting a more academic approach to neo-classical furniture. No longer was it enough to apply classical decoration to eighteenth-century forms – cabinet-makers were attempting to recreate the actual forms of furniture of the ancient world as shown on Greek and Etruscan vases.

For many years philosophers like Rousseau had been decrying social injustice and inequality and the wasteful extravagance of the court and advocating a return to a simpler, more natural way of life. In their eyes the ancient world became the ideal world. Furniture closely copied from the antique, such as chairs with roll-over backs, had been made before the Revolution. The revolutionaries with their admiration for ancient republics found the new taste in furniture very acceptable. Its most celebrated interpreter was the *menuisier* Georges Jacob, under the influence of the leading neo-classical painter David. During the late 1780s David had commissioned Jacob to design a suite of furniture modelled on antique prototypes for his studio. None of it survives, but it can be seen in several of his paintings – 'The Loves of Paris and Helen', 'Brutus', 'Andromache mourning Hector'. It included a bed with a scroll-end head support, a curule-form chair made of bronze with X-supports, mahogany chairs made in the form of the Greek *klismos* chair and a tripod pedestal table which came to be called an *athénienne* after it appeared in a painting by Vien known as 'La Vertueuse Athénienne'. This was to appear in many guises – as a wash hand stand, a candelabra, a vase stand, a plate stand, etc. These studio pieces were eagerly copied by other designers and became popular domestic furniture.

The friendship between David and Jacob was to stand the *menuisier* in good stead during the Terror. David, a prominent revolutionary, gave him protection and through his influence Jacob was commissioned in 1793 to make the furniture for the new conference room in the Palais des Tuileries. Two young architects and designers, Charles Percier and Pierre Fontaine, were introduced by David to design the room but Jacob had over-all command of this enormous project which entailed designing stalls and benches for 760 deputies. Percier and Fontaine were later to become major figures in the formation of the Empire style.

In 1796 Jacob retired, leaving his business, hence to be known as Jacob Frères, to his two sons Georges and François-Honoré. When the elder brother died the younger took the name Jacob-Desmalter and became an outstanding *ébéniste* of the Empire period. Thus the skills of the old regime were passed on to the new. One of Jacob's personal motifs – almost a trade mark – was a marguerite, later adopted by his sons.

The most famous interior of the Directoire period was designed by Percier and Fontaine for Madame Récamier, a renowned beauty and wit whose drawing-room became a meeting place for the leaders of the new regime. The elegant and finely proportioned day-bed, shown in her portrait by David, was modelled on a Grecian couch with roll-over ends. It was immediately copied and became one of the most popular pieces of the day. One version was made with a back.

Symbolism played a large part in late neo-classical furniture design. Many motifs evoked a martial theme – day-beds were modelled in the form of camp beds with tent-like drapes, chairs and stools were made like drums. During the Revolution fasces of arms and Phrygian caps were introduced. Napoleon's Egyptian campaign evoked an interest in Egyptian ornament. Comfort was no longer the dominant factor in design. Comfortable, roomy chairs and settees with plump cushions disappeared. Much of the furniture of the 1790s had a certain starkness after the easy elegance and intimacy of the two preceding decades.

Most of the patrons of the arts, the aristocrats and royalty, were swept away in the Revolution. There was little work for artists and craftsmen – many famous *ébénistes* were prosecuted for their close association with the aristocrats. Not until Bonaparte had crowned himself Emperor in 1804 did conditions allow a revival of fine furniture making.

Outside France, neo-classicism represented a break with French cultural domination which had lasted since the age of Louis XIV and which other countries were beginning to resent.

The second half of the eighteenth century was a period of confidence and prosperity in Britain. Artists and designers flourished under the patronage of those who had accumulated great wealth during the long and prosperous Whig administration, and there was much new building, particularly of fine mansions.

Detail of library ceiling, Harewood House, c.1765

Robert Adam and his influence

Adam design for a stool modelled on an antique cistern, 1768

Mirror, table and tripod designed by Adam for Luton, 1772

Sideboard pedestal and urn, part of a group made by Thomas Chippendale for Harewood House c.1770

Painted commode on blue ground with painted marble top

The major architect was Robert Adam (1728–92), whose effect on domestic architecture, particularly its interiors, was profound. He replaced the predominant Palladian fashion with a lighter, more graceful, mobile style which was to appeal to all classes and influence craftsmen in every branch of the domestic arts.

Like most architects and artists of the time, Adam completed his training in Rome, where an impressive group of French and English avant-gardists had their headquarters, and where he met many of the English aristocracy who were to employ him later. He also met Piranesi, who made a lasting impression on him.

In Adam's eyes the Palladians had failed to distinguish between the interior and exterior decoration of the Romans. Consequently their interior designs were overloaded with heavy entablatures above doors, chimney-pieces and windows, coffered ceilings, etc. In Italy he not only saw the temple architecture which had inspired his predecessors but also became aware that the domestic architecture of the ancient world was very different from its formal public buildings. This neglected area of classical architecture strongly influenced his later work.

He studied the grotesques found among the ancient remains and also the early sixteenth-century painted grotesque work of Raphael and his pupils in the *loggie* of the Vatican and the Villas Madama and Caprarola. The murals excavated at Herculaneum and Pompeii convinced him that he had discovered the classical Roman style of interior decoration. He described the designs of the private apartments as 'all delicacy, gaiety, grace and beauty', qualities he admired and sought to emulate in his own interior designs without slavishly copying the antique forms.

Adam abandoned heavy entablatures and columns except in the most formal rooms and introduced light, delicate moulding. Plaster walls replaced wood-panelling. Colour schemes in pastel shades of blue, pink, green, lilac or grey were relieved by panels of grotesque work executed in low relief plaster and pilasters decorated with arabesques. Heavy coffered ceilings were replaced by flat surfaces decorated with slightly raised geometrical patterns or grotesques. Carpets wherever possible were woven with patterns which echoed or complemented the ceiling decoration. Adam aimed at complete unity in his interiors – a unity probably only realized so completely before in the rococo work of Cuvilliés – and was involved in the design of everything within the house: curtains, pelmets, firegrates and irons, door furniture, wall furniture and 'movables'. Although he probably designed more furniture than any other architect, the amount of work he undertook made it impossible for him to design all the movable furniture in most of his houses. Fortunately a number of talented cabinet-makers of the calibre of Chippendale and John Linnell were able to interpret and produce the 'Adam style'.

Piranesi's etchings of Rome included some illustrations of altars, tripods, candelabra and small articles of bronze and marble. The pedestals with urns which Adam introduced into his dining-rooms to flank the side table were modelled on Roman altars, one of his stool designs was cleverly adapted from an antique cistern, and his various stands and tripods are obviously based upon classical models. There were, however, few surviving pieces of furniture to use as prototypes and he had gradually to feel his way towards a style of furniture which would complement his interiors. At first he resorted to Palladian and rococo forms and applied his repertoire of classical ornament, gathered at first hand, to these. But gradually he rejected the weightiness of one style and the curves of the other and by the late 1760s he had arrived at a mature style of his own. Each piece is smooth, sophisticated and streamlined, classical in proportion and feeling although bearing little resemblance to antique furniture. The form is light and elegant, the decoration rich yet unobtrusive, blending with the decoration of walls and ceilings.

As in France, the cabriole leg was banished and a straight support tapering to the foot was introduced for tables, chairs and commodes. The structural framework was emphasized by the use of friezes, pilasters, etc. Wall furniture – pier tables and glasses, commodes, girandoles and decorative pieces such as tripods, urns and pedestals – dominate Adam's work. Tables had slender tapered legs and their tops were reduced to narrow friezes. The arrangement of the legs in pairs separated by a wide central space to give variety and movement is characteristic of Adam. His later work shows an original treatment for the pier glass and pier table. A tripartite mirror was divided by filigree pilasters or female terms which were laid on to the glass. The top of the central panel was raised in a square or rounded form and ornamented with fanlight tracery patterns to resemble a Palladian window, and the whole was surmounted by urns, medallions, griffins, and festoons. The base of the mirror was brought down to the table top and the four front legs of the table were aligned with the four perpendicular members of the mirror to unify the whole composition.

No Adam house was complete without at least one pair of urns and pedestals. Often they flanked the side table: one pedestal was lined with sheet iron and served as a plate warmer with racks and a stand for a heater, the other probably served as a cupboard for chamber pots (many Georgians were heavy drinkers and sanitary arrangements were still fairly basic). The urns were either containers for cutlery, or water cisterns fitted with taps and lined with lead to hold iced water for drinking or to enable the butler to rinse glasses or cutlery.

The sideboard as we know it today was developed from this ensemble of side table, urns and pedestals by George Hepplewhite. The shallow central section often contained a drawer for linen and was supported on either side by two deep pedestals with cupboards and drawers. One side might contain a water cistern, the other be racked for bottles. The urns soon ceased to be part of the composition. Knife cases were designed to stand independently on sideboard or table.

Adam wine coolers and cellarets, the former lined with zinc to hold ice, the latter compartmented to hold bottles, were usually kept under the side table. They were usually oval in form – some modelled on classical sarcophagi with serpentine fluting and lion's paw feet. Ice was collected in the winter and stored in deep pits, commonly called ice-houses.

The dining-room played an important part in English life at this time. Adam commented, 'The eating rooms are considered as apartments of conversation in which we pass a great deal of our time.' The dining-room, very much the male preserve where the men remained for hours after the women had withdrawn, was functionally furnished in mahogany. The drawing-room however was the ladies' province and was furnished with delicate fabrics and elegant furniture in light satinwood.

Adam designed for the great houses but his ideas filtered down to the middle class and eventually to humbler homes and there was a general demand for lighter, more graceful furniture. Linked with the Adam style and its dissemination throughout the furniture industry are the well-known names of George Hepplewhite and Thomas Sheraton, who adapted and modified the style to suit the tastes of the general public. Their fame rests entirely upon the publication of two pattern books: *The Cabinet-maker and Upholsterer's Guide* (1788) by Hepplewhite, representing the taste of the 1780s (with over 300 different designs for furniture it was the largest publication since Chippendale's *Director*); and *The Cabinet-Maker's and Upholsterer's Drawing Book* by Sheraton, published in parts, 1791–4, showing the taste of the nineties.

For many years these two men occupied a false position in the history of furniture making. They were believed to be major designers – most fine furniture of the correct date was credited indiscriminately to them. In fact, no single piece of furniture has been authenticated as having been made in the workshop of either man, and their names should be used only as a means of categorizing two styles of late Georgian design. The fact that the pattern books were issued mainly for the use of workmen was completely overlooked. They were intended to be of use to 'Countrymen and Artisans whose distance from the metropolis makes even an imperfect knowledge of its improvements acquired with much trouble and expense' and to the minor London makers who did not employ a designer.

Hepplewhite was a lesser member of the trade working in Cripplegate, an unfashionable part of town. When he died in 1786 his widow carried on the business and published the *Guide* two years later. The designs were elegant while remaining practical. There was no novelty furniture – some was strictly utilitarian while some was finely detailed and ornamented in the prevailing taste. Oval, hoop, heart-shaped and the ever popular shield-shaped chair backs were featured prominently, although Hepplewhite was not the first to introduce them. His name is particularly associated with the shield-back and also with the use of the Prince of Wales feathers as a decoration, a motif he probably was the first to use. He also employed many other motifs as fillers – wheat ears, urns, lyre shapes, drapery, honeysuckle.

Hepplewhite was one of the first designers to use japanning, now becoming fashionable again. Chairs of a light framework of beech were japanned or painted to complement the colour scheme of a room. They had cane seats with cushions covered with coloured cotton or linen. Dining chairs were strong and serviceable, probably in mahogany with leather seats. The arm supports of many Adam and Hepplewhite chairs rose from the top of the front legs to just above the seat and then swept back in a pronounced curve to straighten out at the arm rests, which joined the chairback about half way up.

Under the influence of Adam, Sheraton and Hepplewhite, the art of veneer-

Sofa, one of a set of four, by James Stuart; his furniture came closer to classical designs than most English furniture before 1800

Hepplewhite

Sheild-back chair carved with Prince of Wales feathers, in manner of Hepplewhite, c.1785

The fully developed sideboard– from drawing in 3rd edition of 'The Cabinet-Maker and Upholsterer's Guide'

A bar-backed sofa by Hepplewhite, from an engraving 1787

Design for a chamber horse, used by gentlemen for exercising in bad weather. 1793

Designs for chair backs

Sheraton

A sideboard from 'The Cabinet-Maker's and Upholsterer's Drawing Book', 1793

Design for a bidet dressing table by Sheraton, 1793

Sheraton square back chair, mahogany, c.1790

ing, inlay and marquetry reached its zenith of skill and beauty. Painted decoration on furniture went hand in hand with the fondness for light coloured woods. Panels and doors of commodes and cabinets were decorated with figure paintings, either in grisaille or full-colour, in oval or circular medallions set into veneered or painted surrounds. Some were attributed to well-known decorative artists – Pergolesi, Angelica Kauffmann and Cipriani.

Although Sheraton owed much to Adam's influence, his illustrations exemplify the new taste for simplicity in interior decoration which appeared during the last years of the eighteenth century, an inevitable reaction to the intricate decoration of Adam's work. Sheraton established himself in London in 1790 as a drawing master, making designs for the furniture trade and publishing his books – the famous *Drawing Book* and also *The Cabinet Dictionary* and the unfinished *Cabinet-Maker, Upholsterer and General Artist's Encyclopaedia*. He probably never had a workshop of his own or made any furniture under his own name but it is believed that he trained and worked as a cabinet-maker in someone else's business. He certainly understood the techniques of furniture making.

The Sheraton style is individual but has affinities with that of the last years of Louis XVI and the Directoire. A considerable amount of French Louis XVI furniture was brought to England by the first *emigrés* and had appeared on the market by 1790 when Sheraton was working on the *Drawing Book*. He may also have had contact with French craftsmen fleeing from the Revolution. He was certainly indebted to French models for such pieces as the conversation chair and *duchesse*. His drawing book was a distillation of what he considered the best in London design. There is no sharp dividing line between the Adam-Hepplewhite style and that of Sheraton. Both schools used floral inlay or painted decoration on satinwood, painted medallions in the Angelica Kauffmann manner, the inlaid shell-motif and the straight, slender, tapered leg.

On large flat or slightly curved surfaces Sheraton made little use of Adam's decorative motifs but usually enlivened them with contrasting veneers laid in oval or lozenge-shaped patterns set off by black or brass stringing lines and borders of cross-banding. He also introduced brass in the form of galleries on sideboards, desks and worktables (a French fashion).

A characteristic feature of Sheraton chairs is the strong sweep backwards of the arms to meet the back at the cresting rail. The backs were usually lower than those of other contemporary models. Sheraton re-introduced square and rectangular forms into chair backs, sofa backs, mirrors. A simplified version of his square-backed chair, with vertical struts or sticks, became very popular in the country – its simple construction was easy for rural craftsmen to reproduce and it was strong enough to stand up to the fairly rough life of cottage and farmhouse.

Eighteenth-century chairs grew increasingly complicated in form as the century progressed. The shaping of, for example, the shield-back, one of the most beautiful chairs of this period, runs in three directions: the shield shape as seen from the front, the backward rake, and the concave shape as seen in the plan. To produce a harmonious whole out of this compound shaping called for considerable skill. The lower part of the shield, which appears to be made in one piece,

Mahogany urn-shaped 'harlequin' secretaire in the heavy, austere manner of the turn of the century, with rising compartment fitted with drawers. c.1790

Mahogany breakfront bookcase, late 18C

Style of Hepplewhite and Sheraton

Side table, carved and gilded, with a painted panel

Painted cabinet, with medallions of classical figures and floral garlands, c.1790

Moulding disguises joint

Detail of joint of bottom back rail and side part of shield back

Round and D-shaped seats with back legs housed in the curved seat rails

Back legs splay outwards

Shield-back chair – compound shaping requires a lot of wood and labour. Dotted line shows width of timbers

consists of three parts: the two sides, which in fact continue downwards to form the back legs, and a curved bottom rail fitted between them to complete the shield shape. A moulding which runs round the whole shield shape disguises the joins so that it appears as one piece.

The oval-backed chair with a round or D-shaped seat presented further difficulties: because the back legs had to be housed within the curved seat rail they were splayed outwards instead of converging slightly or going straight back. This form was not only difficult to make, it also used more wood – altogether a very costly chair. Many 'Sheraton' chairs had backs with simple shapes which considerably cut down the working costs.

The London furniture trade was organized differently from that in Paris. There were a few shops, run by shopkeepers rather than craftsmen who, like the *marchands-merciers* in Paris, bought their stock from individual craftsmen and small workshops; but in the main the fashionable retail establishments were run by eminent craftsmen such as Chippendale, Hallett, Goodison, Vile and Cobb. They supervised the whole business of designing, manufacturing and selling under one roof. These craftsmen were highly specialized – each man concentrating on a particular aspect of his craft.

Sophie von la Roche, a German visitor, was very impressed to find some four hundred people employed at Seddon's furniture factory in Aldersgate, London, in 1786 – cabinet-makers, upholsterers, mirror makers, gilders, ormolu makers, etc. Each workman in such an establishment supplied his own set of tools and retained a certain amount of independence. The division of labour among the various craftsmen and the improved new tools from Birmingham increased efficiency, but as yet there was no mass production – cabinet-makers had not yet adopted wood-working machinery, although some was in the experimental stage.

Many eighteenth-century Londoners were forced to live in very cramped conditions in order to be near their work, since there was no cheap transport. Many rented unfurnished rooms and bought their furniture on the hire-purchase system by weekly instalments. Lack of space probably accounted for the large number of ingeniously designed, space-saving, dual-purpose furniture which appeared in the cabinet-makers' design books after 1760. Bookcase-wash-stands which folded up to look like desks, bedsteads which resembled wardrobes when closed, and other such innovations enabled a bedroom to be transformed into a sitting-room. These pieces are the forerunners of the constituent furniture of the nineteenth century.

In America, the War of Independence slowed down the importation of European furniture and prevented the introduction of Robert Adam's designs. Cabinet-makers continued to work in the Chippendale style. It was some years before fresh developments appeared, but the ratification of the new American Constitution in 1788 seemed to provide the necessary stimulus for a revitalizing of the arts.

Hepplewhite furniture imported into America became popular enough for local cabinet-makers to imitate. It was closely followed from about 1795 onwards by the Sheraton style. These unpretentious, simple designs, devoid of the heavy elaborate decoration of the previous periods, admirably suited the aspirations of the new republic and the needs of the new senators for stylish furniture and fittings for their neo-classical houses.

For the first time, French styles began to have an impact on American design – an interest probably generated first by the encouragement that France had offered the colonies during the war and later by a fellow-feeling for the French revolutionaries. The cabriole leg was replaced either by the straight leg or by the Directoire sabre leg. Satinwoods, veneers and string banding or painted decoration replaced mahogany and carving.

Although English designs were faithfully followed by some cabinet-makers, others freely mixed Hepplewhite and Sheraton elements; and American decorative motifs such as the eagle, a symbol of American independence, were combined with English to produce attractive and highly individual styles.

Philadelphia, the new nation's capital until 1880, remained an important centre of furniture production with over a hundred cabinet-makers, twenty-one chair makers and various other specialists. She acquired a reputation for distinctive work in the new style. One of her most notable designers was John Aitken who, with other Philadelphia designers, made use of the Sheraton pattern of urns and drapery as infilling for square-backed chairs but introduced individual touches such as a central urn motif between long looped drapes.

Other important furniture centres were developing at this time in Boston, Salem and New York, and each exported furniture. John Seymour, a distinguished British immigrant cabinet-maker, settled in Boston with his son Thomas. They produced elegant, beautifully made furniture, combining veneers and painted decoration to create a distinctive style which became a hallmark of the city's work.

Salem, a small seaport near Boston, grew rich through the 'China trade'. American captains could now trade where they pleased – not only in the south and west of America, but as far away as the Orient. Salem's furniture went far afield, to South America and South Africa. Ship's captains were commissioned to sell the furniture and purchase a cargo of rum, spices, sugar and other goods which could be sold profitably on their return to New England. Among half a dozen fine cabinet-makers in Salem, probably the best known name was Samuel McIntyre, a versatile wood carver who designed houses and furniture. A notable feature of his shield-back chairs, derived from Hepplewhite, was a delicate trailing vine motif tied with a bow which he introduced on the front legs. The town's most distinctive creation was the Salem secretary, a drop-front, kneehole writing desk which combined the functions of bookcase and cabinet. This was the kind of furniture that was shipped as 'venture' cargo.

Gradually Philadelphia lost the leadership in the furniture trade, sustained throughout the colonial days, to New York which grew in importance during the Federal period. More and more furniture makers were drawn there – the most distinguished among them was Duncan Phyfe. Unlike many American furniture makers willing to turn a hand to various carpentry jobs, Phyfe worked in the English tradition. He founded a workshop which prospered until, as New York's

Functional elegance

Three-part dining table of type common in Britain and America

Mahogany cheval dressing table modelled on a Sheraton design in the 'Drawing Book', c.1795

Country chair from Norfolk or Suffolk showing Sheraton's influence

Early American Federal furniture

Martha Washington armchair with high balloon-shaped back, late 18C

Mahogany sideboard in Sheraton style, attributed to John and Thomas Seymour, Boston, c.1810

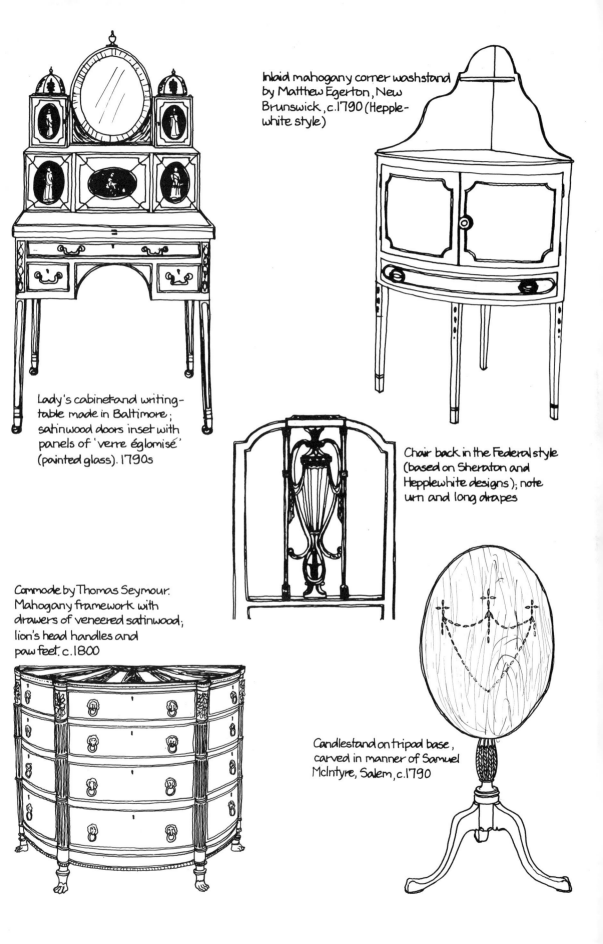

Inlaid mahogany corner washstand by Matthew Egerton, New Brunswick, c.1790 (Hepplewhite style)

Lady's cabinet and writing-table made in Baltimore; satinwood doors inset with panels of 'verre églomisé' (painted glass). 1790s

Chair back in the Federal style (based on Sheraton and Hepplewhite designs); note urn and long drapes

Commode by Thomas Seymour. Mahogany framework with drawers of veneered satinwood; lion's head handles and paw feet. c.1800

Candlestand on tripod base, carved in manner of Samuel McIntyre, Salem, c.1790

leading cabinet-maker in the 1790s, he was employing over a hundred men and had his own timber yard. He was both a fine craftsman and a clever business man. Although he made use of the fashionable satinwood, Phyfe worked mainly in mahogany, a wood which gave his work in the neo-classical style its characteristic but unusual weight and dignity. He was patronized by the fashionable people of the day whose wealth accumulated as New York grew into a prosperous commercial city, and at the same time his clientele spread further afield, particularly to the south.

Some of the most distinctive Federal furniture was produced in Baltimore, where designers were strongly influenced by the work of the French cabinet-makers Carlin and Weisweiler. Instead of Carlin's Sèvres plaques, they introduced panels of *verre eglomisé*, a technique developed almost exclusively in Baltimore: oval or lozenge-shaped glass panels were painted on the reverse with allegorical figures in gold and black. Combined with mitred satinwood veneers inlaid with thin ebony stringing, they made a unique and rich ornament for such specialities as ladies' writing desks.

Modified versions of the English sideboard were popular during the Federal period. The whole carcase was usually occupied by cupboards and drawers, unlike the English version which generally had a kneehole in the centre. The decoration was more restrained – simple stringing in light woods on a dark ground – though McIntyre of Salem produced some attractive versions with carved legs. American dining-tables in the last quarter of the century mostly followed the popular English pattern consisting of three units which could be used independently or clipped together to form one large table. The centre section had rectangular drop leaves, the two end sections were usually D-shaped and could serve as pier tables when not in use. The legs were commonly of square tapered form until the turn of the century when pedestal supports of turned columns and splayed feet became fashionable. Little attention had been paid to the dining-table in France until the very late eighteenth century; until then a simple board covered with a good white cloth served in the grandest of houses. A circular table on a pedestal support, introduced about 1790, proved very popular and soon appeared all over Europe and America.

Sofas in the classical manner became increasingly popular; and the 'Martha Washington', an armchair unique to America, with high narrow back and open arms, was produced in New Hampshire between 1800 and 1810.

The nineteenth century – age of diversity

The nineteenth century was a period of rapid social and technological change throughout Europe and America. The authority of the Church, the rulers and the aristocracy, patrons of the arts and arbiters of taste in previous centuries, was challenged by a rapidly expanding bourgeoisie whose appetite for the good things in life grew as it became wealthier. No longer could the taste of a rich aristocratic minority dominate the fashions of a whole country.

In England, for example, the population more than doubled in the first fifty years of the century. The traditionally organized furniture trade was unable to cope with the expanding market. A new technology had to evolve. Throughout the early years of the century there was a restless search for new manufacturing methods, new techniques and materials, in all areas of industry. Increasingly, domestic objects were designed to be made in several easily assembled parts by machinery. Josiah Wedgwood was the first to introduce new industrial methods – the division of labour and the production line – in the pottery industry. His increased productivity seriously endangered rival businesses. He was soon followed, not only by other potters, but by manufacturers of textiles, wallpapers and decorative ironwork. Cabinet-makers, however, were slow to adopt mechanization, in spite of the remarkable collection of woodworking machinery designed by Sir Samuel Bentham and patented in 1793, which was capable of most of the processes achieved by machinery today – sawing, planing, moulding, grooving, chamfering, etc. Until the middle of the nineteenth century the mechanical saw driven by steam power was the only furniture machinery in general use. One great advantage of steam driven machinery was that it transformed the exacting skill of slicing veneers into a very simple process. Veneered furniture became much cheaper, demand increased, and to some extent it became devalued in the eyes of the connoisseur. Steam was sometimes used to drive powerful lathes, but manual labour was more common and most manufacturers considered the use of woodworking machinery uneconomic even as late as the 1870s.

A speeding up of production was achieved in many large workshops not by the introduction of machinery but by adopting the 'shop method', already started in some establishments in the eighteenth century, in place of the apprenticeship system. Originally young craftsmen learned their trade under the guidance of a master craftsman who instructed them in the whole process of furniture making and was responsible for the finished article; he might also have designed it. Under factory methods each craftsman was responsible only for a limited part of the finished product. Inevitably, standards fell as men lost pride in their work.

The simple, massive forms with plain surfaces favoured during the French Empire and English Regency period of the early nineteenth century were ideal for industrialization. The introduction of French polish, a varnish made from shellac dissolved in spirits of wine, made it possible to achieve a glossy surface quickly, using semi-skilled labour. Previously furniture had been painstakingly polished with beeswax and turpentine or linseed oil to develop a fine patina. With French polish the finest surfaces still had to be built up slowly by hours of rubbing in a rotary direction with a cloth pad, using progressively less lac in proportion to spirit, but little effort was required to obtain a surface acceptable to the new middle-class market. Unfortunately much Georgian furniture was stripped and spoilt by French polishing in the nineteenth century.

During the early years of the century, however, style rather than technology still dominated furniture design. Neo-classicism, adopted throughout Europe, took on different characteristics in France and England. In France under Napoleon's patronage it became the official style, admirably suited to his desire to create an appropriate image for his new regime, to identify himself with the emperors of ancient Rome, and to celebrate his military triumphs. Although after 1799 he had put an end to any further destruction of the nation's cultural heritage, Napoleon disliked the idea of using the furniture of those he had supplanted. As part of his plan to heighten the prestige of the new regime, he ordered the refurnishing of the former royal residences and later the furnishing of new ones acquired outside France. He and the Empress Josephine personally sponsored designers and manufacturers, visiting Gobelins and Sèvres and the work-shops of cabinet-makers. He encouraged luxury, to bolster national prosperity – 'We must lay aside jack boots and think of commerce, encourage the arts, give prosperity to our country.' There was a reflowering of the arts, particularly in the field of furniture. Many cabinet-makers of the *ancien régime* had survived, among them Guillaume Beneman, Jacob and Riesener, to assure a continuity of style and quality despite the trauma of the Revolution.

Several components of the Empire or Napoleonic style had already appeared by the end of Louis XVI's reign. The book by Percier and Fontaine, *Recueil de décorations intérieures* (1802), with engraved plates illustrating the whole repertoire of motifs, crystallized the new style and became the 'bible' of First Empire ornament for cabinet-makers.

Napoleon and Josephine engaged Percier and Fontaine to convert their several establishments, beginning with Malmaison, a house which represents Josephine's taste rather than Napoleon's – a feminine version of the new style. Percier and Fontaine interpreted Napoleon's ideas very successfully, creating a style of austere splendour from the grandeur of the arts of ancient Rome which so much appealed to him.

Furniture took on simple, severe, geometric forms dominated by straight lines. Surfaces were plain with the minimum of ornament. Napoleon disliked fussy ornament and Percier often had to modify his designs. Carving and marquetry disappeared and craftsmen began to substitute gilt bronze decorations which looked well on the rich hard Cuban or Nicaraguan mahogany woods favoured until the English blockade. Prominent among the decorative motifs were imperial and martial emblems such as figures of Victory with outstretched wings, laurel wreaths, eagles, helmeted warriors' heads, winged flambeaux, trophies of lances, fasces and thunderbolts. Much of the ornament was copied directly from Greek or Roman objects. Bees and hives, the emblems of Napoleon's family, appear frequently. The bee motif was first seen at Napoleon's coronation as a substitute for the gold fleur-de-lys which traditionally decorated the ceremonial robes of the kings of France; Napoleon wanted something personal. A capital N surrounded by a laurel wreath was another popular motif, as was the swan, a favourite of Josephine's.

Baron Denon, one of the official artists who accompanied Napoleon on his campaigns in Egypt to examine and make studies of antiquities, published his drawings in 1802 in a fascinating book, *Voyage dans la Basse et Haute Egypte pendant les campagnes du Général Bonaparte*, which was not only of archaeological interest, but of great use to the decorative artist. It aroused interest all over Europe. The Egyptian fashion in furniture was encouraged by Denon who himself commissioned several pieces from Jacob-Desmalter for his own use, among them a pair of armchairs with sides made in the form of standing lions based on drawings he had made at Thebes. Motifs copied from Egyptian temples, tombs and columns were eagerly incorporated into Empire designs, including a variety of animal forms – sphinxes, winged lions, chimeras; monpodia were used as table legs, swans formed the arms of chairs and posts of beds and sofas. Furniture became a blend of Greek, Roman and Egyptian prototypes.

The furniture of Jacob-Desmalter, the son of Georges Jacob, epitomizes the Empire style. He was not only engaged to refurnish the imperial palaces but worked also for prominent socialites, such as the Récamiers and Mademoiselle Mars, and for the general market, running about fifteen workshops. From 1796 he worked with his elder brother under the name 'Jacob Frères, rue Meslée', until his brother's death in 1803. From that time he added 'Desmalter', the name of a small estate of his father in Burgundy, to Jacob.

Empire furniture was conceived as part of an over-all decor to complement the architecture and ensure a pleasing interior harmony. Favourite pieces were the commode, often fitted with a pair of doors to hide the drawers, and the *chiffonnière*, a development of the commode with many more drawers. The *secrétaire*, a similar piece, and the *bonheur-du-jour*, a ladies' desk, were prestige items. The console table, updated with current motifs, was a distinctive piece of Empire furniture. Round tables for various uses were usually fairly accurate copies of antique models. The bed, placed lengthways against the wall rather than in an alcove, took many forms – boat-shaped, *à la turque* with two scrolled ends of equal height, *à l'antique* with a headboard only. A dome or tent-shaped

The Empire style

The bee motif

Napoleon's throne, designed by Percier and Fontaine. The 'N' was removed from within the laurel wreath when the Empire fell

The swan motif as used on an upholstery fabric

Gilt bronze andirons in form of Roman helmet and sword. Metal base has motif of wings and thunderbolts

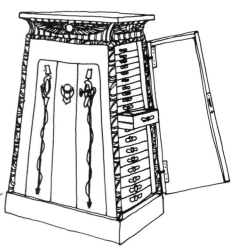

Typical Empire stool with elaborate legs of crossed swords, richly gilded

Napoleon's shield-shaped paper-holder, by Biennais; mahogany with gilt bronze

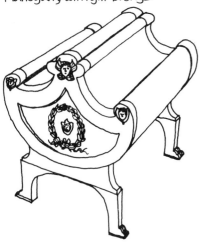

Medal cabinet with Egyptian motifs, by Jacob-Desmalter, after 1802. Mounts by Biennais

Empire chair in the
Egyptian manner

Commode of type designed by Jacob brothers,
with laurel wreath and antique vase bronze
mounts. The door hides a tier of drawers

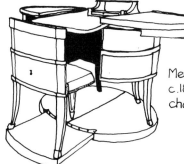

Mechanical desk by Socchi,
c.1810, opens to reveal
chair and writing materials

Meridienne in the Emperor's
study, Château de Compiègne

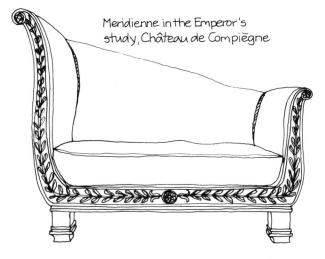

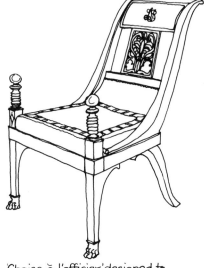

'Chaise à l'officier' designed to
accommodate an officer wearing
a sword. Giovanni Socchi, Florence,
c.1810

canopy was often fixed above the bed, its draped curtains looped around military symbols such as lances or arrows.

The sofa at this time was set against the wall and became a fitting. It was much larger and its wooden frame was often entirely covered by the upholstery – a foretaste of later fashions. An Empire version of the *chaise-longue*, the *saumier*, had a back and two ends of equal height; the *méridienne* had one end lower than the other, with a sloping back. Empire chairs took on many forms. In general those in use at the end of the eighteenth century remained in favour; only their decorative treatment changed. Particularly popular was the gondola chair – its rounded form comfortably supported the sitter's back, the arms and back were combined in a flowing curve down to the seat rail and often incorporated swans, lions, griffins or sphinxes. For chairs and stools the curule form with X-frame supports was popular. Napoleon re-introduced the stool to Court circles, decreeing that armchairs were solely for the use of the Empress, his mother and himself.

The best cabinet-makers produced superb work at this time, but 'everyday' furniture in France was inferior to that of pre-revolutionary days. With the Guilds disbanded, many cabinet-makers lowered their standards.

In England, the first step towards a more severe classicism can be seen in the work of the architect Henry Holland, which was developing along similar lines to that of Percier and Fontaine in France. Although influenced by the French, his work has a distinctive English flavour. His sure grasp of style enabled him to adapt easily for his own use the drawings of ancient Roman furniture and decoration sent to him by his pupil C. H. Tatham, studying in Rome. His best-known furniture designs were those for the Prince of Wales at Carlton House and for Samuel Whitbread at Southill. By the time of his death in 1806 the Regency style was firmly established under his influence.

By now a new name was coming to the fore – that of Thomas Hope, a rich banker, scholar, amateur architect, collector of antiquities and friend and admirer of Percier. He had purchased Sir William Hamilton's remaining collection of Greek vases, bronzes and busts and aimed to transform his London house and his country establishment, Deepdene in Surrey, into a suitable setting for this collection and his other art treasures. He had furniture made to his own designs for the rooms in which they were housed. His narrow archaeological approach, based on sound scholarship, produced close copies of Egyptian, Greek and Roman furniture, and despite the museum-like atmosphere of his houses his designs excited attention. In his book, *Household Furniture and Interior Decoration* (1807), he aimed to provide a selection of designs which would 'associate all the elegancies of antique forms and ornaments with all the requisites of modern custom and habits.' But it was George Smith's derivative pattern book, *A Collection of Designs for Household Furniture and Interior Decoration*, published in 1808, which popularized Hope's ideas and presented them in practical, usable forms. Smith's book became as representative of the classical Regency style as Chippendale's *Director* had been of the mid-Georgian period. It was a style admirably suited to the new, well-proportioned villas and terrace houses springing up in many parts of the country. Some of Smith's designs are in the Chinese taste re-introduced by the Prince of

Council chair, gilt, c.1813. Associated with C.H. Tatham because of his etchings of similar antique seats in marble

Chair in Egyptian taste designed by Thomas Hope for his London house, c.1807

The Regency or English Empire style
The academic approach

Design for bedstead and footstool by Hope. Figures of 'Night' riding a crescent and scattering poppies decorate the pilasters

Armchair in manner of George Smith, painted bronze green and gilded, c.1810

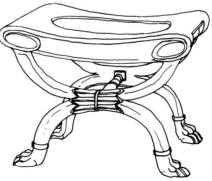

English X-framed stool modelled on ancient Roman curule, early 19C

Drawing-room pier table from Smith's 'A Collection of Designs for Household Furniture and Interior Decoration', 1808

Wales at Brighton Pavilion, others in the gothic, though neither style was used by Hope. The gothic revival owes much to the romantic novels of Sir Walter Scott, whose Scottish house, Abbotsford, was designed in 1816 in a medieval manner; some chairs in this style are known as Abbotsford chairs.

Much Regency furniture was an amalgam of two or more styles. Miss Mitford's description of Rosedale Cottage in *Our Village* is an amusing comment on the eclecticism of the period: 'Every room is a masquerade: the saloon Chinese, full of jars and mandarins and pagodas: the library Egyptian, all covered with hieroglyphics and swarming with crocodiles and sphinxes. Only think of a crocodile and sphinx sofa! They sleep in Turkish tents and dine in a Gothic chapel . . .'

The Grecian revival introduced the popular Greek *klismos* chair – one elegant version was the distinctive and beautiful parlour chair known as the Trafalgar chair, often decorated with rope turning and so called because its design reached a peak in 1805, the year of Nelson's victorious battle. Rope turning, dolphins, sea-shells, anchors and other maritime motifs appeared with each victory: his earlier triumph at the Battle of the Nile popularized Egyptian motifs such as lotus leaves and sphinxes' heads – and introduced such bizarre pieces as crocodile couches.

The Grecian sofa copied from vase paintings was a characteristic Regency piece and its companion, the sofa table, was a highly fashionable Regency innovation beloved by ladies as a needlework or writing table. An interesting new form of writing table, the Carlton House desk, with a superstructure of little drawers and cupboards around the sides and back, proved popular. Circular dining-tables were supported on a pedestal or circular base.

Dark, glossy woods – mahogany and rosewood and boldly figured woods such as zebra wood and amboyna – were favoured. Wood inlay had become too expensive for many people and carving was a dying craft. Brass – cheap, durable, and handsome against the dark woods – became the main decorative medium. It was used in a variety of ways: thin stringing lines and beadings, inlay of sheet brass cut in floral or scroll forms, a more elaborate inlay in the manner of Boulle for expensive pieces, galleries around sideboards etc., wire trellis work in cabinet doors, and castors for chairs and tables.

The Empire style had influenced English design from an early date and soon spread to most of Europe, following swiftly on the heels of Napoleon's conquests in Italy, Sicily, Spain and Holland. Independent nations like Austria, Russia and Sweden were also eager to adopt the new style. Its effect was particularly strong in Italy where Napoleon's family was established in a number of small kingdoms. Little is known of the local craftsmen who were commissioned to work in the Parisian style. Giovanni Socchi of Florence is one of the few whose names survive. He produced some elegant furniture for Napoleon's sister, Elisa Bacciochi, Grand Duchess of Tuscany, and is famed for his mechanical writing desks with extending tops and chairs ingeniously concealed within the structure.

The American 'Empire' style was a mixture of English and French influence. The best furniture of the period was produced in New York where Duncan Phyfe evolved an interesting version of the Regency style and French *emigrés* such as Charles-Honoré Lannuier were working in the Empire style.

Trafalgar chair. Note rope motif on top rail, central motif of anchors, and scimitar legs

Carlton House writing table, probably named after the Prince Regent's London residence

Practical adaptations of the classical style

Chaise longue with inlaid brass work

Large table on central pedestal. Top inlaid with brass, probably by Frenchman Louis le Gaigneur who revived Boulle work. c.1820

Games table; sliding panel covers a well for games equipment. c.1803

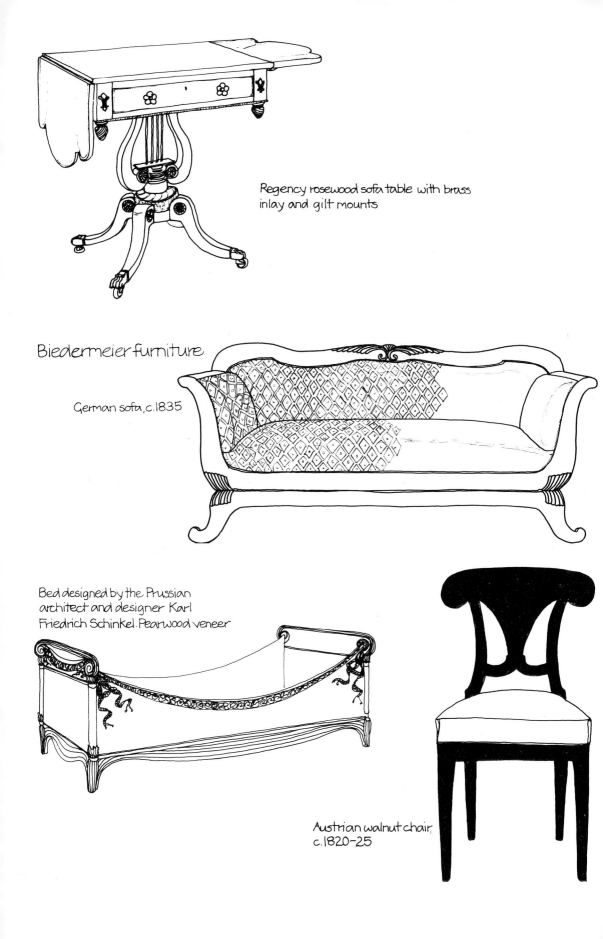

Regency rosewood sofa table with brass inlay and gilt mounts

Biedermeier furniture

German sofa, c.1835

Bed designed by the Prussian architect and designer Karl Friedrich Schinkel. Pearwood veneer

Austrian walnut chair, c.1820–25

An offspring of the Empire style was the simple and attractive Biedermeier furniture made in Austria and some of the German states. Once again, what was at first a derisory label became accepted as the name of a new style. Biedermeier was a combination of the names of two comical characters, Biedermann and Bummelmeier, who represented the self-satisfied philistinism of the bourgeoisie. Not only had the middle classes been impoverished by the war with Napoleon, but the Courts also were short of money. All royal building was stopped; the Austrian Emperor himself practised and encouraged a simpler life style, and the virtues of simple family life were extolled. The more intimate and casual style of Biedermeier furniture, in which comfort took precedence over pomp and circumstance, admirably expressed this mood. The softening of Empire forms also led to a more informal arrangement of interiors. Rooms were sparsely furnished and there were fewer types of furniture – the high-backed, well upholstered sofa was a dominant feature, a round table with a few chairs, long simple mirrors and that symbol of nineteenth century domesticity, the piano, were the main furnishings of the drawing-room. With this new informality came flowers, screens, work tables and various knick-knacks. Bronze mounts disappeared and pale coloured woods like maple, cherry and birch, known collectively as *bois clair* were favoured, particularly in Austria.

Most European countries produced their own versions of Biedermeier furniture, and the stage might well have been set for a new functionalism if other influences had not been at hand. As a reaction to the disciplined conventions of neo-classicism and, perhaps, to increasing mechanization and scientific progress, a romantic revival began to spread through Europe, with a return to past styles. Germany rediscovered first the Middle Ages, then the renaissance and baroque periods. In Austria there was a rococo revival. In France a gothic revival was followed by a return to sixteenth-, seventeenth- and eighteenth-century styles.

British furniture makers, reacting to what was referred to at the time as 'Georgian barbarism', promoted a number of fanciful styles, often imperfectly interpreted, since the study of art history was in its infancy. J. C. Loudon, in his *Encyclopaedia of Cottage, Farm and Villa Architecture and Furniture* (1833), illustrates four styles – Greek, Gothic, Elizabethan and Louis XIV. Other pattern books added several more, among them Louis XV, Pompeian and Moorish. Although taste in furniture in the 1830s and 1840s was catholic and diverse styles were often uncomfortably juxtaposed, the standard of craftsmanship remained high. As new areas of the world were opened up, cabinet-makers had a wider choice of woods than ever before. Also, native woods became fashionable again, and English plants and flowers regained popularity as an alternative to classical motifs.

What might be called the 'association of ideas' came to play an important part in the choice of certain styles for particular uses. The gothic style, thought of in England as a patriotic choice during the Napoleonic war, was considered a sound, sober style suitable for the more masculine, solemn rooms of the house – the library, the hall, and perhaps the dining-room, still the male preserve. The drawing-room, boudoir and other ladies' rooms were often in the more frivolous rococo style. The 'Elizabethan' style, an inaccurate term used to embrace all periods of English furniture from Henry VIII to the Restoration, was highly approved of as representing sturdy national traits. The so-called 'naturalistic' style which evolved from that of Louis XIV was characterized by rich naturalistic carving and swelling forms. Woods were chosen carefully to promote different moods. Light-coloured woods were believed to create a happy, friendly atmosphere for drawing-rooms and bedrooms. Oak and mahogany were considered appropriate for inducing a quiet, restful mood in libraries, dining-rooms and halls.

A distinctive feature of early Victorian furniture was the rounded form of most pieces, whatever their historical style. This is seen particularly clearly on sofas, sideboards, *chiffonnières* and the balloon-back chair, a charming and typically Victorian piece.

During the nineteenth century the machine played its part more in the development of experimental than of traditional furniture. There was a pioneering spirit abroad, eager to develop new materials and overcome technical obstacles. This experimental furniture was often highly original in design and made from materials such as iron, wire, papier-mâché, marble and horn. It is outside the mainstream of historical revivals and stands apart from the 'reformers' furniture of the latter part of the century. Much of it helped to form the background to twentieth-century developments and taste.

The most exciting nineteenth-century development in the furniture industry took place in Austria, where Michael Thonet invented a series of new processes for bending beechwood frames to any required shape by heat and steam treatment to produce his timeless, elegant and functional bentwood furniture. He also invented much of the machinery for adapting these processes to the mass-production line.

Thonet was born in 1796 at Boppard, a few miles from the site of David Roentgen's famous eighteenth-century factory at Neuwied. He set up his own workshop at the age of twenty-three, producing furniture by traditional methods in the Biedermeier style with an emphasis on simplicity and functionalism. It was not until 1830 that he began to look for a new way of making furniture without joints, to save labour and materials. The technique he evolved was partly derived from carriage-making and ship-building methods, in both of which thin strips of wood were bent by heat and water and then laminated together. Thonet took strips of wood of the type used for veneering, bent them to shape, and glued them together to make up the necessary thickness. In subsequent experiments the strips were tied together and then boiled in glue. His earliest experimental furniture was formed almost entirely of laminated wood, with the inner laminations made of ordinary wood, covered by a good veneer on the outside. By 1841 his technique was sufficiently developed to warrant taking out patents in England, France and Belgium, and his work attracted the attention of Prince Metternich, who encouraged him to settle in Vienna. Here, in partnership with Carl Leistler, he provided furniture for the Palais Liechtenstein. His light, elegant chairs made of laminated veneers are forerunners of the solid bentwood furniture of his mature style. In 1849 Thonet founded a firm in his own name. From 1848 Austria was

Stylistic revivals

English design for a carved and painted 'gothic' conversational sofa by L.N. Cottingham, 1840s

Chair 'à la cathedrale'. French neo-gothic style in oak, c.1840

Firescreen in 'naturalistic' style, designed and carved by William Kendal of Warwick, 1858

Chair in mis-named 'Elizabethan' style, c.1845

Middle-class furniture

Dressing-table from Harrods catalogue. Note rounding of forms

Collapsible balloon-back chair, c.1830

Davenport – a popular small desk c.1850

becoming increasingly industrialized – the State supported commercial enterprises and encouraged mechanization. Thonet installed machinery for mass production in his factory in 1856, having by now decided that laminated wood was not the most satisfactory material for his designs – a fact brought home to him when he began to export to the Americas and discovered that humid conditions dissolved the glue.

After more experiment he evolved a method of bending solid wood without breaking it. Beechwood, being pliant, with few knots and long fibres, was ideal. Lengths of timber about 3cm square were sawn mechanically and rounded on a lathe, then made pliable by steaming and attached by clamps to metal straps. Wood and metal were bent together, with the metal on the outside to take the strain, and forced into an iron form. After remaining in a drying-room for several days, the wood became permanently set in the desired shape. The pieces were then dyed, assembled and polished. Skilled labour was required only for weaving the cane seats and backs. This new technique made mass production possible and by about 1859 Thonet's fully-mechanized process was producing functional, light, cheap furniture without any decoration whatsoever. Chair No. 14, the most renowned of his pieces – costing about three shillings or 75 US cents at the time – was made up of only six machine-made parts (see illustration, page 170). It could be transported in pieces and assembled with ten screws on arrival. It was immensely popular in the nineteenth century and is still being made today.

The most graceful and admired of all Thonet's pieces is his rocking chair. The first model, with a buttoned leather seat and back, went into production in 1860, but over the next decade form and construction were refined and the more functional cane replaced the leather upholstery. The proportions of the seat, the angle of the back and the coiled underframing gave it greater support and stability than any other rocker. Rockers were already popular in America; Thonet introduced them to Europe where they were little known. In England the rocker had previously been considered an effeminate novelty for the use of the weaker sex and invalids!

Thonet, the business man and exploiter of the machine, came much closer than William Morris, the reformer, to achieving furniture of beauty and utility for the common man. His furniture was found in palaces and cottages, cafés, hotels, shops, music halls, ships and public buildings throughout the world.

In America another furniture manufacturer, John Henry Belter, was using a similar lamination and steaming process, in a richly decorative neo-rococo style. Rosewood, his favourite wood, was too brittle for carving and difficult to apply as a veneer to curved surfaces, but by his process it could be adapted for elaborately curved and carved pieces. Laminae of rosewood, sometimes as many as sixteen in all, each $\frac{1}{16}$in. (1.5mm) thick, were glued together with the grain of each layer at right-angles to its neighbour, to form a panel. After steaming into the required shape in a mould, this prepared panel could then be carved with elaborate naturalistic designs of fruit, leaves and flowers enriched with piercing, without any danger of splitting.

In 1874 an American patent was taken out for a bentwood chair made of three pieces of laminated wood – one formed a continuous back, seat and front leg, a second strengthened the back and continued down to form the back leg, and a third formed a stretcher between the other two. This process of lamination was not developed further until Alvar Aalto's cantilevered chair of the 1930s.

Metal was another material used by far-sighted designers for experimental furniture. Important changes took place in the iron industry in the first half of the century. Casting processes had greatly improved; it was possible to produce much larger castings, and whole components of furniture could be cast in one piece and then assembled with braces and screws. The Coalbrooke Dale Iron Company of Shropshire were pioneers in this field, producing vast quantities of hall furniture, garden benches and chairs. Cast-iron furniture was recommended for public houses and the entrance halls of houses and hotels. There must have been a considerable export trade; British pieces can still be found in the United States and France. In America cast-iron furniture was manufactured at Boston, New York, Baltimore and Detroit. Functional designs were rare; the Victorians preferred to cover their innovations with an abundance of ornament. Many of the rustic designs, however, have great charm. As early as 1833, Loudon in his *Encyclopaedia* urged the use of iron furniture in farmhouses. The chairs he illustrated are rather stark and unattractive – the legs made of tubular gas piping, the backs of cast iron, and the seats of wood.

Some original and attractive furniture was made of wire, bent cold and twisted into elaborate shapes, by Messrs Barnard, Bishop and Barnard of Norwich – mainly pieces such as jardinières and chairs for the garden or conservatory.

Loudon considered that 'the idea of having iron bedsteads will shock those who have always been accustomed to consider mahogany essential for this piece of furniture', yet the manufacture of metal beadsteads was to become a major industry. The first patent for a metal bed was taken out in 1849. The early beds were rather crude cast iron constructions with a wire or strap metal base for the mattress. In 1856 Henry Bessemer solved the problem of converting pig-iron into steel and, as steel production increased, beds were made of mild steel tubing with a brass casing and sometimes trimmings of solid brass. By the 1880s the catalogues were full of elaborately ornamented brass concoctions. For the mass market the metal bedstead was popular for its cheapness and its obvious hygienic qualities. Its introduction helped to eliminate the bed-bug: eighteenth-century bedsteads had to be taken to pieces annually to keep this unpleasant bedfellow at bay. The cheaper iron beds had a simple functional elegance absent in most contemporary furniture. By the mid-seventies, six thousand iron and brass bedsteads and cots, half for export, were being produced each week in Birmingham by such firms as R. W. Winfield and Peyton & Harlow.

During the 1840s some English manufacturers attempted to use cast iron for rocking chairs but the material was too brittle to withstand the strain of bending. Brass tubing was employed instead for the frame, which supported a continuous upholstered seat and back. This rocker was exhibited at the Great Exhibition in 1851 (and was also reproduced over a hundred years later in the 1960s as a viable commercial proposition). A similar chair was produced later in strap metal

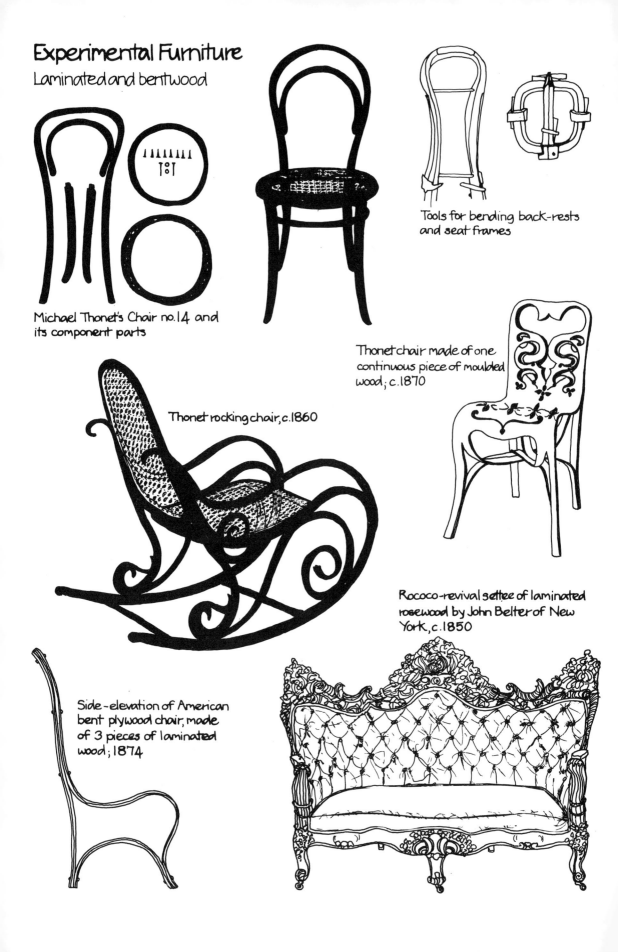

Experimental Furniture
Laminated and bentwood

Michael Thonet's Chair no.14 and its component parts

Tools for bending back-rests and seat frames

Thonet rocking chair, c.1860

Thonet chair made of one continuous piece of moulded wood; c.1870

Rococo-revival settee of laminated rosewood by John Belter of New York, c.1850

Side-elevation of American bent plywood chair, made of 3 pieces of laminated wood; 1874

Metal furniture

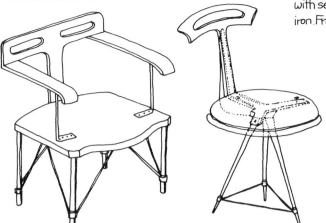

Two metal chairs from Loudon's 'Encyclopaedia of Cottage, Farm and Villa Architecture and Furniture', 1833

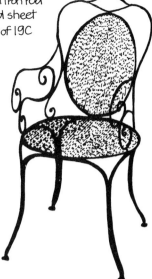

Garden chair of welded iron rod with seat of perforated sheet iron. French, latter half of 19C

Rocking chair of strap brass upholstered in plush. English, c.1850

Cot of twisted iron with net work sides. Heal's, 1853

Brass four-poster bedstead of taper tubing; brass cornice, Heal's catalogue 1853

Design for garden seat in cast-iron. British Patent Office, 1846

decorated with brass inlay. Both had a restrained beauty and fitness for purpose, anticipating the functionalism of the 1920s, but they seem to have provoked little interest at the time.

Probably the most popular of the novel materials used for furniture was papier-mâché. Originating in the Far East, it was known in France and England in the eighteenth century, though at first devoted to the making of trays, mirrors, frames, and panels for carriages. Henry Clay of Birmingham, who patented his process in 1772, grew rich on his products, probably through royal patronage – he is said to have made a papier-mâché sedan chair for Queen Charlotte.

The bulk of papier-mâché was produced in the nineteenth century; in England almost exclusively in the Birmingham area. The major manufacturer, Jennens & Betteridge, began to experiment with the material for furniture-making in the 1820s. Hitherto they had produced tea-caddies and trays, letter-racks, workboxes, coasters and other small articles for which it was eminently suitable. Two processes were used in its manufacture. A superior quality was produced by pasting sheets of wet, porous paper on to a mould and allowing it to dry. Paper pulp pressed between dies under great pressure produced a cheaper version. The resulting substance was durable if kept free from damp. The surface was coated with layers of lacquer – usually black, but green and red were also fairly common – and then decorated with gilt and polychrome painting and mother-of-pearl inlay. The latter was usually used for flower petals and butterfly wings but sometimes as a ground for painting with transparent tints. Floral decorations were the most popular but landscapes and portraits occurred; some were painted by eminent artists, others were of inferior quality painted by child labour. The death of Prince Albert inspired some sombre decorations in greys and lilacs.

Papier-mâché had insufficient strength as a structural material – for ambitious pieces such as beds the panels were mounted on wooden or metal frames. Small tables, light chairs and pole fire-screens seem to have been the most common items but whole bedroom suites were made in this material, even a piano – which unfortunately could not be played as it lacked resonance.

The popularity of papier-mâché is indicated by the fact that Jennens & Betteridge employed sixty-four professionally trained, full-time decorators. Most pieces have gaiety and charm – the method of manufacture kept papier-mâché furniture light and fragile and preserved it from the florid quality which increasingly pervaded furniture made from traditional materials.

A new, versatile material made from the latex of the gutta percha tree came on to the market in 1844. It was suitable for moulding, being highly ductile when heated yet tough and hard when cooled; it was impervious to water and could be made to look like a variety of materials – wood, metal, plaster – and polished to simulate japanning. Its uses were so varied and its popularity so great that by the end of the century latex supplies were almost exhausted and it was no longer a viable commercial material.

Organic materials such as horn and branches or tree roots make up a group of odd, sometimes grotesque, furniture, usually made for country establishments – for use in the hall, conservatory, hunting lodge or garden. The simplest pieces

Papier-mâché

Papier-mâché Canterbury, designed
to hold sheet music, 1830s–40s

Papier-mâché chair
with inlaid mother-of-pearl
decoration, c.1840–50

Organic materials

Wicker garden chair,
American c.1851

Stag's antlers made into
a chair, with buttoned
upholstery seat.
German, mid 19C

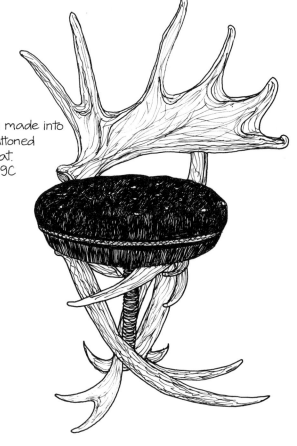

were made from 'found' parts of trees, combined in the semblance of a table or chair and merely nailed together. Furniture made from antlers was popular in Germany and Britain and buffalo horns appealed to the Americans. Elephant tusks were used in a similar fashion and sometimes their feet were made into rather macabre umbrella stands. Some of these pieces have a strange, surrealist quality about them – a complete break with traditional forms and a foretaste of the more extreme Art Nouveau furniture.

The great cabinet-makers of the seventeenth and eighteenth centuries were missing in the nineteenth. As the desire for comfort became a predominant factor, it was the upholsterer who gradually took over the leading role in furniture design.

Early in the century, drapery began to play a greater part in interior decoration. In some interiors, Madame Récamier's bedroom for example, paintings or drapery in the antique manner replaced panelled walls. Painted fabric was in turn replaced by drapes of real material. When designers introduced drapery in the form of a tent enclosing walls and ceilings, as Percier and Fontaine did at Malmaison, the boundaries of the room became undefined. Although the tent room was the exception rather than the rule, other drapery became more conspicuous. The fashionable long windows which now reached floor level were hung with curtains crossed and gathered up in full folds, the upper portion often elaborately cross-draped (*croisée*) and slung over a rod.

By the 1830s the upholsterer, or *tapisier*, who had been concerned originally only with the hanging of tapestries and curtains, dominated the making of seating. A nineteenth-century innovation of major importance was the introduction of spring upholstery. Georg Junigl, a Viennese upholsterer, took out in 1822 the first patent for a new method of upholstery, making use of iron springs. The first English patent for coiled spring upholstery was granted in 1828 to Samuel Pratt of New Bond Street, London, a maker of camping equipment. Deep-sprung upholstery was to change the appearance of the drawing-rooms of Europe and America. It was built around a skeleton of solid wood. In the spaces where a sitting body would need support, i.e. the seat and back, coil-springs supported on a lattice-work of webbing were covered with hessian and layers of horsehair and cotton wadding to produce resilient supporting cushions, the 'flesh' of the chair, which adapted to the sitter's position. Buttoned upholstery was the finishing skin best loved by the Victorians – buttons sunk deep into the thick padding held the layers firmly in place and contributed to the appearance of comfort.

At first the framework of upholstered seating remained exposed but gradually it was covered by the upholstery. To eighteenth-century eyes these pieces would have appeared grossly overstuffed – the form, dictated by bodily comfort rather than appearance, lacked the elegant line of earlier furniture and owed little to past styles. The product of true craftsmen, it was nevertheless 'commercial furniture'.

As the century progressed, furniture began increasingly to invade the centre of the room in an informal manner very different from the 'backs to the wall' principle of the two previous centuries. Many pieces were designed with this in

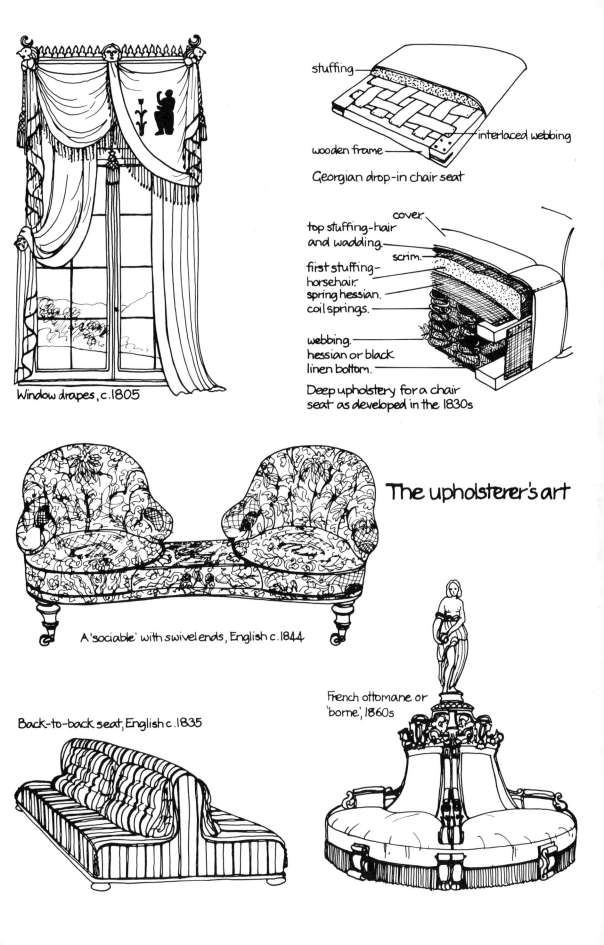

stuffing

interlaced webbing

wooden frame

Georgian drop-in chair seat

cover

top stuffing-hair
and wadding.

scrim.

first stuffing-
horsehair.

spring hessian.

coil springs.

webbing.
hessian or black
linen bottom.

Deep upholstery for a chair
seat as developed in the 1830s

Window drapes, c.1805

The upholsterer's art

A 'sociable' with swivel ends, English c.1844

French ottomane or
'borne', 1860s

Back-to-back seat, English c.1835

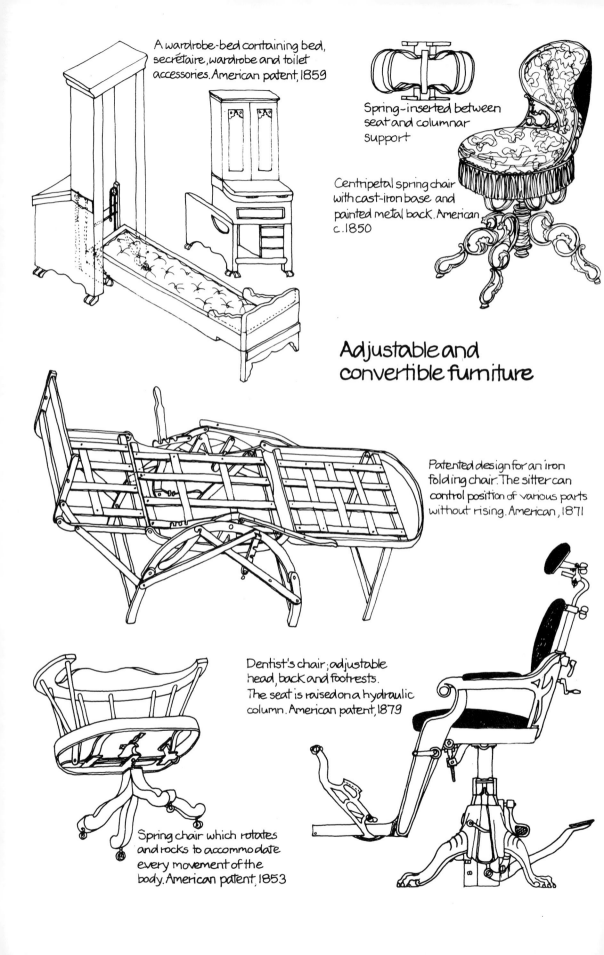

A wardrobe-bed containing bed, secrétaire, wardrobe and toilet accessories. American patent, 1859

Spring-inserted between seat and columnar support

Centripetal spring chair with cast-iron base and painted metal back. American c.1850

Adjustable and convertible furniture

Patented design for an iron folding chair. The sitter can control position of various parts without rising. American, 1871

Dentist's chair; adjustable head, back and footrests. The seat is raised on a hydraulic column. American patent, 1879

Spring chair which rotates and rocks to accommodate every movement of the body. American patent, 1853

mind. French upholsterers were adept at creating a wide variety of exotic seats. A renewed interest in the Orient was first seen in France where cushion furniture first came into fashion. The 'pouf' was introduced in the 1840s; an enormous version called a *borne* ('milestone') became increasingly popular as the centrepiece in large saloons or drawing-rooms, in the foyers of hotels and concert halls, in restaurants or at either end of a ballroom. This circular seat had a central backrest shaped like a truncated cone and was usually of deeply buttoned upholstery with ornate fringes. By mid-century the cone often supported plants, sculpture, lampstands, even fountains. The English version, the ottoman, was usually more restrained in design. There were 'back-to-back' seats like two armless sofas joined at the back, two-seater *confidantes* of S-shaped plan, three-seater *confidantes*, and many other variations of upholstered chair, sofa and chesterfield appeared.

Among the most ingenious and interesting furniture of the nineteenth century was the patent furniture, created not by cabinet-makers or upholsterers but by engineers. Usually these pieces included mechanical devices in their construction and were concerned with adaptability or with posture. Patent furniture was more common in the United States, where thousands of patents were taken out during the latter part of the century. Late eighteenth-century Europe had delighted in ingenious mechanical devices. At the turn of the century the middle and lower middle classes of England and France, living in congested conditions in the towns, were interested in compact, space-saving, dual-purpose furniture but by the 1830s their circumstances had improved and they lost interest. By the 1850s it was the American middle-class families who were facing the problem of trying to live as comfortably as possible in two or three rooms. As a result some very clever, sometimes functionally beautiful and often amusing furniture was produced.

The greatest versatility seems to be found among beds. Some wardrobes served a dual purpose, housing clothes in the front portion, which would pull down from the wall at night to reveal a complete bed, thus converting the parlour into a bedroom. The sofa-bed was a simple conversion. There were many variations on the adjustable chair with several positions between easy chair and bed, including one with the feet raised above the head. There were table-beds and ottoman-beds, but the most extraordinary piece of dual-purpose furniture was surely the piano-bed. One version housed not only a bed but two cupboards to hold the bedding, a wash basin and other facilities.

Posture also influenced the design of patent furniture. A relaxed, lounging posture was popular at this time, and the many positions between lying and sitting were catered for by a number of constructional solutions, applied not only to lounging and invalid chairs but to dentists' and barbers' chairs, surgeons' couches and reclining seats which could be adapted for day and night travel. Railway seating, particularly in America with vast distances to be covered, became the object of much experiment. Inventors were concerned with curving the back rest and seat organically to give maximum support.

The centripetal spring chair introduced in mid-century proved popular. probably as a desk chair. It had a heavy metal spring under the seat, allowing the

Posture

Early wire spring mattress.
British patent, 1865

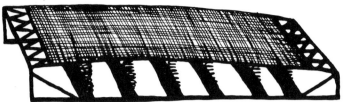

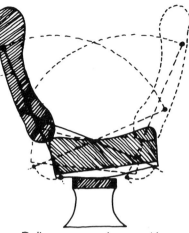

Railway car seat, curved to
support the body. American
patent, 1885

The 'Psyche' chair, curved to support
a reclining body. American, 1830s,
'naturalistic' style

Travelling furniture

Officer's portable iron bedstead
from Heal's catalogue, 1853. Folds
into box 4 ft x 11 ins x 8 ins high

Officer's campaign chest. Top
drawer opens to reveal a
secretaire

angle to be changed by the pressure of the occupant's back – as pressure slackened the chair would click back into its original position. It also rotated. The typist's chair which came later revolved but did not tilt, as a firm back support was needed.

The compact, unadorned furniture made specifically for travellers gives a foretaste of twentieth-century functionalism. An increasing number of people travelled abroad after the Napoleonic war and hundreds made the arduous journey to India each year. Those going abroad for several years or emigrating for good would rent an empty cabin and take as much furniture as possible with them. Some firms specialized in the manufacture of portable furniture – among such pieces advertised were portable chairs 'a dozen of which folded up would fit into the space of two common chairs', armchairs which transformed easily into tent-beds, sofa-beds, and tables large enough to seat twenty people which would fold up into the space of a large Pembroke table. These ideas originated from the camp furniture of officers campaigning in the Napoleonic and Peninsular wars, who took an enormous amount of bulky equipment with them. Clothes and personal possessions were carried from camp to camp in a military chest – a chest-of-drawers made in two parts, the top half sometimes incorporating a *secrétaire* with a fall-front. It was a purely functional, undecorated piece with simple folding handles inset in the fronts of the drawers; brass strips protected the corners and simple turned feet unscrewed for travelling. A bed, and sometimes also a chair and table, folded up and fitted into a box about the same size as the chest.

American camping furniture, designed not for an élite clientele but for common use, was much more compact and practical. A combination camp chest patented in New York in 1864 and illustrated in Gideon's *Mechanization takes Command* was 2ft (61cm) square by 2ft 4in. (71cm) high. It contained a folding frame covered with canvas which served as chair or bed, to which leaves could be attached to serve as tables; there was a cooking stove and utensils, and a drawer for papers and linen.

Aestheticism and reform

Britain led the world in industrialization, becoming the richest and most powerful nation of the nineteenth century in the process. By mid-century a network of railways linking most towns throughout the country had changed the pace of British life as well as the British landscape and more people lived in towns than in the country. By the 1880s London, with a population of two and a half millions, was the world's biggest city.

With the advent of the railways came suburban developments of two-storey semi-detached and terraced houses for the middle classes and white-collar workers. But urbanization did not improve the lot of industrial workers – conditions of work were often appalling, pay was low, thousands lived in squalid, overcrowded, polluted slums. For the poor there was no real home life, and living conditions and furnishings were little better than those of the medieval peasant. By mid-century the middle classes, haunted by the fear of mob violence and disease, were making efforts to improve water supplies and sewerage, and some enlightened employers were building better houses for their workers.

The concept of family life as an almost sacred institution was a middle-class ideal. Solid houses with cluttered rooms full of solid furniture, carpets and heavy curtains, were the status symbols of the prosperous new middle class of the first half of the century. The 'Elizabethan' style of furniture, popular in the thirties, forties and fifties, was an apt choice, for this period in many ways paralleled that of the late sixteenth century when the enterprising and adventurous *nouveau riche* celebrated its prosperity with massive and elaborately decorated furniture.

The Great Exhibition of 1851, housed in Paxton's beautiful and functional iron-and-glass Crystal Palace, was organized by the Society of Arts as a showcase for British industry and a celebration of British pride and power. Commercially it was an outstanding success. To discerning critics it emphasized how far British design lagged behind Continental design, particularly that of France. (To twentieth-century eyes there appears little to choose between them.) English manufacturers excelled in the use of new materials and technology; their craftsmanship was good but their design and decorative work was thought to be poor.

A few people had already become aware of this. Sir Robert Peel's remedy had been to build a National Gallery, housing a fine art collection, to improve the public's taste. A Normal School of Design had been opened in Somerset House in 1837 and eleven branch schools were established in large manufacturing areas. The Society of Arts, with Prince Albert as President and Henry Cole as an active member, made vigorous efforts to promote improved design. Cole, a civil servant, was a zealous reformer with a certain degree of artistic talent who brought improvements and innovations to a variety of areas – the postal system, patent laws, railway gauges, the construction of Grimsby docks, etc. His experience in the pottery industry, while designing a prize-winning teaset, convinced him that 'an alliance between fine art and manufacture would promote public taste'. Unfortunately it was a general misconception of the time that a little 'art' added to manufactured articles would produce good 'design'. Painters, sculptors and architects were considered capable of designing furniture and any other domestic items without any knowledge of the craftsmanship and technology involved in their production. The outcome of their efforts tended to be over-decorated pieces of furniture, particularly after the general revival of the art of carving in the forties. T. B. Jordan's invention of a wood-carving machine in 1845, making it possible to cut several identical pieces of decoration at the same time, contributed to this tendency.

Exhibits at the Great Exhibition were judged by juries of experts from various countries. One of their comments on the furniture section shows that they were aware of the shortcomings of many exhibits: '. . . It is not necessary that an object be covered with ornament or be extravagant in form, to obtain the element of beauty; articles of furniture are too often crowded with unnecessary embellishment, which, besides adding to their cost, interferes with their use, purpose, and convenience; the perfection of art manufacture consists in combining, with the greatest possible effect, the useful with the pleasing, and the execution of this can generally be most successfully carried out by adopting the simplest process.' (*Reports by the Juries – Great Exhibition 1851.*)

Ironically, it was not Cole, the practical and earnest designer, organizer and propagandist for reform who finally swung public taste away from over-elaborate decoration, but the work of a more visionary and romantic group of reformers of which William Morris was the central figure.

At first sight the reformers may seem to have taken a retrograde step, looking even further back into the past for inspiration than other Victorians. Unable as yet to come to terms with the machine, it was necessary for them to clear away the dead wood of Victorian historicism, to ignore the Golden Age of seventeenth- and eighteenth-century furniture design, and to return to earlier forms of construction. It was their philosophy of life and work, rather than many of their products, which inspired the next and future generations of designers.

The reform movement is inevitably linked with the name of Morris but its roots were established early in the 1830s. The writings of A. W. N. Pugin were its earliest manifestos. Although Pugin's conversion to Catholicism in 1835 bound him inextricably to the gothic style, which he felt had evolved to serve the needs of a Catholic world, he developed a rational approach to design projects. He continually emphasized the need for integrity in design. In his book *True Principles of Christian Architecture* (1841), Pugin lays down 'two great rules for design . . . that there should be no features about a building which are not necessary for convenience, construction or propriety', and 'that all ornament should consist of enrichment of the essential structure of the building'. Elsewhere he writes, 'Where use is exiled, beauty scorns to dwell.' Many of his principles were of such sound common sense that they were to inspire artists in many fields and of diverse creeds.

Pugin's interest in furniture design was first aroused when he failed to find any attractive furniture on the open market for his own home. He set up workshops in Ramsgate, employing several assistants to carry out his designs. Shunning contemporary methods of construction, he turned back to a study of the medieval joiner's methods. The constructional features of his own furniture, such as the pegs securing mortise and tenon joints, were clearly shown. This, his major contribution to Victorian design, was to be followed by many progressive designers. His ornament he took from nature. The gothic origin of some of his simpler pieces is barely discernible and some of these had a useful influence on cheap, rational furniture for the mass market. Unfortunately, commercial manufacturers like Morant of London and J. G. Crace & Sons usually borrowed from his more elaborate designs. From 1836 he worked with Sir Charles Barry on the interior of the new Houses of Parliament. He organized the 'Medieval Court' at the Great Exhibition, the only section to gladden the hearts of would-be reformers, which included the gothic furniture designed by Pugin and made by J. G. Crace which was to inspire the later gothic revival.

Pugin felt none of John Ruskin's dislike of machinery – he saw steam as 'a most valuable power for sawing, raising and cleaning stone, timber and other materials.' The machine, if properly used, should not interfere with integrity of design.

Ruskin, although not himself a designer, shared Pugin's view that a reform of the arts could only be realized by a change in society. Pugin found his solution in his Catholic faith, but for Ruskin the only possible remedy was complete social reform. He wanted a return to the basic attitude to work of the gothic world rather than a revival of medieval forms. In his book *The Seven Lamps of Architecture* (1849), 'the lamp of sacrifice', meaning the dedication of a man's work to God, came first. Second was 'the lamp of truth' – meaning honesty in construction, making by hand, which would be 'making with joy'.

Division of labour was to him a hateful thing – 'It is not, truly speaking, the labour that is divided, but the men: – divided into mere segments of men – broken into small fragments and crumbs of life; so that all the little piece of intelligence that is left in a man is not enough to make a pin, or a nail, but exhausts itself making the point of a pin or the head of a nail.' (*The Stones of Venice*, 1851.)

To Ruskin it appeared that Cole and his group had failed in the reformation of design because they were concerned only with material things. He believed that the best designs of the past had been endowed with the personal stamp of their creators and that this would again become evident once men were freed from the

Exhibition work

Bracket made of gutta percha, Great Exhibition

Elaborately decorated piano by Collard & Collard, London, shown at the Great Exhibition, 1851

Bronze bell-pull shown at Great Exhibition

Pugin and his influence

A trade interpretation of Pugin's ideas, from 'The Victorian Cabinet Maker's Assistant' by Blackie & Son

Carved oak armchair with imitation leather upholstery by Pugin, c.1837

Carved oak cabinet with brass mounts by A.W.N. Pugin, made by J.G. Crace, 1851

impersonality and the deadly precision of the machine. Machines might be used to perform necessary jobs of drudgery, but he feared that mechanical production on any large scale would inevitably mean that a few men would plan or design the work which the majority would carry out. He stressed the importance of education for all men according to their capacity. He felt it was essential for artists and craftsmen to work in beautiful surroundings with nature constantly before them, in an atmosphere of peace and kindliness, so that they might take pleasure in their work. These ideas were developed in *The Stones of Venice* (1851). One chapter in particular, 'On the Nature of Gothic', later became the basis of the Arts and Crafts Movement. It was reprinted in pamphlet form for the students of the newly established Working Men's College, where Ruskin started teaching in 1854. Among his fellow teachers were members of the Pre-Raphaelite Brotherhood whose work he had already praised in print; and it was Burne-Jones's friend from Oxford days, William Morris, who was to become the prime mover in a bid to turn Ruskin's theory into practice.

When Morris moved into the Red House, designed for him by his associate Philip Webb in 1860, some of his Pre-Raphaelite friends were also furnishing new accommodation. From their fruitless efforts to find aesthetically pleasing furniture and fabrics grew not only the idea of designing these themselves, but eventually the concept of the firm of Morris, Marshall and Faulkener – basically an artists' co-operative. Morris's aim was to make all kinds of household articles 'in a thoroughly artistic and inexpensive manner'. A man of dynamic energy, he was not only artist, craftsman and poet but social reformer. In the thirty-five lectures given between 1877 and 1894, he spoke of art in its broadest sense; 'I don't want art for a few, any more than education for a few, or freedom for a few . . . What business have we with art at all unless we all can share it?' Unfortunately, instead of turning his creative ability to improved designs for cheap, mass-produced goods for the majority, he urged a return to handicraft and set up workshops for the revival of old crafts. Each of these he brought to a high standard of design and production; but he admitted, 'All art costs time, trouble and thought.' Inevitably most of his products, too expensive for the average man, were bought by rich connoisseurs. His own special interests were tapestry, weaving, textile printing, carving and typography. Although he took little interest in furniture himself he stipulated that 'Our furniture should be good citizen's furniture, solid and well made in workmanship, and in design should have nothing about it, that is not easily defensible, no monstrosities or extravagancies, not even of beauty, lest we weary of it. As to matters of construction, it should not have to depend on the special skill of a very picked workman or the super excellence of his glue, but be made on the proper principles of the art of joinery: also I think that except for movable objects like chairs, it should not be so very light as to be nearly imponderable, it should be made of timber rather than walking-sticks.'

Two categories of furniture were produced by the Morris firm; the first, 'necessary workaday furniture' as Morris called it, included rush-seated furniture based on the traditional Sussex cottage chair, either stained green or ebonized. These cheap and popular chairs were almost the only product of the firm to fulfil

Wardrobe designed by Philip Webb and painted by Burne-Jones, 1858-9; a wedding present for Morris

Morris and his associates

Oak table of simple 'revealed' construction by Philip Webb, c.1865

A sophisticated example of the 'Sussex' chair, produced by Morris & Co. and designed by D.G. Rossetti, c.1865

Another successful adaptation of a 'Sussex' chair: the Morris adjustable back chair by Philip Webb, 1866

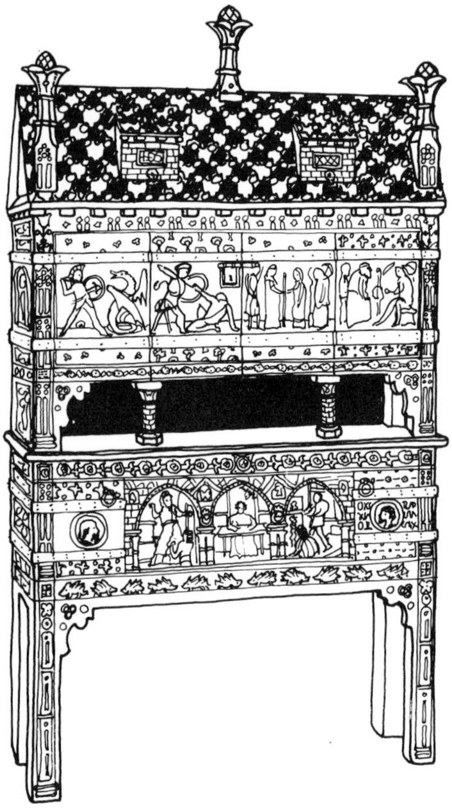

Writing cabinet of painted and
gilt wood by William Burges,
shown at the 1862 Exhibition

Other progressive designers

Oak sideboard made by Gillow & Co.
from a design by Bruce Talbert in
'Examples of Ancient and Modern
Furniture'

Cradle of carved oak with
painted and gilt decoration
by Richard Norman Shaw, 1861

Drawing-room chiffonnier made by
Jackson & Graham from
a design by Charles Eastlake.
A simplified version of
reformed furniture

Morris's ideal of 'art' for everyone. The other type, 'state furniture', was in the massive gothic style of the thirteenth century, mainly in oak with revealed construction; some of the large pieces had painted panels in the medieval manner by Morris, Burne-Jones and others.

The firm's work was first introduced to the public at the 1862 International Exhibition at South Kensington. Their painted furniture, tapestry and stained glass were favourably received and they were awarded two gold medals. Morris's great contribution to the field of design was the new respect which he engendered for artist-craftsmen working with their hands, at a time when manual work was looked down upon by the upper classes. He inspired many craftsmen to set up small hand-craft industries – indeed the studio-craftsman of today is his direct artistic descendant. He and his followers were to have a profound influence upon the Modern Movement.

Two other notable reformers, the architects William Burges and Norman Shaw, who shared the interest in early gothic, also exhibited at the 1862 Exhibition. Burges made careful research of thirteenth- and fourteenth-century France and England and believed that his massive furniture with its painted decorations and insets of various materials was an accurate reconstruction, although there was little surviving evidence, of the furniture of the period.

Although the solid core of the middle class took little interest in the work of the reformers, middle-class interiors were changing gradually. For the first time a collection of Japanese objects was exhibited, at the 1862 Exhibition. It made a strong impression on the public, who were fascinated by the sophisticated techniques of the Japanese. Arthur Lazenby Liberty, a young man of eighteen, was so affected by this collection that he persuaded his employers, the retailers Farmer and Rogers, to start an oriental department. The growing enthusiasm for oriental goods enabled Liberty to open his own shop in Regent Street, London, in 1875. Leaders of the cultural and artistic world patronized Liberty's and the interest created by the oriental patterns, subtle colours and soft fluid fabrics began a reform of women's clothes, away from the heavy fabrics and constricting styles hitherto fashionable. Softer drapery and lighter colour schemes of soft greens, greys, apricots and blues found their way into interiors. The Aesthetic Movement, as it came to be known, flourished during the 1870s. To some people it appeared foolish, to others offensive. Du Maurier satirized 'aesthetic' attitudes and fashions in *Punch*, Gilbert and Sullivan poked fun at all things Japanese in *The Mikado* and ridiculed the whole Aesthetic Movement in *Patience*.

'Art furniture' was one of the more concrete expressions of the artistic revolt among younger members of the prosperous middle class against the claustrophobic world of their fathers. From the late 1860s until the 1880s many 'art furniture' manufacturers appeared who considered themselves apart from the ordinary or commercial furniture makers. The origins of art furniture are diverse – the lingering Gothic influence, a strong interest in Japanese design, and also a general interest in Georgian design, hitherto disliked by the Victorians and now collectively and wrongly termed 'Queen Anne'. These interests were expressed in a general fining down and lightening of furniture forms – in straight lines and slender turned supports, often with incised lines picked out in gold which contrasted well with the ebonized wood popular at this time. Large pieces such as cabinets often had coved tops in the medieval manner, or galleries of turned spindles. There were many shelves for the display of knick-knacks, blue and white oriental vases, etc., and what-nots and overmantels became popular additions to drawing-rooms. Painted panels with human figures or floral motifs were preferred to carving.

The major propagandist of this furniture was Charles Eastlake whose influential book *Hints on Household Taste in furniture, upholstery and other details* was first published in 1868, the year in which the term 'art furniture' first appears to have been used. Eastlake deplored the way in which household goods were chosen for their newness and novelty rather than fitness for purpose and aimed 'to suggest some fixed principles of taste for the popular guidance of those who are not accustomed to hear such principles defined.' His practical 'down-to-earth' approach dispelled many established ideas about taste. Although not himself a craftsman, he understood the materials and technology of furniture making. He advocated cheap, simple rectangular furniture, panelled and boarded in the gothic manner, with pegged joints, no glue, staining or French polishing and hardly any decoration. Unlike that of earlier gothic reformers, it was well suited to domestic interiors. At a time when the Victorian middle class, with its passion for self-improvement, was eager for advice on the practice and appreciation of the arts and crafts, etiquette, home decoration, household management, fashion etc., Eastlake's *Hints* was well received in Britain and America and had a strong influence on the Arts and Crafts movement.

One of the earliest professional designers to achieve a national reputation was Bruce Talbert, whose ideas became known through his book *Gothic Forms applied to Furniture, Metalwork and Decoration for Domestic Purposes* (1867). His work, like that of Burges and Shaw, tended to be of massive proportions. Talbert disliked the rounded forms and elaborate carving of mid-Victorian furniture. He used a basic framed construction and decorated his work with inlaid geometrical decoration and low-relief metal panels. He introduced a fashion for bold, gothic metal hinges. He deplored, as many other designers did at this time, the use of shiny veneers as a cheap covering for inferior work. (In *Our Mutual Friend* Charles Dickens named his family of social upstarts 'the Veneerings'.)

The architect E. W. Godwin, who at first shared other reformers' predilections for medieval art, began around 1867 to design highly original and elegant furniture in the Japanese manner. The hallmark of his work is functional simplicity. He favoured ebonized wood and rectilinear forms with attenuated supports. A characteristic feature – what he called 'grouping of solid and void' – is best seen in his famous sideboard, c.1867, of ebonized wood with inset panels of 'embossed leather' paper on the cupboard doors and silver-plated fittings. His work excited much attention abroad, particularly in Austria and Germany where he is considered the first pioneer of modern design.

Godwin also introduced an entirely new form of interior decoration, with light coloured walls, painted not papered, Japanese matting on the floor, plain

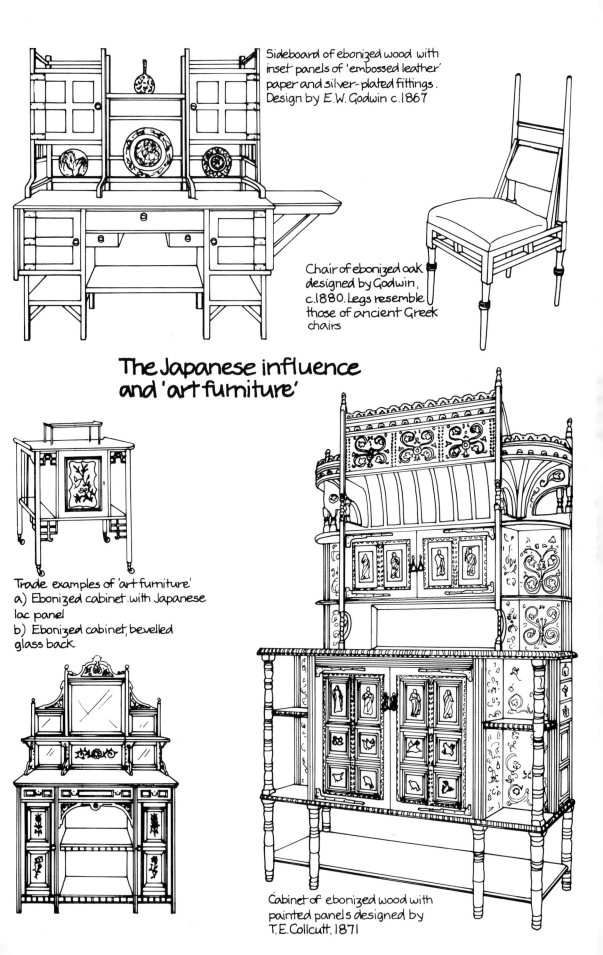

Sideboard of ebonized wood with inset panels of 'embossed leather' paper and silver-plated fittings. Design by E.W. Godwin c.1867

Chair of ebonized oak designed by Godwin, c.1880. Legs resemble those of ancient Greek chairs

The Japanese influence and 'art furniture'

Trade examples of 'art furniture'
a) Ebonized cabinet with Japanese lac panel
b) Ebonized cabinet, bevelled glass back

Cabinet of ebonized wood with painted panels designed by T.E. Collcutt, 1871

undraped curtains hung in straight folds, a few paintings or etchings simply framed, some Chinese pots, and very little furniture.

During the last twenty years of the century there was a rapid proliferation of Arts and Crafts groups, as many designers felt that little could be achieved in the way of reform by artists working alone. In the main they followed the lead given by Pugin, Ruskin and Morris and most groups adopted the medieval title of 'guild'. The first was the Century Guild founded in 1882 by architect A. H. Mackmurdo 'to render art the sphere, no longer of tradesmen but of the artist'. The Guild's publication *The Hobby Horse* was the first magazine to present English ideas on the arts to the continent, and was later to inspire *Studio* magazine and a variety of periodicals on home improvement and decoration produced at the turn of the century. This Guild, unlike those which came after, employed firms of professional cabinet-makers to carry out its furniture designs. Mackmurdo's own furniture, although not original in form or construction, was the first to incorporate what were to become Art Nouveau motifs. The fret-work panels of his chair backs and also his textile designs had a restless flame-like quality.

In 1883 a group of Norman Shaw's pupils and associates formed a discussion group, the St George's Art Society, from which grew the Art Worker's Guild a year later. From a desire to hold selective exhibitions came the idea for The Arts and Crafts Exhibition Society, founded in 1888 to show the public not only the work of leading designers but also the ideas of the movement. Many designers had been frustrated by the current definition of 'art' in terms of the fine arts only and the title 'Arts and Crafts' suggested by T. J. Cobden-Sanderson seemed an ideal choice, and gave a name to the whole British and American movement of reform. It also suggested the derisory term 'arty-crafty' coined by its critics.

In 1888, to substantiate his belief in a co-operative society, Charles Robert Ashbee formed his Guild of Handicraft, noteworthy both as a social experiment and for the work it produced. Its aim, which germinated in Ashbee's classes for young people at Toynbee Hall in London's East End, was to recreate, as closely as possible, the working conditions of a medieval guild. A later move to pleasanter surroundings at Chipping Campden in the Cotswolds proved economically disastrous, and in 1914 the guild disbanded. Perhaps because of its hopeless struggle against modern methods of manufacturing, Ashbee broke away from what he was then calling the 'intellectual Ludditism' of Ruskin and Morris, and the first principle of his last two books published after 1910 is that 'Modern civilization rests on machinery and no system for the endowment, or the encouragement, or the teaching of art can be sound that does not recognize this.'

There were about fifty workmen in the Guild of Handicraft, producing mainly metal work, jewelry, pottery and furniture. Ashbee encouraged collaboration between the crafts. Probably the most exciting project of the Guild was the complete decoration of Magpie and Stump, the house which Ashbee built for himself in Cheyne Walk, London, in 1895. It achieved not only national but international fame. It was reviewed and illustrated in the *Studio* in 1895 and Hermann Muthesius discussed it in an article in *Dekorative Kunst* (1898).

Muthesius, an architect, was attached to the German embassy in London to carry out research into English housing and design; the Germans were most interested in the Arts and Crafts movement. The result of his studies was the three-volume *Das Englische Haus* published in 1905. The Grand Duke of Hesse sent a special envoy to see Ashbee's house and as a consequence the Guild was invited to make furnishings for his Darmstadt Palace. These were carried out to M. H. Baillie Scott's designs. The Guild was later to prove an inspiration for Josef Hoffman's Vienna Workshops.

The furniture of the architect C. F. A. Voysey, first produced in the late 1880s, shows the influence of Mackmurdo, Godwin and the Japanese in its clean lines, simple forms and the long, thin shafts supporting his cabinets. His work was much admired on the continent and, although he detested the style, his influence was acknowledged by several European Art Nouveau designers.

Among the younger designers at the turn of the century who were influenced by the teachings of Morris were three architects, Ernest Gimson, Sidney Barnsley and Ernest Barnsley. They set themselves up in a peaceful Cotswold village and attracted fine craftsmen around them. Their work showed a feeling for wood in the English tradition – it was of simple design but superbly made with sophisticated detailing. Gimson in particular had a marvellous flair for bringing out the beauty of each material, whether wood, brass, silver or steel: every detail was given meticulous consideration. The example of these three men greatly inspired young designers in the early years of this century – Gordon Russell, Ambrose Heal and others.

In the United States, although there were no philosophers or reformers of Pugin's, Ruskin's or Morris's stature, the English Arts and Crafts movement was enthusiastically taken up towards the end of the century and several groups of skilful craftsmen followed Arts and Crafts ideals. In 1876 Philadelphia held an International Exposition, inviting the world to join in a celebration of one hundred years of Independence. Visitors were impressed by the industry exhibited but appalled by the standard of design. By the end of the decade, however, New York had replaced Philadelphia as the artistic and cultural centre and its furniture industry was revitalized, strongly influenced by the art furniture of England. Two English publications, Talbert's *Gothic Forms applied to Furniture* and Eastlake's *Hints on Household Taste* each ran to several American editions and were highly influential. In the United States a so-called 'Eastlake style' of simple rectangular forms, well made and richly decorated, was disowned by the author in his fourth edition.

A Japanese Bazaar at the Philadelphia Exhibition and a Japanese showroom which opened in New York engendered an interest in Japanese design. As in England, Japanese motifs were frequently incorporated into art furniture. The leading New York firm, Christian Herter, catered for the wealthy of the late nineteenth century until the rise of Tiffany's, America's greatest interior decorating firm of the twentieth century. Herter's superbly made art furniture, laced with an oriental flavour, paralleled the best of English design.

As in England, the number of Arts and Crafts organizations mushroomed in

The 'Manx' piano designed by M.H. Baillie Scott

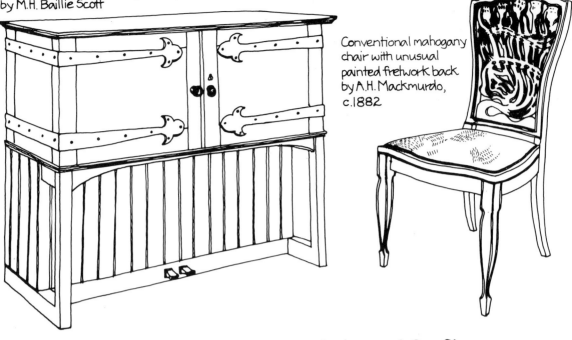

Conventional mahogany chair with unusual painted fretwork back by A.H. Mackmurdo, c.1882

Painted music cabinet designed by Baillie Scott and made by the Guild of Handicraft for the Palace of Darmstadt, c.1898

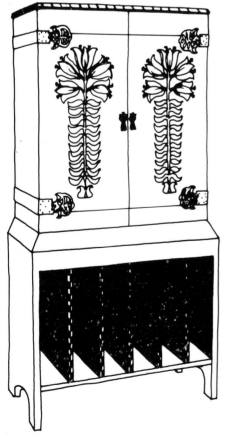

The Arts and Crafts Movement

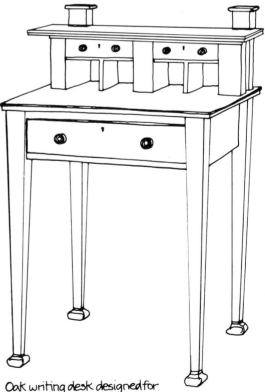

Oak writing desk designed for the Century Guild by Mackmurdo

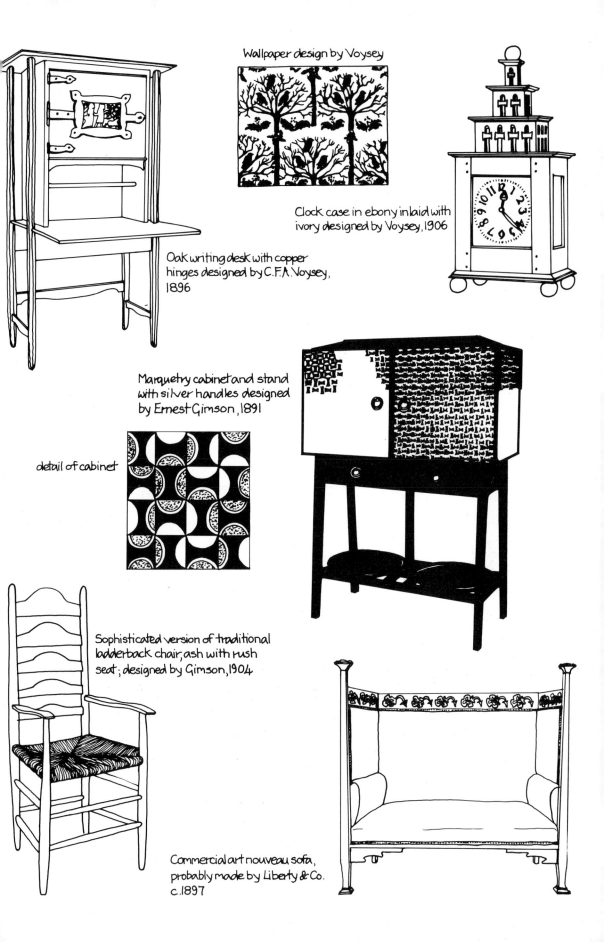

Wallpaper design by Voysey

Clock case in ebony inlaid with ivory designed by Voysey, 1906

Oak writing desk with copper hinges designed by C.F.A.Voysey, 1896

Marquetry cabinet and stand with silver handles designed by Ernest Gimson, 1891

detail of cabinet

Sophisticated version of traditional ladderback chair; ash with rush seat; designed by Gimson, 1904

Commercial art nouveau sofa, probably made by Liberty & Co. c.1897

the nineties. Two of the most influential designers of this era were Gustav Stickley and Elbert Hubbard. According to Stickley the movement stood for 'the simplication of daily life and a more reasonable way of living'. After a visit to Europe in 1898, where he met Voysey and other leading designers, he set up the Craftsman Workshops near Syracuse, New York. His furniture was in direct contrast to the mass of cheap, over-decorated, factory-made furniture churned out in the mid-West to satisfy a rapidly expanding population. It was hand-made by craftsmen, simple, basic and of sturdy construction, with no references to historical styles but a slight suggestion of rectangular Art Nouveau. When other designers became interested in his simple style and began to make similar furniture, Stickley distinguished his products by adding the motto, 'Als ik Kan', borrowed from Jan van Eyck by way of Morris, to his trade name 'Craftsman' and his device of a joiner's compass. The spread of 'craftsman' furniture throughout the country, and its great popularity, was no doubt due to a small monthly magazine, *The Craftsman*, which developed into a platform for opinions on the latest developments in the arts and crafts – it helped to spread Stickley's ideals not only to many furniture firms but to amateurs as well. There were articles on architecture and city planning and a monthly feature on tasteful houses. Stickley's furniture, like most products of the Morris firm, was priced beyond the pocket of the masses by labour and material costs and found its way into the houses of a discerning moneyed elite, but he did attempt to present his ideas to a wider market by his 'do-it-yourself' manuals.

Stickley's own furniture was not particularly distinguished but Harvey Ellis, a designer of note working at United Crafts (the co-operative scheme which Stickley promoted), produced a less aggressive, more subtle type of furniture. His severe forms were relieved by inlaid designs of simplified, elongated floral motifs in pewter and copper.

Stickley's contemporary Elbert Hubbard was the keystone of another group of workers, The Roycrofters, in East Aurora, New York. He had fallen under Morris's influence on a visit to Kelmscott in 1894. He established the Roycroft press and shortly after produced his own magazine, *The Philistine*. A bindery followed, then a leather shop, and eventually a whole artistic community including workshops producing a variety of hand-made goods. An apprenticeship scheme evolved, with workers moving from shop to shop to learn each craft. Roycroft furniture was of simple, massive form in oak and mahogany – usually rectilinear and undecorated. Hubbard propagated his ideas by his writings, his magazine and his lecture tours. Robert Judson Clark describes him as 'a cultural Messiah to thousands of Americans . . . who popularized a severe, if sometimes plebeian, version of the ideals of William Morris.' In the Roycroft catalogue of 1901 a Morris chair is listed.

The most original graphic artist of the nineties, illustrator and typographer Will H. Bradley, shared Arts and Crafts ideals of making everyday life more pleasant for everyone. He set up the Wayside Press in Springfield, Massachusetts, and published a small magazine, *Bradley: His Book*, which was concerned with art, literature and fine printing and had similar aspirations to the English *Studio*.

Oak settle with leather cushion designed by Gustav Stickley at the Craftsman Workshops, c.1909

Inlaid panel from a table made by Herter Bros, leaders in the field of 'art furniture', c.1880

The Arts and Crafts Movement in America

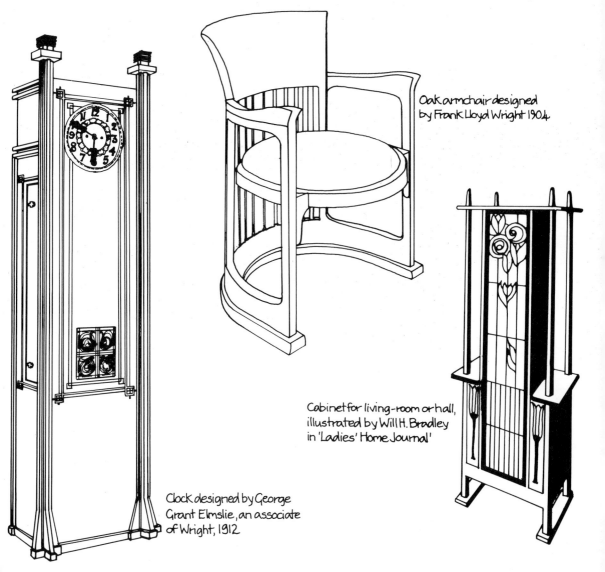

Oak armchair designed by Frank Lloyd Wright 1904

Cabinet for living-room or hall, illustrated by Will H. Bradley in 'Ladies' Home Journal'

Clock designed by George Grant Elmslie, an associate of Wright, 1912

Bradley's next venture was to contribute designs for a series of interiors for the *Ladies' Home Journal*, an influential magazine edited by Bok. Bradley's designs for modest, cosy suburban homes aimed for unity in design, with each piece of furniture related to the room it occupied and the house as a whole. The colours were warm earth colours, yellows and browns, with greens. In an effort to promote good domestic architecture Bok featured a series of designs for moderately-priced homes designed by a number of the country's leading architects, including Frank Lloyd Wright.

The Arts and Crafts movement appealed to the general public of America, with its rugged pioneering tradition, much more than it had to the English people as a whole. In spite of this, it had little chance of survival, and as the country moved closer to full mechanization in many areas, it became little more than a pleasant hobby for the amateur.

While the Arts and Crafts movement flourished in America, an interest in the past and the designs of the colonial period was growing, along with a new nationalism. Tiffany and others encouraged the use of indigenous materials, motifs based on native flora and fauna, and an interest in American Indian art.

Chicago was one of the major Arts and Crafts centres. Much of the inspiration of the Prairie School of architects was drawn from the movement – their emphasis on simple, uncluttered interiors, a natural blending of exterior and interior and a rectilinear and geometric style, their respect for natural materials, and their interest in oriental art.

Frank Lloyd Wright, a major architect coming to the fore at this time, while sympathizing with many of the precepts of the Arts and Crafts groups, is remarkable for his early acceptance of the machine. As he said in his manifesto, *The Art and Craft of the Machine* (1901), 'The machine is here to stay. It is the forerunner of the democracy that is our dearest hope. There is no more important work before the architect now than to use this normal tool of civilization to the best advantage instead of prostituting it as he has hitherto done in reproducing with murderous ubiquity forms born of other times and other conditions and which it can only serve to destroy.'

The furniture he designed for his houses was intended to be an integral part of the architecture – to blend with it, in the same way that his 'organic' buildings were designed to harmonize with the surrounding countryside. In his words, 'The most truly satisfactory apartments are those in which most or all of the furniture is built in as a part of the original scheme. The whole must always be considered as an integral unit.' (*In the Cause of Architecture*, 1908.) This was by no means an original concept when one remembers the built-in furniture of earlier ages, but it was born of a different need: a desire for harmony and simplicity. His furniture, with its emphasis on simplicity, lends itself to machine production, and although not made entirely by machinery, it has the appearance of being sympathetic to the machine age.

Another group of furniture makers in America who shared with the Arts and Crafts designers a desire for simplicity and purity of form were the Shakers, though there was no link between the two. Shaker furniture was a physical expression of the religious aspirations of this austere and very strict religious sect. In recent years their products have achieved international recognition as superb examples of functional design flourishing long in advance of the modern concept of functionalism.

The Shaker community, founded in England by its self-appointed priestess, Mother Ann Lee, emigrated in 1774 and established its first settlement at Watervliet, near Albany, New York. This was run on pure communistic lines – with no individual ownership of property and all goods dedicated to the common fund. In spite of the strict life of self-denial and the vow of celibacy, the sect grew until mid-nineteenth century, by which time there were eighteen communities totalling six thousand members. The group's name was derived from the ritual shaking dance performed at the Sunday religious services, the only relief allowed from hard work. The narrow, enclosed life of the Shakers might have curtailed all progressive design; but among their many inventions can be numbered the threshing machine, the circular saw, the automatic spring, the metal pen-point, the flat broom, the apple corer and the clothes peg. For more than seventy years after founding the communities, they managed to ignore the worldly influences of the fast-growing, materialistic culture around them. What they considered cardinal virtues – regularity, harmony and order – guided the work of the furniture makers, and its increasingly restrained functional style was based on Mother Ann's precepts: 'Whatever is fashioned [let] it be simple and plain . . . un-embellished by any superfluities which add nothing to its goodness or durability.' – and, 'Do all your work as though you had a thousand years to live, and as you would know you would die tomorrow.' Simplicity was considered an attribute of purity. Many contemporary pieces such as canopy beds and cabinets were rejected as too ornate or complicated. Although there was no shortage of wood, all parts were fined down to the minimum – chair posts were rarely more than an inch in diameter, with tapered legs; turning was allowed only for functional purposes, dovetailing was exposed, no veneering was permitted; the beauty of the wood had to remain revealed. All surfaces were made as smooth as possible and all parts were finished as perfectly as possible, whether or not exposed to view.

The standard Shaker chair was a refinement of the traditional ladder-back with a seat either of rush or of a woven tape made by the women. There was a ready market for these beautifully made and cheap chairs, far superior to anything else available, and thousands were sold outside the settlements. The rocking chair was a particular favourite – indeed the Shakers are said to be responsible for the popularity of the rocker in America. An interesting addition to the side chair was a ball and socket device fitted to the back legs so that the chair might be tilted easily without toppling backwards. A unique Shaker dining-chair had only one slat, low enough to push under the table when not in use. Large communal dining-tables were of trestle form. Chests and cupboards, often built in as permanent fittings, were austerely plain with turned wooden knobs for handles. Beds were simple cots, easily moved on castors or rollers for cleaning.

During the 1890s the style now known universally as Art Nouveau swept through Europe and America so rapidly that it is difficult to tell where it

Sewing desk or workstand

Shaker furniture

Shaker slat back rocking chair

Turned maple 'buttons' used on Shaker tilting chairs

Round stand, c.1820

Art Nouveau in America

'Fancy' chair by Charles Rohlfs, one of the few Americans working in the art nouveau style, c.1898

Table and lamp made by Tiffany Glass & Decorating Co. and Tiffany Studios, 1890–1905

originated. Considered revolutionary at the time because it aimed to sever all links with the past, in retrospect tenuous links can be perceived with rococo designs, the work of Blake and the Pre-Raphaelites, Celtic art and Japanese painting and prints. *L'Art Nouveau* was the trade name of a shop opened by Samuel Bing, a Hamburg dealer, in Paris in 1895, which became an influential art centre. Bing traded not only in works of art from the Far East but collected paintings, *objets d'art*, furniture and textiles for the decoration of modern interiors. He was closely associated with a renaissance of French furniture, which had endured a period of little artistic merit during the Second Empire. The rich bourgeoisie had encouraged a return to various sixteenth-, seventeenth- and eighteenth-century styles; there were no outstanding designers, and the upholsterer almost eclipsed the cabinet-maker as the fashion for all kinds of upholstery and excessive drapery flourished. In mid-century Comte Léon de Laborde, fearing that the machine was a threat to design standards, had urged a return to nature and fine craftsmanship. The Union Centrale des Arts Décoratifs, formed in 1877, aimed to put into practice Morris's ideal of art for all and to bring together designers and manufacturers. Paris and Nancy were the two outstanding centres of the re-birth of French design; each in its own distinctive fashion rivalled in quality the best products of the eighteenth century.

Emile Gallé, a glass designer who also experimented with cabinet-making, was the central figure of the Nancy School, but the major figures in this field were Louis Majorelle, Victor Prouvé and Eugène Vallin. More robust and provincial in character than the Parisian Art Nouveau, their inspiration came directly from nature. Sinuous lines reflected the roots, growing limbs and stems of trees and plants, and regional motifs such as cow parsley, thistle, cyclamen, butterflies and dragon-flies were favoured.

Working under the patronage of Bing in Paris, the cabinet-makers Eugène Gaillard, Eugène Colonna and Georges de Feure became famous at the Paris Exhibition of 1900 for which each designed complete room settings. But it was the architect-decorator Hector Guimard who produced one of the most spectacular achievements of the whole Art Nouveau movement – a block of exclusive flats, the Castel Béranger, in the smart Auteuil quarter of Paris. The whole building and its contents – furniture, bronzes, lamps, etc. – unite in free-flowing sculptural forms. His furniture, which often gives the impression of having a veil or skin drawn tautly across its forms, was usually modelled first in clay, and craftsmen had the difficult job of interpreting its sculptural forms.

Bing sought out talented foreign artists and introduced their work to Paris. He became the sole agent for Tiffany's beautiful glassware. He employed the Belgian artist Van der Velde to design rooms for the shop. From here Van der Velde went on to Germany where his work was a great stimulus to architects and designers. For a time he was Professor at the School of Decorative Arts at Weimar. His work was obviously influenced by Arts and Crafts precepts but his pieces are united by sweeping, all-embracing lines; form rather than decoration is all-important.

It was in Belgium, a highly developed industrial country with a newly-founded Socialist party in power, that Art Nouveau found full expression. Brussels

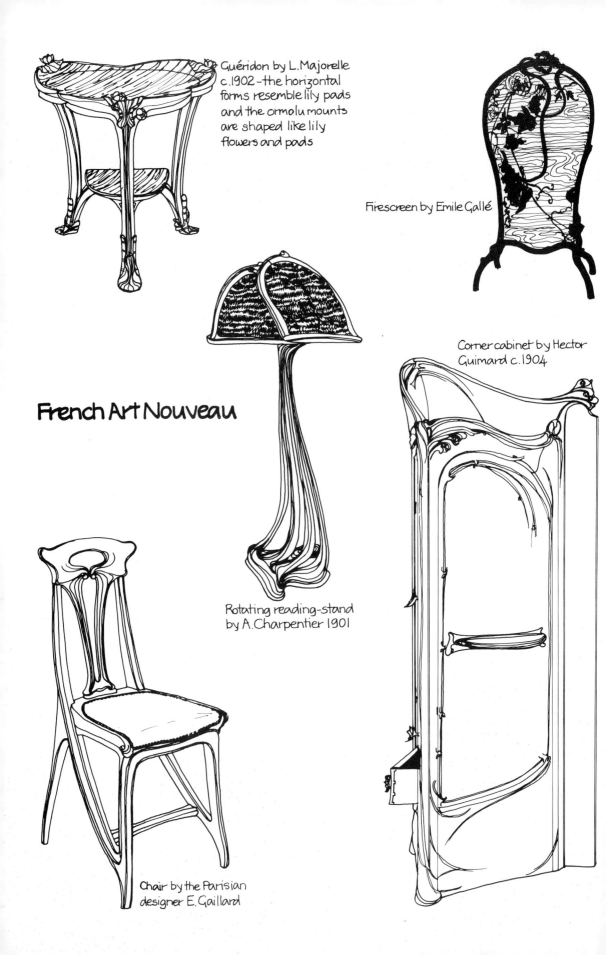

Guéridon by L.Majorelle
c.1902 - the horizontal
forms resemble lily pads
and the ormolu mounts
are shaped like lily
flowers and pads

Firescreen by Emile Gallé

Corner cabinet by Hector
Guimard c.1904

French Art Nouveau

Rotating reading-stand
by A.Charpentier 1901

Chair by the Parisian
designer E.Gaillard

Furniture designed by Victor Horta for his own house, c.1898

Belgian Art Nouveau

Armchair of Burmese sandalwood with batik upholstery by H. Van der Velde

Lady's desk in oak by G. Serrurier-Bovy c.1900

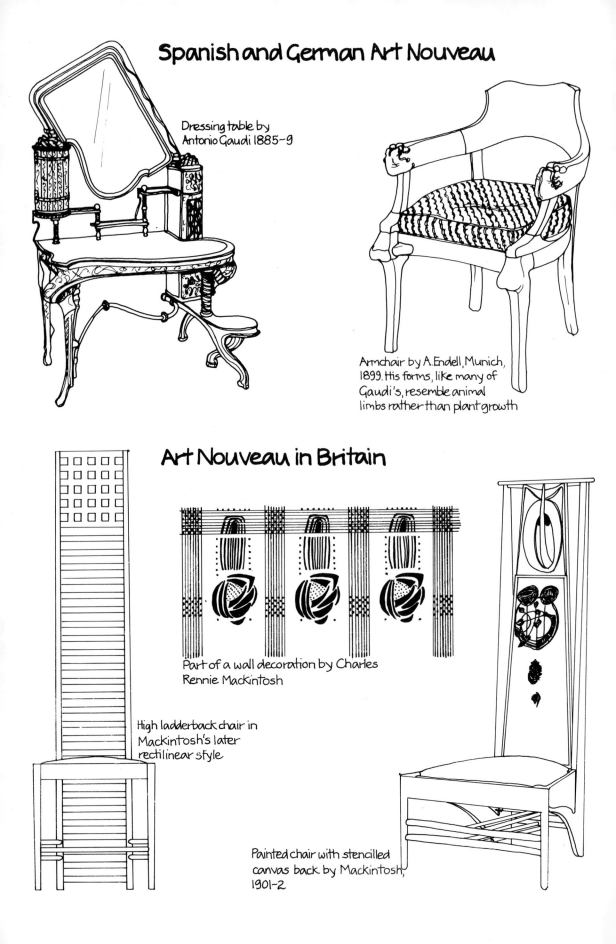

Spanish and German Art Nouveau

Dressing table by
Antonio Gaudi 1885~9

Armchair by A. Endell, Munich,
1899. His forms, like many of
Gaudi's, resemble animal
limbs rather than plant growth

Art Nouveau in Britain

Part of a wall decoration by Charles
Rennie Mackintosh

High ladderback chair in
Mackintosh's later
rectilinear style

Painted chair with stencilled
canvas back by Mackintosh,
1901-2

provided a stimulating atmosphere for intellectuals – an air of experiment which encouraged new approaches to the arts. The most spectacular and exciting examples are found in the work of Victor Horta. His Hôtel Tassel in Brussels (1892) shows an exciting use of new materials: iron and glass with long, sinuous, curving lines as the dominant features of the decoration. In a later house, the Hôtel Solvay (1895), every detail of furniture and furnishing was designed by Horta, all complementing the sinuous 'eel' style of the decorations which united ceilings, walls and floors in a manner reminiscent of rococo. His work is the most complete expression of the Art Nouveau style to be found anywhere in Europe.

Standing somewhat apart from the Art Nouveau mainstream was the work of the Spanish architect Antonio Gaudí. The undulating forms of his buildings were echoed in his furniture, which had an organic, 'growing' quality.

Although Mackmurdo had probably produced the first example of European Art Nouveau and helped to shape the style, it had little appeal for the British who considered it fanciful and tasteless. The most sophisticated British furniture in the new style was created by Charles Rennie Mackintosh, leader of the Glasgow school of designers. His exteriors have an almost puritanical structural integrity, but in the interiors of his Glasgow tea-rooms and the houses he built around the city he saw a legitimate field for non-structural decoration. He and his wife were very free in their treatment of everything within these interiors – carpets, silver-ware, appliquéd textiles and long, attentuated furniture (often painted in pastel shades). Their light, delicate colour schemes – off-white and pearl greys with accents of pink and lilac – and their flowing linear decoration struck a new, refreshing note.

In his later work Mackintosh developed a rectilinear style which was to have enormous influence abroad. The methodical Germans with their love of precision and order found in Mackintosh what they could not find in Van der Velde or the fanciful unrestrained French brand of Art Nouveau. The Weiner Secession was launched in 1897 by a group of Viennese artists eager to break away from the conservatism of their contemporaries and bring a new look to the arts. The inscription above the doorway of the Secession building – 'To each time, its own art: to that art, its freedom' – was interpreted literally by its members who believed that not only architecture, painting and sculpture but the design of everyday objects needed to be re-evalued. In the work of the Wiener Werkstätten established by Joseph Hoffmann in 1903 and modelled on Ashbee's Guild of Handicraft, there is a severer and more functional approach to design. Secession exhibitions gave pride of place to British exhibits.

As the century waned the design initiative passed from Britain, which had prepared so much of the groundwork for the modern movement in design, and America which had contributed so many inventions and innovations, to the continent of Europe. With a few exceptions, such as the work of Gimson, the Barnsley brothers, and the younger designers they inspired, British design slumped back into historicism. America followed a similar pattern and her inventiveness was channelled into streamlining and making functional domestic service areas such as kitchens and bathrooms.

The modern movement

A general uneasiness pervaded Europe at the beginning of the twentieth century; social and religious problems divided some countries; the major industrial nations – Britain, France and Germany – shared a mutual distrust, while Italy, only recently unified, struggled to establish a modern industrial society. In the arts, this unstable situation was reflected in a restless search for a new ideology.

It was inevitable that the exotic, hot-house bloom of Art Nouveau should be shortlived. Its flowing lines and subtle forms were unsuitable for machine production. The best pieces were hand made and exclusive, and even its leading designers tended to sacrifice construction to decoration. As a reaction, the British architect C. F. A. Voysey introduced a plain functional style of architecture and furniture and Mackintosh and the Vienna Secessionists returned to straight lines and geometric forms and patterns.

In February 1909, a memorable year in the history of the arts, the first manifesto of the Italian Futurist movement was published in Paris. Although Italy lagged a hundred years behind the three great powers in industrialization, progress was greatly accelerated in the first decade of the century and this led to a national mood of confidence and aggression. Futurism was not just a movement of the visual arts; it aimed to reform life as a whole. Led by the poet Marinetti, its driving ambition was to re-establish Italy as a cultural and political power. Old institutions, academies, museums and works of art were condemned. Rome, Venice and Florence were seen as 'suppurating sores' of the national disease, complacency. A new culture, inspired by scientific and technological achievements, was required to reflect the dynamism of modern life. Obsessed by the beauty of speed and the power of the machine, the Futurists set out to capture in painting and sculpture the impressions of life in a modern city – the noise, the speed, the changing lights and the violence. Their attempt to develop a new art failed, since their ideas were literary rather than visual, but their propaganda spread rapidly throughout the west, inspiring the English Vorticists and Russian Cubo-Futurists, and reached America and even Japan.

In 1909 also, the first performances of Diaghilev's Ballets Russes were given in Paris. Received with rapturous applause, they opened up a whole new world of colour and splendour and presented a new theatrical experience in which dancing, music and décor achieved a new unity. The stage designers, responsible for posters and programmes as well as costumes and sets, master-minded each production. New, rich colour schemes were introduced by the painters Benois, Larionov, Goncharova and Bakst. Bakst's use in *Scheherazade* of two violent colours, red and green, produced an effect of glowing barbaric splendour that immediately influenced the world of fashion and interior decoration. Well into the twenties the decorating firm of Martine, founded by the great couturier Paul Poiret in 1909, was producing 'Scheherazade' interiors. The decorator Paul Iribe was also notably influenced by the Ballets Russes.

The pale, pastel shades of Art Nouveau were replaced by vivid jade greens, reds, oranges and purples; huge, shapeless cushions placed in heaps on the floor and vast sofas fringed and tasselled in the oriental manner became the fashion. Diaghilev employed many west European musicians and avant-garde artists – among them Matisse, Picasso, Braque, Derain and Rouault – and his ballets made the general public aware of Fauvism, Cubism and other new art movements which were also to make an impact upon interior and furniture design.

From about 1905 a number of artists in Paris and Berlin became aware of the art of Africa and Oceania and found this so-called 'primitive' art in sympathy with their conviction that fine art and all forms of design must be simplified and rid of inessentials. In 1907 Picasso's 'Demoiselles d'Avignon' effectively began the Cubist movement.

Moscow at this time became the meeting place of most revolutionary movements in European art – Cubists from Paris, Marinetti's Futurists, the Munich 'Blaue Reiter' Expressionists, all made an impact upon the Russian art world. Russian artists developed several schools along these lines and there was a continuous exchange of ideas from all over Europe until, with the outbreak of the First World War, they were thrown back upon their own resources. Their isolation lasted throughout the war and the ensuing revolutionary period until the break in the blockade in 1921. The Revolution in 1917 acted as a catalyst for the various artistic movements. The Bolshevik regime promised a new society transformed by the machine and industrialization. The former painters Rodchenko, Popova and Stepanova tried to become artist-engineers, turning their skills to furniture design, textiles and graphics. Their furniture was experimental, with little sophistication. In structure it reflected the architecture of the movement with its noticeable diagonal lines. The most interesting piece produced was a bent-tube chair by Tatlin. The angular forms of Melnikov's USSR Pavilion at the Paris Exhibition of Decorative Arts in 1925 aroused considerable interest.

The First World War wrought cataclysmic changes, both spiritual and physical, throughout Europe. Many of the surviving young were filled with a deep hatred of war and wanted to change drastically their lives and their environment. The desire for experiment and change, as strong in western Europe as it was in Russia, had at first three centres – Holland, France and Germany.

The Dutch, spared the war, were the first to project the new artistic ideas of abstraction into furniture design. The architect Gerrit Rietveld, a member of the

Cabinet inlaid with mother-of-pearl,
Josef Hoffmann, Vienna Secessionist.
Early 20C

'L'atelier français'. The influence of the Ballets Russes
lasted well into the twenties

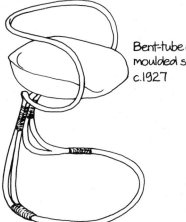

Bent-tube chair with a
moulded seat by Tatlin,
c.1927

New trends

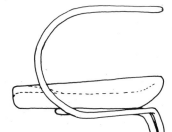

Modern version of Tatlin chair
in chromium-plated tubular steel
with padded leather seat

Rodchenko's design for adaptable fittings for a
worker's club: rostrum, screen, display bench

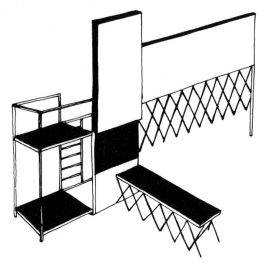

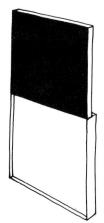

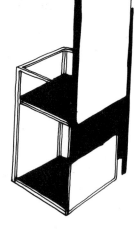

avant-garde group whose ideas were expressed in a magazine called *De Stijl* first published in 1916, from which the group took their name, had been working during the war years on designs completely different from anything seen before. Whereas Morris had sought a revival of medieval handicrafts and to some extent turned his back on machine production, De Stijl saw the machine as a spiritual force and a medium for social liberation. In 1923, Van Doesburg and Van Eesteren wrote in *De Stijl*, '. . . Under the supremacy of materialism, handicraft reduced men to the level of machines; the proper tendency for the machine (in the sense of cultural development) is as a unique medium of the very opposite, social liberation.' Piet Mondrian, the leading painter of the group, wrote in the first issue, 'The life of contemporary cultivated man is turning gradually away from nature; it becomes more and more an a-b-s-t-r-a-c-t life.' In his work Mondrian eliminated curves and any forms or colours which might express personal emotions. He used only primary colours and non-colours – white, black and grey. The rectangle was the basic form and compositions were asymmetrical.

Rietveld aimed to put the ideas of the group into three-dimensional form. He felt it necessary to strip furniture down to its basic forms and re-think each piece as if no furniture had ever been made before. The chair in particular, endowed through the centuries with various extraneous attributes, had to be conceived anew. A chair must have a seat, a back and something to support these elements. The construction of his Red-Blue chair of 1917–18 was brutally simple: two flat rectangular pieces of plywood set at an open angle to each other formed the back and seat; the supporting framework consisted of square- or rectangular-sectioned members set at right angles to each other and screwed together without dove-tailing. There was no upholstery and the original chair was in unstained natural beech. In the house that he designed and equipped for Mrs Schröder-Schräder, Rietveld painted the back red, the seat blue and the framework black, all square-cut ends were picked out in yellow, and it was placed on a black floor against a black wall so that the main elements, the back and seat, appeared to hover in mid-air. Although simple to make, fairly cheap and reasonably comfortable, it was much too stark for conventional manufacturers priding themselves on skilful craftsmanship.

Rietveld produced several other equally memorable pieces of furniture. His sideboard of 1919 exposed clearly every single piece of wood in its construction as a separate element. The pieces appeared to be laid upon each other as a child assembles building bricks. In his extraordinary Zig-Zag chair he aimed to create a form which would occupy as little of the volume of the room as possible – four legs appear to occupy much more space. Rietveld originally intended to make it from one piece of material but found this technically impossible. None of his designs were taken up commercially at that time.

The basic ideas of the De Stijl group were adapted by and incorporated in the Bauhaus, the new design school formed in Germany after the war. Hermann Muthesius, inspired by the British Arts and Crafts movement, had founded the Deutsche Werkbund in 1907 in an attempt to relate design to technology, but it was not wholly successful. Not until 1919, when Walter Gropius, the youngest of

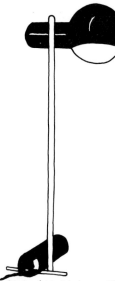

Rietveld table lamp, 1924, chromium-plated and painted metal

Cover design for first number of 'De Stijl' magazine, published June 1917, from a painting by Vilmos Huszar

End table by Rietveld, 1923; blue square top and red circular base are connected by a black and white rectangle

De Stijl

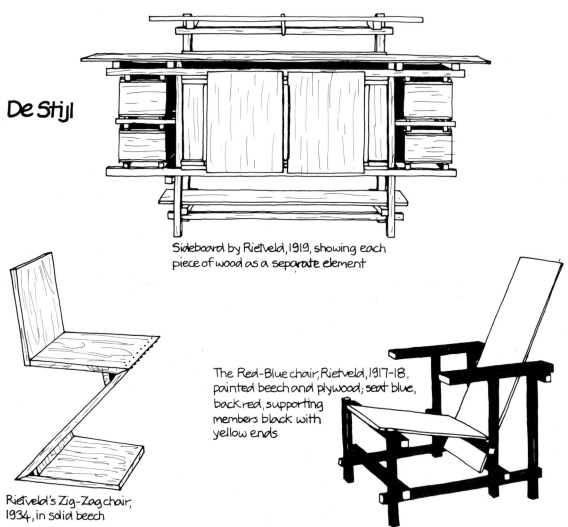

Sideboard by Rietveld, 1919, showing each piece of wood as a separate element

The Red-Blue chair, Rietveld, 1917-18, painted beech and plywood; seat blue, back red, supporting members black with yellow ends

Rietveld's Zig-Zag chair, 1934, in solid beech

the Werkbund designers, amalgamated the Academy at Weimar with the local Arts and Crafts School to form the Bauhaus, did the problems of designing for industry begin to be solved.

Six months after war ended Gropius sent an exhilarating Manifesto to the students of all German art schools, acknowledging their war-time experiences and offering them new hope: 'Let us create a new guild of craftsmen, without the class distinctions that raise an arrogant barrier between craftsman and artist. Together let us conceive and create the new building of the future . . .'

Bauhaus students of industrial design were trained to combine the talents of craftsmen, creative artists and designers. They learnt that the hand tool and the industrial tool differed only in scale, not in kind, and that it was necessary to understand the relationship between the tool (whether hand or machine) and the material used and to seek a functional solution, using the most suitable material and technique, to each design problem. Past styles were abandoned. The work of the Bauhaus received international recognition. Unfortunately the rise of the Third Reich halted all modern development and in 1933 the Bauhaus was forced to close. Many staff and students emigrated, some to England, many more, including Gropius, Mies van der Rohe, L. Moholy-Nagy and Joseph Albers, to the United States where they were welcomed by universities. Their ideas became more widely known, particularly in America, where the ground was already prepared. For some time European art had been represented in American collections and a few young Americans had been training at the Bauhaus since 1928. American furniture design, dormant for so long, was poised to take on a new lease of life.

The tubular steel cantilevered chair is as characteristic of the Bauhaus period as are cantilevered slab floors and walls of glass; part of a general desire to create a lightweight, hovering structure, visually occupying as little space as possible. At the Bauhaus the production of tubular steel chairs was a natural extension of the experiments made into the nature of this material. Marcel Breuer, a student who after only four years was made head of the Furniture Department, first experimented with tubular steel in 1924–5. He is said to have first thought of using this material for furniture while looking at his bicycle. Using a non-resilient chrome tubular steel, he produced a number of new forms – chairs, stacking stools, the famous Wassily armchair and a nest of occasional tables. In 1926 the Dutchman Mart Stam designed the first cantilevered chair and Mies van der Rohe produced another, more elegant version; it was 1928 before Breuer, who originated the idea, produced his own more practical version. With two legs instead of four, the cantilevered chair introduced a new dimension to furniture design, a transparent see-through effect. It also combined strength with lightness. Breuer's chair became the prototype for countless versions in the following years. It combined beauty and comfort with the minimum of materials, labour and cost. The firm of Thonet was by this time a vast organization exporting bentwood furniture to all parts of the world. It was relatively easy for them to make the transition from bending wood to bending metal tubing, and they produced thousands of pieces of metal furniture for schools, canteens, public halls, gardens, etc., from designs by

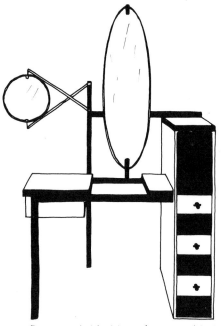

Dressing table, Marcel Breuer, 1923

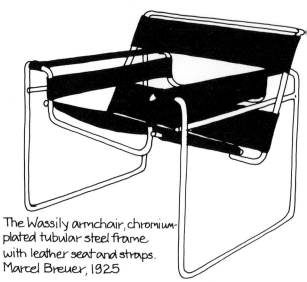

The Wassily armchair, chromium-plated tubular steel frame with leather seat and straps. Marcel Breuer, 1925

The Bauhaus

Table, chromium-plated tubular steel with black lacquered top. Mies van der Rohe, 1926

Electric table lamp, Wilhelm Wagenfeld, 1924

The first cantilevered chair: chair S33 by Mart Stam, 1926; plated tubular steel frame, canvas seat and back

Cantilevered chair; chromium-plated tubular steel frame, cane seat and back. Mies van der Rohe, 1926

Leather couch, Mies van der Rohe, 1931

The Cesca cantilevered chair, Marcel Breuer, 1928. Chromium-plated tubular steel frame, cane back and seat

Barcelona chair and stool, Mies van der Rohe, 1929; chromium-plated steel frame, leather-covered cushions

Reclining chair and stool in bent laminated birchwood with latex foam seat and back, designed for Isokon by Marcel Breuer, 1936

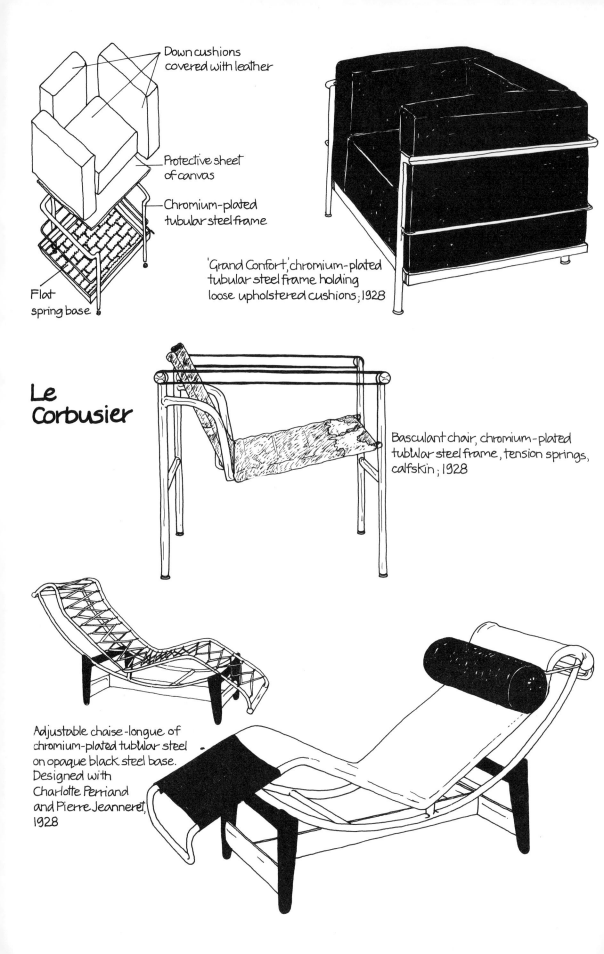

Down cushions
covered with leather

Protective sheet
of canvas

Chromium-plated
tubular steel frame

Flat
spring base

'Grand Confort,' chromium-plated
tubular steel frame holding
loose upholstered cushions; 1928

Le Corbusier

Basculant chair, chromium-plated
tubular steel frame, tension springs,
calfskin; 1928

Adjustable chaise-longue of
chromium-plated tubular steel
on opaque black steel base.
Designed with
Charlotte Perriand
and Pierre Jeanneret,
1928

Breuer, Mies, Le Corbusier and others, but few people found it a suitable material for the domestic interior.

In 1929 Mies van der Rohe designed his most beautiful piece of furniture, the Barcelona chair with its accompanying stool. The supporting frame was made of two crossing curved bars of solid stainless steel on each side. Their slim sweeping lines gave it greater elegance than the tubular steel chairs in spite of its broad seat. Upholstered cushions of leather-covered latex foam supported on leather straps made it a very comfortable chair which fitted unobtrusively into a domestic setting. Industrial methods are used in the manufacture of this chair, but for precision rather than mass-production. It is a luxury piece which requires hand finishing despite the simplicity of its form.

The invention of latex foam, derived from experiments in the motor industry in 1928, brought about a revolution in upholstery techniques; upholstery units could now be moulded in one operation, either in the form of loose cushions or pre-formed units which were then bonded to the frame of the chair. The *chaise longue* designed by Marcel Breuer for Isokon shortly after he arrived in England in 1935, which combines latex foam with preformed bent plywood to produce a sophisticated new form, is an excellent example of the new possibilities opened up by this material. Because of its high cost of production, however, it was not widely used at the lower end of the industry, where traditional fillings persisted.

During these experimental years Le Corbusier and Charlotte Perriand in France were also designing metal furniture, following similar lines to the Bauhaus designers. Le Corbusier's attitude to furniture differed from that of the Germans; he saw furniture as equipment, reducing it to three categories – chairs, tables, and shelves either open or enclosed. He felt that furniture should perform an anonymous function within an architectural framework and should adjust to a variety of uses. For each category he designed various forms: a multi-purpose table, standardized sectional cabinets and seating for different uses – a chair with an adjustable back, an easy chair, a *fauteuil* and a *chaise longue*. Having produced these standard models which could be used in any of his buildings, he designed no more furniture. He regarded it as part of the equipment of the house, part of 'the machine for living in'. This phrase sounds rather cold and inhuman and is often misinterpreted. Le Corbusier wanted houses and flats to be convenient, comfortable and functional. None of his own furniture had been made in time to be included at the Paris Exhibition of 1925 in his Pavillon de l'Esprit Nouveau which he designed as a protest against the accepted interior decoration of the day. Plain coloured walls were hung with Cubist paintings and all the furnishings were chosen for their simplicity and functionalism – Bedouin carpets with simple, abstract patterns; stage flood lights or store window lights rather than fussy chandeliers; laboratory jars instead of decorative vases; simple café wine glasses. Since his own furniture was not yet available he chose Thonet chairs, acknowledging their purity of form.

Le Corbusier's most striking contribution to furniture design is his *Grand Confort*, a compact design for an armchair in the form of a cube (1928). The normal method of chair construction, in which the upholstery clothes the supporting framework, is reversed by putting the skeleton of chromium-plated steel tubing on the outside, like a cage, to support four large cushions of soft down which form the seat, sides and back. The cushions are not fixed and can change positions so that they wear evenly; the outer framework prevents damage. Though interesting as a design solution, it is not as functional as it looks – the soft cushions have a tendency to sink and deposit the sitter on the floor.

Probably because of the public's lack of enthusiasm for metal furniture, many architects and designers in the thirties began to experiment with plywood. Formed plywood was already being used in the aircraft industry, and the pressures of the First World War had brought about great improvements in the structure of plywood, a relatively cheap material. The old method of sawing veneers was wasteful of wood; but improved techniques made it possible to slice veneers as thinly as 0.6mm in a continuous sheet from a revolving log, a method which makes seasoning unnecessary. Cuts of wood that are of no use to the cabinet-maker can be used for plywood. Laminated board and blockboard, made by similar techniques but of a heavier gauge, also came into use after 1919.

Alvar Aalto was the first to develop the use of plywood for furniture design, and to exploit the natural spring of the material in the manner that Breuer and Mies had exploited the spring of metal. With a personal conviction that the human body should only come in contact with organic material, he began to experiment with various ways of moulding plywood, making use of the natural moisture content of birchwood, his favourite material, instead of bending by steam alone as Thonet had done. His first experiments coincided with the opening of his native Finland's new timber industry, which produced ample supplies of plywood.

Aalto's first chairs had moulded plywood seats supported on tubular steel legs – later replaced by laminated wooden ones. His first notable breakthrough was his lounge chair of 1930 – the result of three years of experiment with plywoods made by the designer himself. The seat and back were formed of a single sheet of plywood bent in sweeping curves and supported on a laminated birch frame. *The Architectural Review* commented in 1933, 'Though buoyant as a spring cushion the seat-back is virtually unbreakable . . .'

Equally comfortable and of a far more subtle form was his cantilevered chair no. 31, shown in an exhibition of Finnish design sponsored by the *Architectural Review* in London in 1933. The bent plywood back finished with Masur birch was supported by cantilevered combined arm-leg pieces of laminated birch bent by steam, in forms, into wide curved slabs and then sawn into sections of the correct width. Laminated wood was used rather than plywood, because plywood is built up with the grain of each layer at right angles to that of its neighbour and can only be used in a rigid form, whether pre-formed or flat. Laminated wood, however, is formed of thicker layers than ply with the grains all running in the same direction. This, combined with the synthetic resins used to form and set the material in its final shape, give it greater strength and spring.

With his wife Aino and Mairea Gullichen, Aalto established the Helsinki firm of Artek in 1933, both to manufacture his furniture and as a 'centre for contemporary furniture, home furnishings, art and industrial art'. He continued to

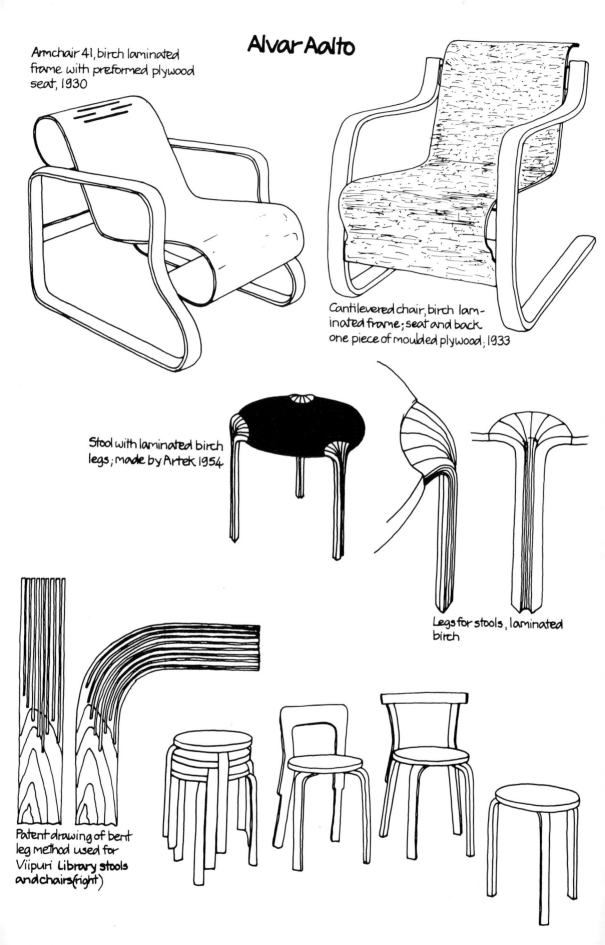

Alvar Aalto

Armchair 41, birch laminated frame with preformed plywood seat, 1930

Cantilevered chair, birch laminated frame; seat and back one piece of moulded plywood; 1933

Stool with laminated birch legs; made by Artek 1954

Legs for stools, laminated birch

Patent drawing of bent leg method used for Viipuri Library stools and chairs (right)

develop the possibilities of laminated birch, and Artek has manufactured shelf-unit brackets, tables, stools and chairs. Particularly noteworthy is the shaping of the legs where they join the seat or table top, opening out like a fan in a gentle curve – a reference both to architectural forms and organic growth. Aalto has called the furniture leg 'the baby sister of the architectonic column' and his furniture in general 'accessories to architecture'.

New dry bonding methods using resin glue and electricity replaced steaming and made possible the moulding of plywood into shapes which curved in two directions. From 1939 the Institute of Design in Chicago made extensive studies into the use of plywood and a variety of plywood chairs were produced.

Scandinavian countries came late and gradually to industrialization, without the upheaval experienced in many countries. With their low density of population they avoided mass building projects and shoddily produced factory furniture. English furniture imported during the eighteenth and early nineteenth century had had a strong influence. Sweden had also been influenced by the Napoleonic style. The high standards of craftsmanship and fine proportions established in the eighteenth century have been maintained without a break. Even when Art Nouveau reached Scandinavia her craftsmen were influenced by the Viennese school rather than the more extravagant versions and took their motifs from ancient Nordic ornaments. Scandinavian designers have never broken completely with the past; they have learned from traditional forms, adapted and improved on them. Long, hard winters and the isolation of small communities in earlier years have given the home a vital role in Scandinavian life and the furniture reflects a democratic, homely life style. It is well made, practical, elegant and unpretentious, designed to blend well with any setting.

Carl Malmsten, who set up a cabinet-making business in Stockholm before the First World War, was strongly influenced by the English Arts and Crafts Movement. A teacher, philosopher and artist like Morris, he had no liking for industrialization; nevertheless his aim was to adapt old forms to twentieth-century needs. He founded several schools where students studied not only their own subject but also music and gardening and other crafts such as pottery. During the years when the international style was developing Malmsten was considered by some a reactionary for speaking out against 'sterile formalism'. He fought for friendly, warm and individual environments. His work is now highly appreciated for these very qualities, and his 'series' furniture for the manufacturing firms Karl Andersson and Soner and Svenska Mobelfabrikerna is well known.

Kaare Klint in Denmark was similarly no revolutionary, but working in traditional ways with traditional materials he made a very valuable contribution to the field of furniture design. He set about analysing the uses to which various traditional pieces of furniture were put, whether they were still functional for present requirements, or too large and cumbersome for smaller houses probably run without servants. One design for a sideboard, in the late twenties, was based upon an assessment of the crockery, glassware, cutlery and napery needed by the average middle-class household and the number and size of compartments

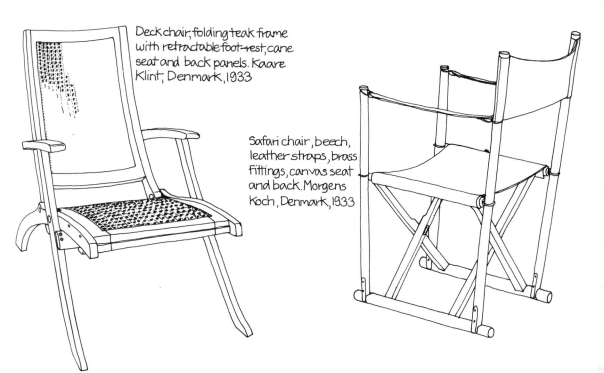

Deck chair, folding teak frame with retractable foot-rest, cane seat and back panels. Kaare Klint, Denmark, 1933

Safari chair, beech, leather straps, brass fittings, canvas seat and back. Morgens Koch, Denmark, 1933

Other Scandinavian designers

Chest inlaid with various woods. Carl Malmsten, Sweden, 1929

Sideboard, Kaare Klint, late 20s

required to store them. It was half the size of the average model then on the market.

In 1924 Klint became Professor of the newly established Furniture School of the Danish Academy of Art. He and his students continued with his 'scientific function studies'. The starting point in designing any piece of furniture was to establish its function and its proportion in relation to the human figure. Once these facts were known, construction methods, materials and appearance could be considered. One of Klint's most important contributions to Danish design was the standardization of the height of tables and chairs and the size of drawers. He advocated the use of natural materials – untreated wood neither painted nor varnished, untreated leather and simple textiles preferably of black, white, grey or brown wool.

Elsewhere in Scandinavia, particularly Sweden, similar efforts were being made to rationalize furniture design. By the thirties, architects and designers were producing designs for functional, utilitarian furniture using new technology and new production methods. The various standard units could be mixed and matched for different requirements.

The decorative arts of the twenties and thirties stand apart from the work of the progressive architects and designers. The Art Deco style had started as early as 1910 and had in many ways passed its best by 1925, the year of the Paris Exhibition of Decorative and Industrial Arts from which it took its name. This was the first international exhibition for over a century to be devoted entirely to the applied arts, and it gave a new generation of decorative artists, as well as those already established, an opportunity to display their work. A condition of acceptance was that exhibits should make no reference to past styles and must be truly representative of the contemporary way of life. Paris became the centre of a feverish regeneration of the decorative arts in France.

The extravagant flowing forms and pale colour schemes of Art Nouveau lost favour early in the century. In contrast much Art Deco furniture is reminiscent of the austere forms of the Directoire and Consulate periods, using strong colours in the Ballets Russes manner. Simple basic forms and smooth surfaces were chosen to enhance the extravagant materials used by cabinet-makers to produce the finest luxury goods – woods, chosen for their surface beauty and distinctive markings (rosewood, mahogany, palm, macassar ebony, elm, violet wood, sycamore); leather both plain and stamped; parchment, ivory, lacquer, glass, sharkskin, shagreen (imitation sharkskin – almost a trademark of art deco), tortoiseshell, mother-of-pearl and metals. Certain motifs appear repeatedly in these designers' work – sprays, swags and baskets of stylized flowers; geometric forms, particularly octagonal panels; stylized tree and fountain forms.

The work of Emile-Jacques Ruhlmann, interior decorator and furniture designer, is probably the most memorable and distinguished of the twenties and early thirties in France. He worked exclusively for the very rich, using only the most sumptuous materials and demanding the highest standards of craftsmanship from his workmen to achieve absolute perfection of finish. Some of his pieces not only rivalled but surpassed the technical finish of the eighteenth-century masters.

Art Deco

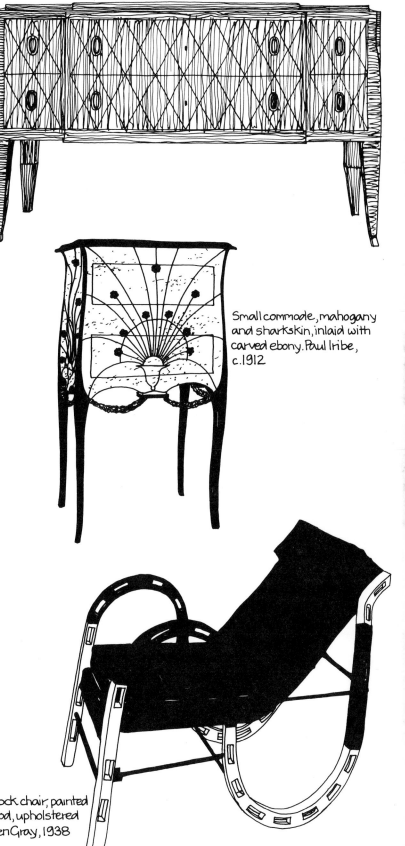

Chest of drawers, macassar ebony veneer and ivory. Emile-Jacques Ruhlmann, 1924

Small commode, mahogany and sharkskin, inlaid with carved ebony. Paul Iribe, c.1912

Lady's writing desk, painted stylized decoration of fruit and flowers, probably by Paul Follot, 1920s. Bronze and ivory ornament by Chiparus

Folding hammock chair, painted laminated wood, upholstered in canvas. Eileen Gray, 1938

Dining-table - a thick sheet of opalescent glass supported on four glass columns on a solid glass base. René Lalique, c.1931

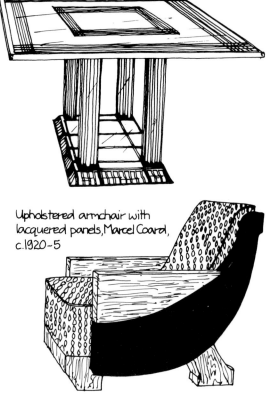

Cubist influence

Interior design from advertisement for Hamptons, London, 1936. The 'clinical look'- plain walls, concealed lighting, geometric forms

Upholstered armchair with lacquered panels, Marcel Coard, c.1920-5

Popular Art Deco

Silver bronze clock in the form of Egyptian-styled Cleopatra headdress. Albert Cheuret, 1930

Marble clock with typical art deco motifs-stepped face, gazelles, sunrays, reclining figure of Amazon

Surrealism

'Mae West lips', upholstered in shocking pink, designed by Salvador Dali, c.1936

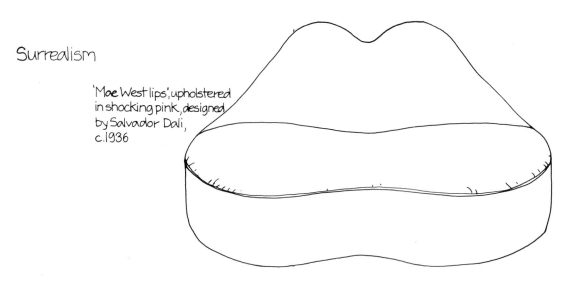

Such was the demand for his work that he was able to establish a large workshop in spite of his exorbitant prices. The possession of a Ruhlmann interior or a piece of his furniture became a status symbol. His early forms were delicate with slender, tapered, ivory-tipped legs, but in later years he favoured more massive forms. He preferred the distinctly marked woods of macassar ebony and Caucasian burr walnut, enriched with decorative details in ivory, sharkskin, silver and other metals. Fabrics were often specially designed for individual pieces of furniture.

The oriental influence was strong in much Art Deco work: a general lowering of seating height at this time may be due to this influence, and certainly the low coffee- or cocktail-table which appeared at this time was often oriental in character. There was also a revival of lacquer work, usually with modern motifs rather than the traditional oriental ones. Probably the best lacquer work ever produced in Europe was made in the period between the wars. Two major designers in this material – an English architect, Eileen Gray, and a Swiss metalworker, Jean Dunand – were both working in Paris and learned the correct oriental technique from the Japanese artist Sugawara. Eileen Gray achieved great skill in lacquering, applying it to furniture, screens, etc., but treating it as an entirely new material without reference to traditional designs. Her highly individual style, based mainly on geometrical shapes, had a limited appeal.

Dunand worked on a surprisingly large scale for lacquer-work, with large plain areas of colour on which any flaw would clearly show. As many as forty layers of lacquer were used to achieve the mirror-like surface he demanded. To prevent the wood of his screens and panels warping, each layer of lacquer had to be applied to both sides at once and allowed to dry evenly. Each layer was smoothed to a perfect surface before applying the next. In spite of this elaborate process Dunand produced many screens, wall panels and inset panels for other designers' furniture including that of Ruhlmann. His largest commission was for door and wall panels for the French liner *Normandie* in 1935.

As people began to tire of the richness of Art Deco, a modified version of Cubism with simple clean lines and muted colour schemes became acceptable in interior decoration. Designers tried, not always successfully, to reconcile the public to the use of metal – for example, with central metal columns supporting dining tables. Metal framed chairs were covered with leather, fur and other materials to avoid contact with the metal, which so many people disliked.

Unfortunately, it is the popular, mass-produced Art Deco, rather than the luxury version, with which we are more familiar today. Its sources were more varied: Cubism, the Orient, African art, pre-Columbian art (particularly the Aztec ziggurat shape), Futurism, and a taste for the Egyptian style revived by the opening of Tutankhamun's tomb in 1922. Blériot's flight across the Channel and the growing interest in fast travel by air, rail and road encouraged images of speed and streamlined forms in the thirties. Rounded corners and edges are a notable feature of thirties furniture.

In England the first specialist interior decorators appeared between the wars.

Best-selling piece of
furniture, 1937

Sideboard in Bombay rosewood with
elm inlay. Gordon Russell, 1935

English design

Unpolished oak
dresser and plate rack,
Ambrose Heal, 1906

Mahogany sideboard, influenced by
Paris Exhibition, 1925. Charles Richter

Bedroom writing table,
veneered in walnut with
burr figure on drawer
fronts; tassles of flame-
coloured silk. R.W. Symonds
and Robert Lutyens

Bedroom by Serge Chermayeff, 1928

Before 1914 the big 'furnishing houses' had their own design studios and were responsible for most of the work. Their style was sound but traditional, and lacked individuality; the choice was limited to Tudor or Georgian. Almost the only large established firm to show an interest in contemporary design and produce pleasant functional furniture was that of Heal & Son, run by Ambrose Heal, himself a talented furniture designer who attracted other good designers in all facets of interior design to work with him from *c.*1900. Within a few years he had modernized the firm, and in the twenties and thirties it was producing and selling not only hand-crafted furniture and the ultra-modern continental tubular steel furniture, but good quality 'series' furniture made by traditional methods, with traditional materials, but using modern factory methods for the mechanical jobs of sawing and planing, etc. Waring & Gillow also updated their decoration department in 1929 and stocked continental furniture. Gordon Russell was another cabinet-maker who established a business geared to factory production of high quality furniture, after the First World War, in Broadway, Worcestershire. He also produced fine hand-made furniture.

The introduction of plywood aided quite considerably the uncluttered look aimed for by decorators in the thirties. Built-in cupboards with doors which would not shrink or warp replaced large wardrobes too cumbersome for the smaller flats and houses now being built. Bathrooms with fitted units did away with washstands in the bedrooms of richer houses.

A new social habit, the cocktail party, introduced an entirely new piece of furniture to house all the paraphernalia of cocktail-making. The cocktail cabinet in the modernistic interior was often a very showy piece lined with mirror glass and fitted with lights. Glass, particularly mirror glass, was a popular material in the thirties, introduced into all kinds of furniture but rarely used on its own. A few glass tables were made around 1930 by the French designer Réné Lalique, and Pilkington Brothers in England produced a bedroom made entirely of glass as an advertising stunt in 1933.

In France a much greater gap existed between the very rich and the moderately well off than in England, with a consequently greater demand for luxury furniture. In Britain the most notable designers of the thirties, Serge Chermayeff, Robert Lutyens and R. W. Symonds, were designing for middle class clients. They shared a liking for strongly marked woods and an interest in geometric forms.

The bulk of the furniture produced between the wars, however, was in neither Art Deco nor Modern International style but was inferior factory-made furniture in a poor interpretation of past styles – neo-rococo in France, Queen Anne or 'Jacobethan' in Britain and a mixed assortment of styles in America. A certain amount of 'modernistic' rubbish also appeared, with flashy chrome trimmings.

The 1940s onwards . . .

Great Britain's impact upon the world of design was negligible during the early decades of this century. It was not until the Second World War that a comprehensive re-evaluation of furniture design took place and an attempt was made to raise standards. This was forced upon the country by the circumstances of war and was not entered into gladly by the furniture manufacturers. In 1939 timber was in short supply. Britain produced little of her own and there was a serious shipping shortage. Craftsmen also were in short supply, either seconded to war work or conscripted. Less than ten per cent of the pre-war workforce remained in the furniture industry. Although furniture stocks were high at the outbreak of war, they were soon depleted – the services needed furniture, as did newly-weds and homes damaged by bombing.

To overcome the problem of demand an allocation system was devised which allowed those who could prove real need to buy a certain amount. The Utility scheme was introduced to control the price and quality not only of furniture but of other household goods such as sheets and blankets, and of clothes. Never before had there been such complete state control of the design, quality and supply of a basic commodity as there was at this time in the realm of furniture production. From November 1942, all designs were standardized. The only furniture that might be produced, throughout the country, was a single 'Utility' range controlled by the Utility Furniture Committee chaired by Gordon Russell. Their only brief from Hugh Dalton, President of the Board of Trade, was that the furniture should be pleasant in design, well made, of the best materials available, and must be produced quickly to cope with the growing shortages.

At last the climate was favourable for good design and craftsmanship to be built into the industrial system, and functional, practical standards could direct the taste of the whole nation. Hitherto, a return to honest craftsmanship had been equated with hand-craftsmanship, and therefore the prerogative of the affluent; the poorer classes, thought by manufacturers to have a taste for the over-decorative, had had to put up with shoddy goods. The first Utility furniture, produced by trade designers Mr Cutler and Mr Clinch of High Wycombe, was a solid undecorated range in the manner of Gimson's plainer work; it was considered too progressive by most of the trade, and reactionary by the *Architectural Review*. With the return of craftsmen after the war it was possible to produce a lighter, more sophisticated range which met with general approval.

The enforced introduction of the Utility range brought simple, functional furniture into the homes of those who would neither have considered buying nor have been able to afford Gimson-type furniture in pre-war days. It contributed to a general raising of people's expectations of what they might be able to buy for their homes, and it did much to dissipate consumer apathy to modern design and to prepare the ground for a reformation of British furniture in post-war years.

The 'Britain Can Make It' Exhibition in 1946 was intended 'to intensify the interest of manufacturers and distributors in industrial design, and their aware-ness of the desirability of rapid progress; to arouse greater interest in design in the minds of the general public, as consumers . . .' Although quickly renamed by the public the 'Britain Can't Have It' Exhibition, since most of the exhibits were unobtainable, it marked the turning point of the general public's awareness of design.

Three main areas have dominated furniture design in the post-war years – Scandinavia, the United States and Italy. Wartime occupation hardly affected the craftsmen of Scandinavia; new industrial techniques were developed and new designs for furniture produced. Much of the industry had been co-operating with first-class architects and designers to produce good, timeless furniture since the 1930s and Scandinavia's reputation for fine design was well established. During the war years Borge Mogensen had taken up and developed the ideas of Kaare Klint and was producing modern functional furniture in Denmark. He was in charge of furniture design for the Danish Co-operative Society which opened its first furniture shop in Copenhagen in 1944. With the cessation of hostilities it was to Scandinavia that war-torn Europe looked for the goods its people could not buy in their own countries. To those starved of beautiful things, Scandinavian furniture was new and exciting, although mainly traditional in flavour. Danish cabinet-making in particular seemed superb in the fifties. This little country, with no wood of its own, led the world in fine furniture manufacturing and was soon exporting half of its products. Demand was met by making use of power tools for the cutting and basic shaping of the various furniture components, but hand finishing by craftsmen retained the high standards established before the war. These high standards were and still are encouraged by the common practice of each major designer working with one particular craftsman and his workshop, who understand and can sympathetically interpret his designs. Among such successful collaborations are those of Arne Jacobsen and cabinet-maker Fritz Hansens, and Hans Wegner and master craftsman Johannes Hansen. These leading designers are also responsible for products produced entirely by machine, so that high standards are retained throughout the industry at every level. There is continuous quality control; everything is tested and inspected before leaving the factory or workshop. The superbly finished hand-made products of the small craft workshops still have the greatest appeal on the international market – the warmth and beauty of natural uncarved wood, the satiny sheen of hand-rubbed,

Utility furniture in Britain

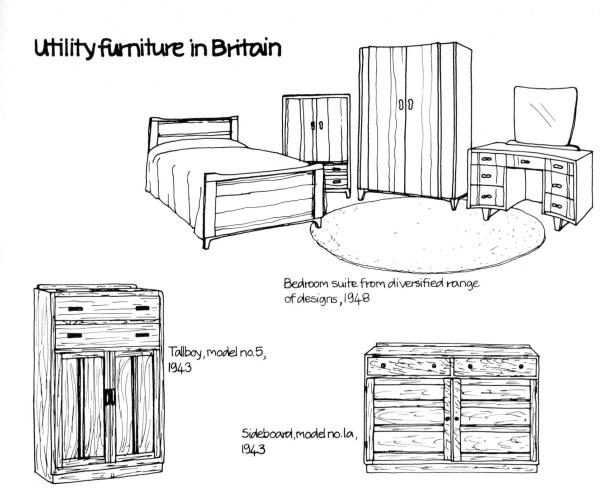

Bedroom suite from diversified range
of designs, 1948

Tallboy, model no.5,
1943

Sideboard, model no.1a,
1943

Scandinavian design after 1940

The Boligens Byggeskabe ('BB'Cabinet) designed by
architects Borge Mogensen and Grethe Meyer, Denmark,
1957. Interchangeable units adapt to changing needs

'Chinese' chair in cherry wood with
leather seat pad, Hans Wegner,
Denmark, 1944

Stacking chair, moulded plywood with chromium-plated tubular steel legs. Arne Jacobsen, Denmark, 1945

Series of office furniture designed by Finn Juhl - tables, chairs and interchangeable cabinets and shelving. Prize-winning desk, 1957

Easy chair, lacquered and oiled teak frame, upholstered in handwoven wool, Finn Juhl, Denmark, 1945

Hammock chair, stainless steel frame, handwoven cane seat and back; adjusts to slightest movement. Poul Kjaerholm, Denmark, 1965

Plastic forms

The 'Egg' chair; moulded glass-fibre shell, covered in leather or fabric, swivelling on aluminium base. Arne Jacobsen, Denmark, 1958

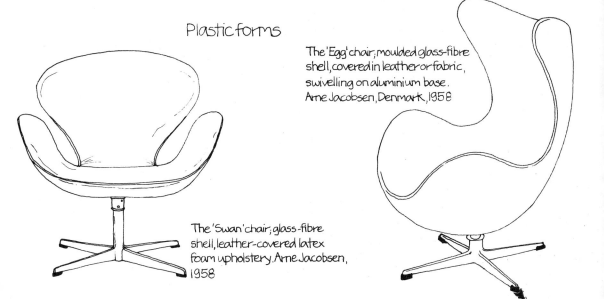

The 'Swan' chair; glass-fibre shell, leather-covered latex foam upholstery. Arne Jacobsen, 1958

untreated surfaces, the smooth beautiful joints and natural leather seats have an enormous appeal in our industrially orientated society. Designs range from the rugged, 'backwoods' forms of Borge Mogensen and the finer classical lines of Ole Wanscher to the more sculptural and romantic forms of Finn Juhl, Hans Wegner and Arne Jacobsen. Some of these designers have also experimented with and exploited most cleverly the new technology of the plastics industry, as an alternative to the 'teak' style.

The greatest changes in furniture design in the post-war period were due neither to style nor to ideology but to the introduction of plastics, a new range of synthetic materials. Research into the development of synthetics had been going on since bakelite was produced in America in 1916, but it was not until the Second World War that plastics came to be recognized as a new class of material with unique properties, which could be developed and produced on a large scale. The wartime demand for lightweight materials that could easily be moulded and were strong enough to support considerable weight produced a plastic that was also suitable for furniture making. Previously, the most commonly used plastic was a rigid laminate, developed in the United States in 1913 and known as Formica; made from two resins bonded together and backed with plywood, it presented a hard, heatproof, waterproof, wipe-clean and almost scratchproof surface, ideal for table tops and work tops. The nature of plastic, its almost complete malleability, demanded a new aesthetic – a challenge which was taken up by leading designers in the late forties and the fifties. The exciting shapes that designers had struggled to achieve in the twenties and thirties were now within the bounds of possibility.

The International Style in Germany had been stifled by the rise of Hitler. The little that remained of Germany's furniture industry after the war had no resources with which to develop new technology or new ideas. The rest of Europe, apart from Scandinavia, was in a similar position. Across the Atlantic, however, there was a vital industry whose designers were eager to 'beat swords into ploughshares' and direct the formidable resources of American technology, developed under wartime pressure, towards the domestic scene. Several Bauhaus architects and designers, Gropius and Breuer among them, who had fled from Nazi restrictions, were now in prominent teaching posts in America and already strongly influencing American architecture and furniture design. Some of them were closely associated with two leading American furniture manufacturing firms – the Herman Miller Furniture Company, which had directed its interests towards modern design about the time that the Bauhaus people were arriving in the States, and Knoll International founded in 1945. Hans and Florence Knoll, themselves talented designers, collaborated with Mies van der Rohe and produced and distributed his pre-war furniture designs.

It was the Herman Miller Company which helped Charles Eames, one of the native designers coming to the fore at this time, in his early experiments, and manufactured all his early designs. Eames was the joint winner with another young architect, Eero Saarinen, of the prize for seating and other living-room furniture in a competition for Organic Design in Home Furnishing, held by the

Museum of Modern Art, New York, in 1940. The Museum had just set up a department of industrial design which was to have a profound influence on the design of domestic goods and also on the fine arts. Eames's and Saarinen's revolutionary design was for a chair in which seat, back and arms were united in one multi-curved shell made up of strips of veneer laminated and moulded in a cast-iron mould by the new electrical method, using new bonding resins. Requiring the minimum of materials, the design broke away from the geometrical approach of the Bauhaus; it has a more fluid and friendly form, with a greater regard for comfort, than many of the Bauhaus models. The shell form was covered with a thin pad of rubber and then fabric. Although the seat was designed to stand on four slender aluminium rod legs, wooden legs had to be substituted and the form of the shell modified because of wartime restrictions and production difficulties – the welding process required to attach the aluminium legs was reserved for military projects. It was not until after the war that the significance of this design was fully realised.

In 1946 Eames produced the famous DCW chair ('dining chair wood'), now known as the 'Eames chair', with seat and back made of two pieces of plywood moulded to fit the body comfortably. Not only was the form innovative but the plywood pieces were shock-mounted to the metal rod frame by thick rubber cushions which gave the chair resilience. New glues made it possible to glue the rubber to the plywood, so that the junctions were not visible on the front surface. A variation of the DCW chair, known as the DCM because of its metal legs, proved most popular. It was lightweight and easy to move around.

After the war Eames was eager to apply the new methods that had been developed for shaping metal sheets, and the products of the plastics industry, to furniture production. From 1946 he experimented with a series of shell forms which were a development of the 1940 prize-winning design, making use of these new materials. At first he used sheets of steel, stamped out in a shell shape to form a seat, back and arms in one piece and coated with neoprene. Soon, however, he turned from this to experiment with a more attractive material – polyester reinforced with glass-fibre; and in 1949 he produced the first chair with a seat moulded in this material – the first commercial use of glass-fibre reinforced plastic for a consumer product. This chair, the DAR, was developed from a design that Eames and other members of the Engineering Department at the University of California submitted for an International Competition for Low-Cost Furniture Design sponsored by the Museum of Modern Art in 1948. The material, now generally known as GRP, had only just become available. During the next twenty years its toughness, the ease with which it could be moulded into a variety of shapes, its lustre and its colour tempted many designers to use it. Chair manufacturers realized the advantages of moulding techniques for long production runs but had to balance against this the disadvantages of the high cost of 'tooling up' and of the glass-fibre itself. The making of GRP shells has for this reason tended to be based on 'hand lay up' methods and small production runs, producing chairs of a relatively high price.

Some highly original chairs with exciting new profiles have been produced in

LCM chair, developed from prize-winning
design; moulded plywood and chromium-
plated rods. Charles Eames, 1949

Side elevation and back view of LCM
chair showing rubber pad and screw
attaching frame to back

Post-war American design

One of the prize-winning designs by
Charles Eames and Eero Saarinen
in the Organic Design Competition, 1940

DAR chair, Charles Eames, 1949 –
the first chair with a moulded
glass-fibre seat

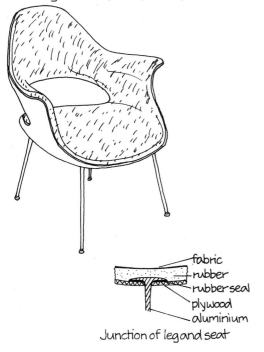

fabric
rubber
rubber seal
plywood
aluminium

Junction of leg and seat

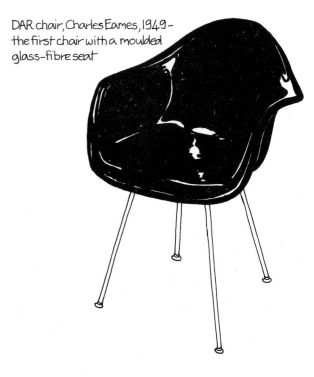

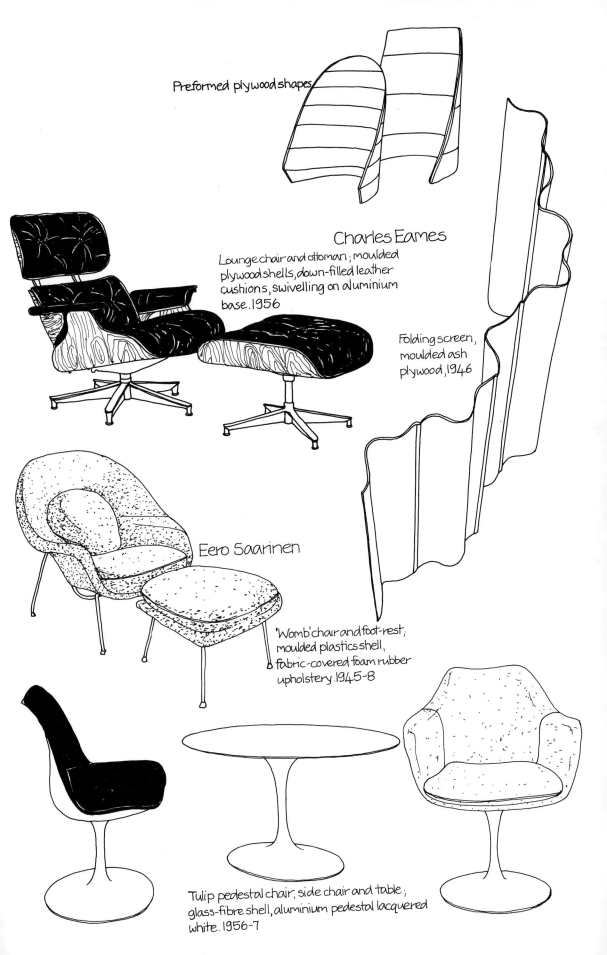

Preformed plywood shapes.

Charles Eames

Lounge chair and ottoman; moulded plywood shells, down-filled leather cushions, swivelling on aluminium base. 1956

Folding screen, moulded ash plywood, 1946

Eero Saarinen

'Womb' chair and foot-rest; moulded plastics shell, fabric-covered foam rubber upholstery. 1945-8

Tulip pedestal chair, side chair and table; glass-fibre shell, aluminium pedestal lacquered white. 1956-7

this material – notable among them the Tulip pedestal and side-chairs of Eero Saarinen and the Egg and Swan swivelling chairs of Arne Jacobsen of Denmark which have a fluid sculptural quality. These beautiful chairs are unfortunately expensive productions. The costs of 'tooling up' and materials are high. To produce such forms requires the use of glass-fibre mats reinforced by soaking in special resins. Variations in the thickness of the forms are built up by hand spraying, and this considerable amount of hand work makes these chairs almost collector's pieces.

Charles Eames's luxurious lounge chair no. 670 with its accompanying ottoman, produced in 1956, updates the traditional armchair, combining comfort with masculine good looks. Down-filled leather cushions are fastened to moulded plywood shells veneered with rosewood and supported on a metal swivel base. Eames has also designed a series of collapsible tables of plywood and plastic tops held firm by ingeniously braced slender metal rod legs. Among his other designs are storage units, radio cabinets and a charming undulating screen of moulded ash plywood made in sections so that it may be folded up small.

Eero Saarinen, Eames's collaborator in the 1940 competition, developed the experience gained from that work into what became known as his Womb chair. He, like Eames, saw the need for a large comfortable chair to replace the old-fashioned, over-stuffed armchair but realized that people liked to sit lower than their Victorian forebears and to slouch, and that they needed to be able to change position frequently. In his own words, 'The Womb chair attempts to achieve a psychological comfort by providing a great big cup-like shell into which you can curl up and pull up your legs (something which women seem specially to like to do). A chair . . . should not only look well as a piece of sculpture in the room when no-one is in it, it should also be a flattering background when someone is in it – especially the female occupant.' The Womb chair is a glass-fibre reinforced plastic shell of generous proportions with fabric-covered foam rubber upholstery, mounted on a simple chromium-plated tubular steel leg frame. This design was followed in 1957 by Saarinen's Tulip chairs and tables, one of the most beautiful sets of furniture so far produced in the twentieth century. The fluid sculptural forms of the chairs are of plastic reinforced with glass-fibre, mounted on slender aluminium pedestals lacquered white. The table tops of white plastic laminate are similarly supported. Saarinen was disappointed that it proved impossible to cast the table and chairs entirely in plastic; he had hoped to create a completely plastic chair. The seat pad is covered in a woollen material. This series shows mass-production methods and synthetic materials combined to produce furniture of great elegance and memorable form.

Saarinen, fully engaged as an architect on some of the most exciting buildings erected since the war, was unable to design much furniture. He concerned himself only with tables and chairs; as an architect he did not favour other forms of movable furniture, believing that they should be part of the fabric of the house – a trend followed in many modern interiors.

Saarinen's designs are carried out by Knoll Associates – he had begun working for them as early as 1943. Knoll expanded in the fifties, opening branches of the firm in Germany in 1951 and France in 1955, and their influence spread. Other gifted designers joined them. One of the most imaginative was Harry Bertoia who also shared a common twentieth-century desire to create weightless see-through furniture. Primarily a sculptor, he was engaged by Hans and Florence Knoll in 1950 with an open brief to experiment either within the furniture field or outside. The outcome of his experiments was an exciting range of chairs (and related furniture) using welded lattice wire shells mounted on chromium-plated steel rod frames. The see-through forms on their slender legs appear to float. Bertoia himself provided the best description: 'In the sculpture I am concerned primarily with space, form, and the characteristics of metal. In the chairs many functional problems have to be satisfied first . . . but when you get right down to it, the chairs are studies in space, form and metal too. If you look at them, you will find that they are mostly made of air, just like sculpture. Space passes right through them.' Unfortunately many designers were attracted to wire mesh who had little understanding of its potential and the fifties saw a glut of rather unattractive spindly furniture.

Ernest Race, who came to the fore in Britain during the fifties when materials were still in short supply, adapted to furniture design the technology with which he had become familiar in the aircraft industry during the war. With great economy of materials he combined laminated plywood and wire to produce his attractive, lightweight Antelope chair, used with great success at the Festival of Britain in 1951.

A breakthrough came in 1954 when Professor Natta, working for the Shell Chemical Company in Britain, discovered polypropylene, a new plastic produced from gases. This tough material made it possible to use the technique of injection moulding for chair production. Until then there had been nothing strong enough to use without reinforcing for such large mouldings. Polypropylene does not need reinforcing; it is rigid and strong with a clear, fresh-looking surface which does not scratch, stain or chip and which can be wiped clean. A product can be manufactured in this material for half the cost of glass-fibre reinforced plastic.

Robin Day, the designer of the first polypropylene chair in 1963 for the firm of Hille, wrote in 1970, 'The invention of polypropylene seemed to me to offer exciting possibilities for the development of a new chair. Its low cost, great strength and suitability for injection moulding made it ideal for a mass-produced one-piece back and seat, which could be mounted on various frame-types for different purposes . . . A single mould can produce as many as 4,000 shells per week, at the rate of two shells every three minutes.' This chair is now being exported to or made under licence in at least twenty-three countries.

Although the production rate is fast and labour costs are low on such a production, large capital outlay is involved in the initial 'tooling up'. The moulds may have to be carved out of solid steel and may cost over £10,000 each; this has to be recovered from the selling price of the object and necessitates production in very large numbers. 'Custom built' polypropylene injection moulded furniture is therefore an impossible luxury.

Polyprop stacking chair, the first
injection-moulded polypropylene
chair, on chromium-plated base.
Robin Day, 1963, for Hille & Co., London

Polyprop stacking
open armchair

Developments in the use of plastics

Panton stacking chair, moulded
glass-fibre shell. Verner Panton,
Switzerland, 1960

Child's chair, polyethylene-coated
laminated paperboard, made in one
flat piece. Peter Murdoch, England, 1964

Wire furniture

Side chair; welded lattice wire
shell mounted on chromium-
plated steel rod frame. Harry
Bertoia, USA, 1951

'Antelope' chair; plywood seat,
steel rod frame. Ernest Race,
England, 1950

A technical breakthrough of the sixties was the Swiss Verner Panton's stacking chair. The first single-form plastic chair produced by a single industrial process, it exploited to the full the latest developments in technology. It is strong and comfortable with a pleasing, flowing line.

Another important British invention in the seventies made it possible to produce at the same time, by one process, a core of rigid plastic with a synthetic upholstery cover.

Italy unexpectedly became one of the dominant forces in the design field in the sixties, with a boldness of style that had been lacking in this area since the thirties. Fascism had fortunately had a less damaging effect upon design and architecture in Italy than Nazism had in Germany. Some worthy designs had been built under Mussolini who, like Bonaparte, favoured a functional classicism in architecture. Furniture tended to perpetuate the neo-classical type of Art Deco. The liberation brought a refreshing zest and excitement back to Italian design as her industries revived and prospered. In the industrial design field a number of interesting, well-designed products appeared, such as the Vespa and Lambretta motor scooters in 1948 and 1949 and the Olivetti typewriters of Marcello Nizzolli, and these began to interest the rest of Europe in Italian design. In an attempt to promote original furniture design a Milan department store, La Rinascente, began awarding the *Compasso d'Oro* prize for modern furniture. This gave an enormous boost to Italian products.

The Italians seemed to have the ability to approach all design problems without preconceived ideas. The strictly functional approach of the Bauhaus gave way to a new aestheticism, and highly individual sculptural forms replaced rigid geometrical ones. Design in Italy has been too varied to classify easily. Some designers have continued to refine and develop traditional forms, making imaginative use of new materials – laminated wood and plywood have been used with great panache. Bold use has been made of colour – lacquer is a favourite medium. These designers have been mainly preoccupied with the aesthetic attributes of individual pieces.

Some have been concerned with giving their furniture the appearance of sculpture. The Dondolo rocking chair designed by Cesare Leonardi and Franca Stagi is impressive first an an exciting sculptural form, second as something upon which to sit.

Some designers appeared to 'cock a snook' at established design and to be influenced by 'kitch' and 'pop' art; some have designed furniture whose appearance gives no clue to its function – as, for instance, the 'Joe' sofa designed by Paolo Lomazzi, Donato d'Urbino and Jonathan de Pas in 1970 in the form of a giant baseball glove made of polyurethane covered in leather; the *Pillola* (Pill) lamp in the form of four brightly coloured plastic capsule shapes standing on end in a row; *I Sassi* (The Rocks), a set of polyurethane seats in varying sizes made to resemble rocks, by Piero Gilardi; and Ettore Sottsass's cupboards and wardrobes in brightly coloured and striped rectangular forms resembling nothing so much as gigantic Liquorice Allsorts.

The Italians began experimenting with plastics from a desire to produce

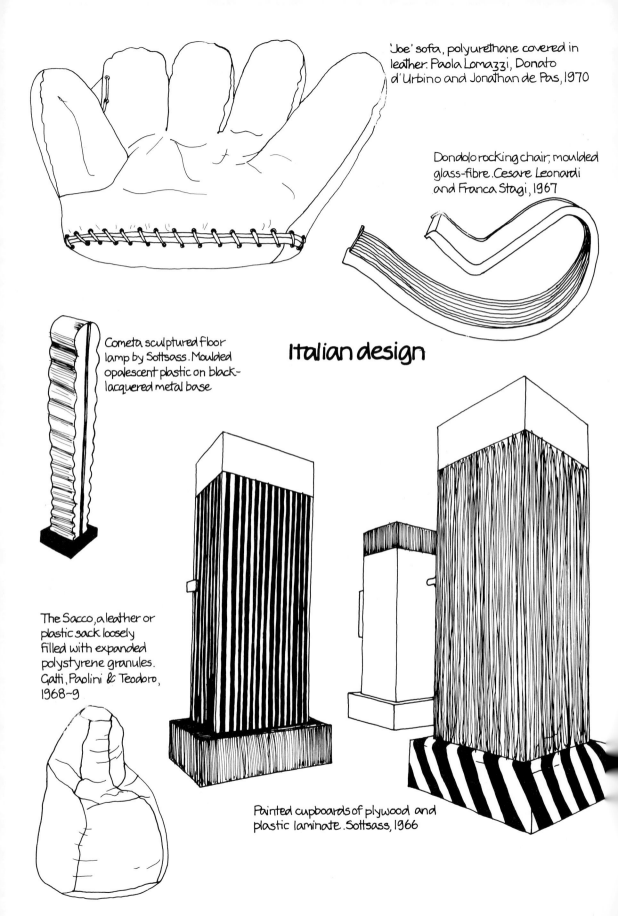

'Joe' sofa, polyurethane covered in leather. Paola Lomazzi, Donato d'Urbino and Jonathan de Pas, 1970

Dondolo rocking chair, moulded glass-fibre. Cesare Leonardi and Franca Stagi, 1967

Cometa sculptured floor lamp by Sottsass. Moulded opalescent plastic on black-lacquered metal base

Italian design

The Sacco, a leather or plastic sack loosely filled with expanded polystyrene granules. Gatti, Paolini & Teodoro, 1968~9

Painted cupboards of plywood and plastic laminate. Sottsass, 1966

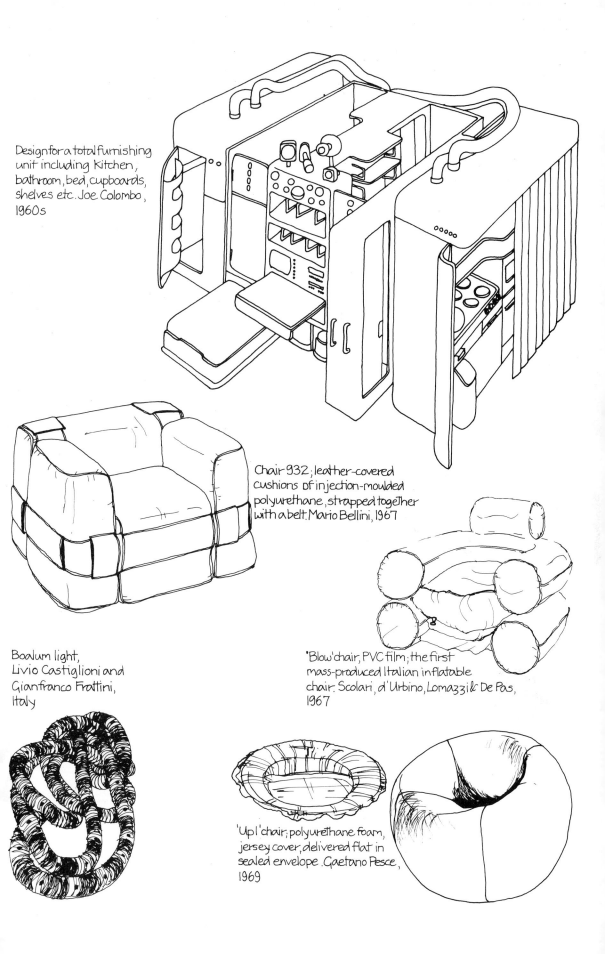

Design for a total furnishing unit including kitchen, bathroom, bed, cupboards, shelves etc. Joe Colombo, 1960s

Chair 932; leather-covered cushions of injection-moulded polyurethane, strapped together with a belt. Mario Bellini, 1967

Boalum light, Livio Castiglioni and Gianfranco Frattini, Italy

'Blow' chair, PVC film; the first mass-produced Italian inflatable chair. Scolari, d'Urbino, Lomazzi & De Pas, 1967

'Up1' chair; polyurethane foam, jersey cover, delivered flat in sealed envelope. Gaetano Pesce, 1969

cheap, well-designed furniture and in an attempt to lessen the sharp division between the very rich and the poor – much greater in Italy than in other European countries. Because of the growing cost of traditional materials they also turned their attention to less permanent forms of furniture, particularly in the area of seating. Into this category fall the Sacco and the Blow chair. The Sacco, resembling an enormous beanbag, is a sack partly filled with plastic granules which adapt to the contours and movements of the sitter's body. It stands firmly on smooth or uneven surfaces and is very light. The Blow chair, made of PVC film seam-welded by radio frequency, was the first Italian inflatable chair to be mass produced. It could be easily inflated or deflated and was adaptable for use in the home, the garden or on the beach. Although fashionable for a time, this type of furniture did not really fulfil people's needs. Far more successful were sofas and armchairs made of expanded plastic foam sheathed with fitted covers, such as the Bibambole furniture designed by Mario Bellini, which could be made in established shapes but much more cheaply than traditionally upholstered furniture, since they dispensed with a rigid frame and springs. The method of construction gave them an up-to-date appearance. Falling partly into this category, by nature of its construction, is Bellini's de luxe Chair 932, which was obviously influenced by Le Corbusier's *Grand Confort*. It is made up of large, leather-covered cushions of injected-moulded foam polyurethane simply belted together by a broad strap slotted through loops in the cushions, without any supporting structure. Such cushions can be arranged in a variety of ways to make up settees or even large areas of seating.

The concept of flexible furniture known as 'environmental ensembles', which could be adapted to a variety of uses and arrangements, became popular in the sixties. As living areas became smaller, they allowed a more informal life style. Mario Bellini's Chameleon, an unlimited cushion system, consists simply of base cushions and back cushions of fabric-covered polyurethane foam which may be arranged at will.

The Up 1 chair by Gaetano Pesce is an amusing idea which, although unconventional, will fit into most interior schemes. Made of polyurethane foam of a precisely controlled density, with a stretch nylon jersey cover, it overcomes the difficulties and cost of shipping in a unique way: the chair is placed between two sheets of vinyl in a vacuum chamber and, as the air is withdrawn, it compresses to one tenth of its expanded volume. The vinyl is then heat-sealed to form a protective, airtight envelope which packs into a flat box. When the vinyl cover is removed, the foam expands to its former size and shape unaided. The chair travels easily and remains clean and undamaged until released from its envelope.

Some modern Italian furniture is dual-purpose, recalling nineteenth-century convertible furniture (although not in appearance) – wardrobe-beds which resemble simple cubes of lacquered wood when folded, beds which fold into low tables, etc. A composite unit designed by Alberto Seansearo contains a bed, a table, a wardrobe, a toilet and a variety of shelves. The individual parts fold or slide into the central core to form a rectangular block of painted wood and

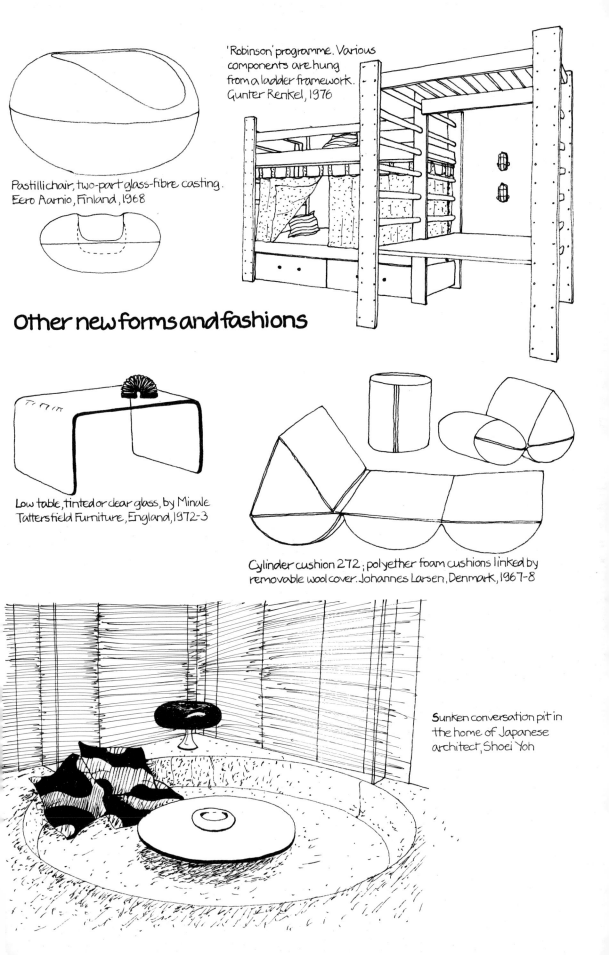

Pastilli chair, two-part glass-fibre casting.
Eero Aarnio, Finland, 1968

'Robinson' programme. Various components are hung from a ladder framework. Gunter Renkel, 1976

Other new forms and fashions

Low table, tinted or clear glass, by Minale Tattersfield Furniture, England, 1972-3

Cylinder cushion 272; polyether foam cushions linked by removable wool cover. Johannes Larsen, Denmark, 1967-8

Sunken conversation pit in the home of Japanese architect, Shoei Yoh

chrome steel. A similar unit by Joe Colombo is illustrated on page 237. From the late sixties and throughout the seventies flexibility has been a key factor in furniture design in Europe and America.

In the late 1920s, Bauhaus designers were predicting that within a few years furniture would radically change – that the conventional chair might disappear and our bodies be supported by cushions of warm air, and that furniture might be held in position magnetically, without legs. In the sixties, minimal artists and others were again suggesting that traditional forms of furniture would soon be gone – storage furniture replaced by interchangeable factory-made units which would probably be built into the house, even chairs and tables made to unfold from the wall or come up through the floor. But there seems to be little danger of furniture becoming merely anonymous, efficient equipment; shops are still stocked with the same types of furniture as they were selling during the fifties. Certain pieces that were common earlier in the century have disappeared – the washstand and the pot-cupboard have gone from the bedroom, thanks to improved plumbing; the large radiogram has gone from the sitting-room. In many houses central heating has replaced the fireplace and its associated furniture and the focal point of the living-room has moved, perhaps to a large picture window or, more likely, to the television set, a new challenge for the furniture designer. Another new piece, the music centre, is fast becoming the latest status symbol in the furniture hierarchy.

People still need to personalize their environment by their choice of furnishings and the objects with which they surround themselves. Standardized units and equipment are acceptable and welcome in kitchens and bathrooms, not only because they are labour-saving and hygienic but because it does not offend us if these rooms appear impersonal. For living-rooms and bedrooms, however, different criteria come to the fore: the furniture for them is chosen in much the same way as we choose our clothes, not just for its functional qualities but as an extension and expression of our personalities and to create the kind of atmosphere in which we feel at ease.

The appeal of the 'conversation pit' or 'lounge pit', introduced from time to time by designers since the first one designed by Saarinen's architectural practice in the late fifties, has been limited. The 'pit' is a sunken area upholstered and cushioned for reclining in comfort; apart from an occasional central table, all furniture including the chair is banished. Some designers have raised part of the floor around the pit in a series of stepped platforms, carpeted to blend with the rest of the floor and sometimes containing storage areas. Cushions placed on the steps serve as seats. This use of space may be pleasant in large rooms but in a confined area it allows less freedom than lightweight, versatile furniture.

Fixed cupboards, unless built into the fabric of the house, have become less popular in recent years. Variable units which can be assembled and reassembled easily in several ways, to stand against the wall or project into the room, reflect the contemporary life style. Many people no longer want or can afford single-purpose rooms filled with traditional, single-purpose furniture. 'Knock-down' cash-and-carry furniture (chairs, tables, bunk beds, storage units) bought direct

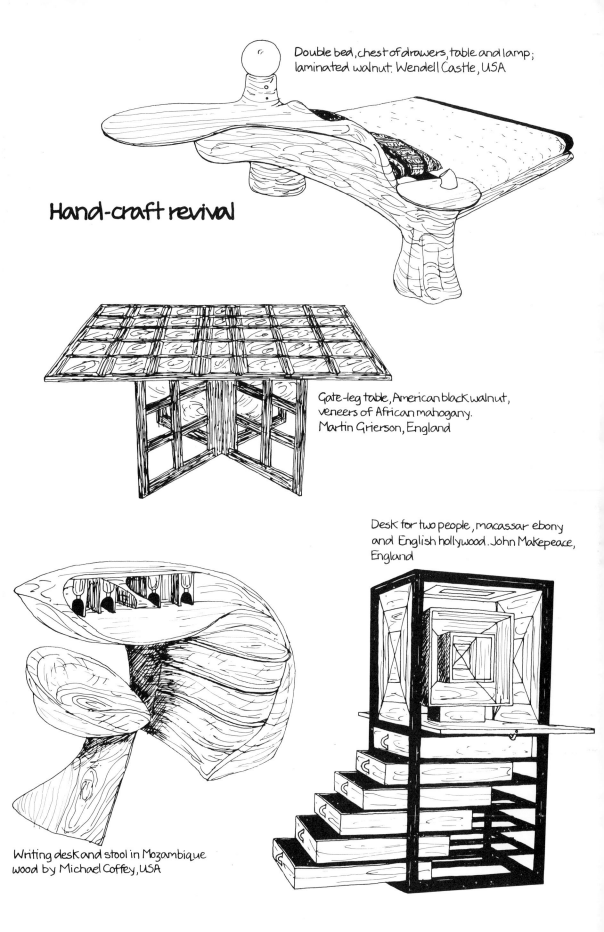

Double bed, chest of drawers, table and lamp; laminated walnut: Wendell Castle, USA

Hand-craft revival

Gate-leg table, American black walnut, veneers of African mahogany. Martin Grierson, England

Desk for two people, macassar ebony and English hollywood. John Makepeace, England

Writing desk and stool in Mozambique wood by Michael Coffey, USA

from store or warehouse in easily-transported boxes and assembled at home, has great appeal for young people living in small apartments. 'Home assembly' effectively reduces the cost and allows more frequent changes in the domestic landscape.

Although there may have been a paucity of skill in the fine arts in recent decades, there has been a strong revival of fine craftsmanship, particularly in the field of hand-made furniture. In England this can be seen in the work of designers like John Makepeace, whose workshops are producing furniture impossible to rival with the machine; Makepeace's unusual gothic chair of 1978 was made up of thousands of pieces of ebony. In the United States the powerful and superbly made organic forms of Wendell Castle have visually much in common with the creations of Gaudí.

High quality wood is becoming a very expensive, almost semi-precious material and certain woods are almost unobtainable. There are, however, many indigenous woods and woods from emergent nations which can be used. Fine craftsmen can and will adapt their skills and surmount these difficulties – as did the ancient Egyptians, producing superb pieces out of a miscellaneous variety of woods over three thousand years ago.

Select bibliography

World Furniture edited by Helena Hayward; Hamlyn, London, New York, Sydney, Toronto, 1969

The Complete Guide to Furniture Styles by Louise Ade Boger; Allen & Unwin, London, 1961; Charles Scribner, New York, 1969

Cabinet Makers and Furniture Designers by Hugh Honour; Weidenfeld & Nicholson, London, 1969

The Dictionary of English Furniture (3 vols) by Percy Macquoid and Ralph Edwards; Country Life, London, revised edn. 1954

Furniture in the Ancient World, Origins and Evolution 3100–475 BC by Hollis S. Baker; The Connoisseur, London, 1966

Ancient furniture. A history of Greek, Etruscan and Roman furniture by G. M. A. Richter; Oxford University Press, 1926

Guide to Early Christian and Byzantine Antiquities; British Museum, London, 1921

Furniture 700–1700 by Eric Mercer; Weidenfeld & Nicholson, London, 1969

Mediaeval Furniture: Furniture in England, France and the Netherlands from the Twelfth to the Fifteenth Century by Penelope Eames; The Furniture History Society, Victoria & Albert Museum, London, 1977

Furniture and Interior Decoration of the Italian Renaissance by Frida Schottmüller; Hoffmann, Stuttgart, 1928

Printed Furniture Designs Before 1650 by Simon Jervis; The Furniture History Society, Victoria & Albert Museum, London, 1974

Chinoiserie by Hugh Honour; John Murray, London, 1961

Furniture by F. J. B. Watson; Wallace Collection Catalogue, London, 1956

The Age of Rococo by A. Schönberger and H. Soehner (trs. D. Wood); Thames & Hudson, London, 1960

The Age of Neoclassicism; Arts Council of Great Britain exhibition catalogue, London, 1972

Empire Furniture by Serge Grandjean; Faber, London, 1966

English Furniture Design of the Eighteenth Century by Peter Ward-Jackson; HMSO, London, 1958

Adam, Hepplewhite and other Neo-Classical Furniture by Clifford Musgrave; Faber, London, 1966

Regency Furniture Designs from Contemporary Source Books, 1803–26 by John Harris; Tiranti, London, 1961

An Outline of Period Furniture by Katharine M. McClinton; Clarkson Potter, New York, 1971

The Cabinetmakers of America by Ethel Hall Bjerkoe; Doubleday, New York, 1957

American Furniture of the Queen Anne and Chippendale Periods by Joseph Downs; Macmillan, New York, 1952

The American Shakers and their Furniture by John G. Shea; Van Nostrand Reinhold, New York, 1972

Nineteenth-Century American Furniture and Other Decorative Art; Metropolitan Museum of Art exhibition catalogue, New York, 1970

Bentwood Furniture – The Work of Michael Thonet; Bethnal Green Museum exhibition catalogue, London, 1968

Nineteenth-Century English Furniture by Elizabeth Aslin; Faber, London, 1962

Art Nouveau by Robert Schmutzler; Thames & Hudson, London, 1979; Harry Abrams, New York, 1964

Mechanization Takes Command by Siegfried Giedion; Oxford University Press, New York, 1948

Pioneers of Modern Design by Nikolaus Pevsner; (new edn) Penguin, London, 1960 and New York, 1964

Furniture from Machines by Gordon Logie; Allen & Unwin, London, 1947; Macmillan Co., New York, 1948

The Knoll Index of Contemporary Design; Knoll Associates, New York, 1950

Modern Scandinavian Design by Ulf Hård af Segerstad; Studio Vista, London, 1963

Pionniers du XXe Siècle; Musée des Arts Décoratifs exhibition catalogue, Paris, 1971

Bauhaus; Royal Academy of Arts exhibition catalogue, London, 1968

Index

mechanical chair of, 34
Thonet, Michael, 166, 168, 209, 213, 214
thrones, 34, 43, 60, 63, 125; of Dagobert, 43; of Maximian, 34; of Tutankhamun, 15
Tiffany, 191, 196, 199
tools, 18, 23, 31, 45, 84, 91, 150, 197, 209, 225
torchères, 106, 127
tortoiseshell, 60, 91, 93, 116, 194, 218
tripods, 27, 121, 143, 144
truckle-bed, 41
tulip wood, 113
Turkey work, 78
turners, 78
turning, 78, 100, 104, 197
'turtlebacks', 104

Ucello, 54
Udine, Giovanni da, 53
upholstery, 100, 120, 129, 150, 174, 199, 238, 240; beds, 94, 97; buttoned, 174, 177; chairs, 94, 112, 169; Elizabethan, 78; French, 93, 106, 109; leather, 71; methods of attaching fabric, 112; sofas, 97, 112, 160; spring, 174, 177
Urbino, Donato d', 235
'Utility' furniture, 224, 225

Vallin, Eugène, 199
van der Velde, Henri, 199, 203
Van Doesburg, 207
Van Eesteren, 207
van Leyden, Lucas, 71
van Riesenburgh, Bernard, 113
varnish, 15, 87, 112, 113, 119, 156

veneering, 88, 91, 94, 100, 108, 121, 140, 151, 154, 188, 197, 232; banding, 85, 87, 119; Egyptian, 15; intarsia, 60; laminated, 166, 168, 229; oyster, 85; rococo, 116; Sheraton, 145, 148; technique, 84, 85, 214; use of mechanical saw, 155
vernis Martin, 113
verre eglomisé, 154
Versailles, palace of, 82, 88, 91, 93, 94, 105, 106, 137
Vile, William, 150
violet wood, 218
Vitruvius *De Architectura*, 53
Vorticism, 204
Voysey, C. F. A., 191, 194, 204

wainscot, 45, 52; w. chair, 104
wall-hangings, 10, 13, 34, 45, 58, 87, 125
wall paintings, 27, 57, 58, 60
wallpapers, 87, 129, 140, 155
walnut wood, 45, 58, 61, 71, 85, 100, 119, 121; American black walnut, 132; Caucasian burr walnut, 221
Wanscher, Ole, 228
wardrobe, 63, 91, 93, 121, 223, 235, 238
Waring & Gillow, 223
wash hand stand, 141, 150, 223, 240
Webb, Philip, 184
Wedgwood, Josiah, 137, 155
Wegner, Hans, 228
Weisweiler, Adam, 137, 154
wickerwork, 31
Wiener Secession, 203, 204, 216

Wiener Werkstätten, 191, 203
William and Mary, 94, 100
willow wood, 15
Winckelmann, Johann, *Geschichte der Kunst des Altertums*, 133
wine coolers, 144
wire, 166, 169, 233
wood carving, 52, 57, 157, 162, 181, 184; American, 104, 151; Anglo-Flemish, 73; baroque, 79, 82, 84; Byzantine, 32, 34; Georgian, 121; Grinling Gibbons, 100; neo-classical, 134, 137; Queen Anne, 120; renaissance, 61, 63, 66, 73, 75; rococo, 109, 116, 125, 127; romanesque chip, 43
wood, 15, 45, 84, 100, 121, 166, 218, 224, 242; blockboard, 214; *bois clair*, 165; ebonized, 184, 188; laminated, 166, 168, 169, 214, 235; plywood, 213, 214, 216, 223, 232, 233; for veneering, 85, 112, 113, 168
Woodforde, Revd. James, *Diary*, quoted, 129
work tables, 137, 148, 165
Wright, Frank Lloyd, *The Art and Craft of the Machine*, 196
writing desks and tables, 37, 67, 73, 93, 108, 113, 120, 137, 140, 150, 151, 154, 157, 162

zebra wood, 162